FINGERS CROSSED

HOW MUSIC SAVED ME FROM SUCCESS

MIKI BERENYI

NINE
EIGHT
BOOKS

NINE
EIGHT
BOOKS

NEB 010 PB

First published in the UK in hardback in 2022
This paperback edition published in 2023 by Nine Eight Books
An imprint of Bonnier Books UK
4th Floor, Victoria House, Bloomsbury Square, London, WC1B 4DA
Owned by Bonnier Books, Sveavägen 56, Stockholm, Sweden

@nineeightbooks

@nineeightbooks

Paperback ISBN: 978-1-7887-0557-8
eBook ISBN: 978-1-7887-0556-1
Audio ISBN: 978-1-7887-0531-8

Publishing director: Pete Selby
Senior editor: Melissa Bond

Cover design by Paul Palmer-Edwards
Cover image © Jurgen Ostarhild
All images in the plate sections courtesy of the author
Typeset by IDSUK (Data Connection) Ltd
Printed and bound in Great Britain by Clays Ltd, Elcograf S.p.A

1 3 5 7 9 10 8 6 4 2

Text copyright © Miki Berenyi, 2022

Nine Eight Books is an imprint of Bonnier Books UK
www.bonnierbooks.co.uk

MIX
Paper from
responsible sources
FSC® C018072

Praise for this book:

Rough Trade Book of the Year
Resident Book of the Year
A *Rolling Stone* Book of the Year
A *Mojo* Book of the Year
A *Sunday Times* Book of the Year
★★★★★ *Record Collector*
★★★★★ *The Sun*

'So relatable, so poignant, so emotionally intense, it's an irresistible rush of a book.' – **Rolling Stone**

'A great memoir requires an extraordinary life story and the ability to write it. Miki has been blessed with both. Compelling. Funny. Vivid.' – **Mojo**

'A remarkable, revelatory memoir.' – **The Times**

'Fiercely honest and emotionally acute . . . *Fingers Crossed* breaks the mould of music memoir . . . Berenyi's writing is characterised by arch humour and a delight in the absurd.' – **The Guardian**

'*Fingers Crossed* provides a salutary corrective to a much-mythologised musical era; it's often extremely funny. But it's also a nuanced portrait of personal survival.' – **The Observer**

'This is quite the revelation . . . infinitely superior to the average rock autobiography . . . the most candid, full-disclosure demystification of the indie scene you'll ever read. This is special, a superbly written book about a vanished world and so much more.'
– **Record Collector**

'Miki writes beautifully with soul and humour. A brilliant, engaging read.' – **Classic Rock**

'A beautifully written memoir.' – **Stylist**

'Intelligent and searingly candid.' – **Grazia**

'By far the best music memoir of 2022. An utterly riveting peek into an extraordinary early life.' – **The i**

'A great life story combined with excellent recall and refreshingly honest writing is a bonus when it comes to any memoir, but the superb *Fingers Crossed* achieves brownie points by delivering details with real dexterity.' – **Irish Times**

'A powerful, emotional journey intensely well told. All other autobiographies should be judged against it.'
– **Louder Than War**

'Few autobiographies depict the highs and lows with quite the merciless clarity as *Fingers Crossed*.' – **The Monocle**

'You will laugh, you will cry, you might never, ever form a band.' – **Virgin Radio**

'Honest and brilliantly written.' – **We Are Cult**

'I felt like I was on the roller coaster with Miki, from making mixtapes with her school friends to the wild dream of making it as a pop star. It's a gripping and delightful read, even as, without an ounce of self-pity, the bright energy of Miki's star is always tailed by darkness . . . A thrilling, moving and essential book for anyone who grew up in love with pop music.' – **Samira Ahmed**

'Extremely colourful and dramatic.' – **Mark Ellen**

'Brave and forthright. It instils in you the thing most necessary from a musician's memoir: the urgent need to play the records again.' – **John Niven**

'Beautifully and movingly written, this is a hugely entertaining read.'
– **Shaun Keaveny**

'A really incredible book.' – **Skin, Skunk Anansie**

'This is extraordinarily good. A memoir that reads like a novel, full of vivid characters, wild highs and lows and brutal honesty. And it's the single best thing I've read on the sexism and toxicity at the heart of Britpop.' – **Matt Osman, Suede**

'Miki tells it like it was, warts and all.' – **Steve Rippon, Lush**

For Moose and Stella and Ivan

CONTENTS

PART TWO

INTRODUCTION

My father's favourite parenting anecdote, delivered with side-splitting guffaws, described him bundling the two-year-old me out of my depth and tossing my thrashing body into the Mediterranean. The crash-course swimming lesson was, however, scuppered by a group of muscle-bound sunbathers alerted by the alarmed screams of my bikini-clad mother, whereupon I was scooped up and deposited, hysterical with terror, back onto the sandy beach. Dad's moral of the story was that, if Mum hadn't made such a fuss, I would have had a bright future as an Olympic swimmer and not be piddling about with rubber rings and armbands, too nervous to abandon flotation devices for several years thereafter.

There's a lot of my childhood in this event: Dad determined that I run before I could crawl; Mum on a distant shoreline, a helpless spectator to machismo; my disappointing failure to exhibit (literal) buoyancy in the face of a challenge, relying on strangers to provide rescue because my own parents, though well intentioned, had no fucking idea how to bring me up or keep me safe. Also, glamour and drama – the sun-sparkled splendour of the Med, the peacocking display as Dad fended off a beating

1

from the men, the damsel in distress (Mum, not me). And how reckless behaviour provides excellent material for a colourful story.

Dad's mantra when discussing my upbringing was 'I always treated you like an adult', implying he didn't patronise me and had faith in my abilities. Mum's tactic was to praise me for being impressively grown-up and capable, which was encouraging, but also allowed her to abandon any maternal responsibility since I seemed to be doing so well on my own. My own guide to life became 'What doesn't kill you makes you stronger' – another cliché that can be interpreted in two ways. Picking yourself up from a pounding and getting back on your feet brings resilience, but it's also true that terrible experiences cause damage and then you're saddled with the fallout, having to try to fix what should never have happened. Still, a smooth road to easy success makes for a dull story, so I hope that mine will at least be entertaining to read.

I never intended to be in a band. I didn't grow up having music lessons or enjoying rousing sing-songs around the piano, I didn't get taken to concerts or even *listen* to anything but background music with my family. As a kid, films, books, drawing and gymnastics vied equally for my attention. It wasn't until I reached adolescence, when I needed more than childish distractions and fantasy to provide solace and escape, that I really got sucked in. Music gave me hope and distraction: rhythm and noise that could change or enhance my mood; lyrics that provided reassurance that someone out there understood me or that there were other, better ways to feel. The players – real people, not just fictional characters – embodied possibilities: alluring, confident women I dreamed of becoming; sensitive, artistic men

2

I might one day love and be loved by; exciting and interesting performers who could end up becoming my friends. And, if their backstories were sad or tough, they offered hope that I, too, might escape whatever crap I was stuck in and one day be lauded and adored.

When I started going to gigs, I'd immerse myself in the crowd, roiling among the sweaty bodies and thrown around to the songs. Though the moshpit would often become violent, I felt numb to the blows and would be surprised by the bruises that would emerge the following day, covering my arms in a polka-dot of purple (this, too, feels like an apt metaphor). It was the ultimate high to be subsumed, a part of something bigger and enveloping. And if it was this wonderful to be the listener – the audience – imagine how amazing it might be to be the instigator. To have the gift and the power of creating that magic yourself.

The miracle of music, of all creativity, is making something from nothing. Stringing notes together, adding depth with lyrics, breathing life into a song by playing it with a band, finessing it through the recording process, then sharing it with an audience, spreading all that emotion and connection and joy – all born from a bedroom, a guitar and a voice. Happiness from sadness, a ticket out of loneliness and loserdom, escaping a bad place to beat a path to somewhere better.

And it was bands in particular that I connected with. I never craved the life of a solo artist, celebrated but alone. I wanted the camaraderie of a gang. A family. Imagine being with your mates, having a laugh, playing wonderful music to crowds of people who are all communing to celebrate together in one great big party. Never lonely, always together and looking out for one another; uniquely appreciated and being loved for what you do.

I mean, I know that's all bollocks – I know that *now* – but at the time it felt like a dream that could be realised.

So I wasn't driven to form Lush by an inborn talent I wanted to showcase. I fell into music, grabbed onto it like a lifeline. Meeting Emma, being part of the gig scene, joining a band – it was more luck, opportunity and need that made me follow that path, rather than a lifelong ambition. I was escaping the craziness and disruption of my childhood surroundings, beckoned towards a world that accepted damaged people, celebrated them even. I didn't much care for the trappings of success – global fame and immense wealth weren't on the agenda. And I've never had much truck with hero worship and the cult of the solitary genius. It was my *lack* of faith in any inborn talent, the punk-rock ethic that anyone can have a go, that inspired me to jump into the fray. I just wanted to be a part of something, in the middle of it, willing to try to hope for the best. Throw myself into the sparkling sea and, fingers crossed, this time I'll swim.

PART ONE

1

IVAN

I cling to Dad like a monkey, wrapping myself around his leg, squealing like a chimp, carried along as he walks. He holds my two hands and I walk my feet up his body until I flip over. I stand on his feet and we dance.

In the summer, when Dad lies out in the sunny garden, reading and smoking on a blanket, I lounge on his hot back like Mowgli on Baloo.

At the swimming pool, I place my foot in the cradle of his interwoven fingers and he hurls me high in the air. I hold his shoulders as he butterflies through the water with thrilling speed and splash. We duck underwater for a whole half-length.

When we drive around the wide curve of Sidmouth Road, he lifts me from the passenger seat into his lap and I steer the car while he operates the pedals. It's exciting but I have to fight an instinct to randomly jerk the steering wheel and slam into the oncoming traffic.

Dad holds his palms up for me to practise boxing. He tells me to always go for the gut and avoid the face, as haymakers rarely connect.

Sometimes I sit astride his lap, planting tiny kisses on his face wherever he points. Dad carries me up to bed on his shoulders – I squash right down to avoid the door frame, my feet braced under his armpits, my face buried in his neck.

My father, Ivan Paul Berényi, was born in 1933 and came from what he called 'seven-plum-tree nobility', which in his parlance implied a modest bourgeoisie with laughable airs and graces. However, the framed family photographs of little Ivan decked out in a sailor suit and Dad's casual references to the German-speaking servants suggests a level of privilege beyond the average citizen of the era. Indeed, his mother Nora (born Eleonóra Vörös) loved nothing better than to reminisce about the glamorous balls and Viennese palaces she had frequented in her youth, where she claimed she was inundated with offers of marriage from dashing men of good stock. I have a university photo in which she is the only female in the graduating class, so she must have been a pioneer of sorts, but, if she really did have the pick of the eligible bachelors, she made a poor choice in my grandfather, Paul Berényi. Though his family's fabulous wealth made him a good bet, Paul was, by Dad's account, an incorrigible gambler and womaniser whose reckless antics caused such disgrace and ruin that he was eventually packed off to Australia by both his own and Nora's families, with instructions to never darken their doorsteps again.

The enforced separation didn't seem to bother Nora much. She was glad to be rid of her wayward husband and only ever spoke of him with disparaging venom. I suppose bringing up her son was unexacting since little Ivan was fussed and cossetted by her own mother and the servants. Even the imminent threat of the Second World War had its upsides in the form of lively parties of visiting Nazi officers, keen to enjoy the lakeside hospitality of the family's 'Hungarian Riviera' villa. Granny claimed that she had marriage offers aplenty from high-ranking Nazis and broke their hearts by refusing them all, insisting that she could never 'betray' her son – whatever that means. Personally, I'm not convinced that as the shadow of war fell across Europe, a thirty-year-old single mother was quite the catch she claimed and Nora was certainly bitterly resentful that her convivial socialising was brought to a close by the outbreak of armed conflict and the eventual defeat of the Axis powers. She remained a loud and unapologetic admirer of Hitler for the rest of her life.

From Dad, I got only fleeting details of his wartime boyhood. Most of his anecdotes described the horrors of Soviet occupation: the crescendo of screams as Red Army thugs went house to house, raping women and ransacking property; a cousin shot in the head following an attempted escape from arrest; the fortuitous treasure of scavenging an orange peel, discarded by a soldier walking ahead of him on the street, which he and Nora used to brew tea for a week; and the near miss of surviving a random roadblock where passing pedestrians were filtered either left or right and those in the 'wrong' line were loaded into trucks and never seen again.

Dad's teenage recollections focused on disappointment and thwarted ambition. Under communist rule, Ivan's privileged background branded him a 'class alien' and disqualified him from pursuing his preferred academics of literature and law. His only degree option was to attend agricultural college, in an ideological effort to turn him into a grounded son of the soil – an entirely fruitless endeavour, since Ivan would laughingly recount – with some pride – his utter incompetence at riding a horse and mastering the details of crop cultivation.

The regime was, however, big on sport. All youngsters were offered the opportunity to participate and rewarded if they excelled. Dad was a strong swimmer, having had access to the vast waters of Lake Balaton throughout his childhood, but his dreams of sporting success as a water polo player (the Hungarian team was world renowned) were dashed when he got dropped from the national squad. By seventeen, he had married his schoolmate Zsuzsa – dazzled initially by her intelligence (she had apparently published a novel at the age of sixteen) but quickly demoralised by the domestic dead-end of their life together.

A turning point came during a student protest on the streets of Budapest. What started as a spirited gathering ended in gunfire and slaughter and, in describing the revolution that ensued, Ivan would become animated about the street battles and toppling of statues, then sombre about the chaos of violence on all sides, describing the horror of a Soviet soldier, younger than himself, beaten to death by the enraged mob. Amid the chaos, there had been an air of triumphant hope that the Russians could be permanently ousted. But this was not to be. Dad would bitterly curse the lack of support from the British and Americans who, preoccupied with the Suez Crisis, deserted the revolutionaries in their hour of need. As the Soviets redoubled their control of their wayward satellite, Dad determined to abandon Hungary, fleeing on foot for the border and eventually making it to Britain as a refugee.

Ivan was always rather cheerful about the welcome he received, though he frequently took the piss out of 'snobby English types' while harbouring a dark distrust of the working-class left, who he suspected of allying ideologically with the loathed Russians. But being European and middle class – and tall and good-looking, to boot – must have been a big help in assimilating into life in the UK. He certainly seemed to have a high time of it, racking up exploits with new-found friends and fellow Hungarian refugees, recklessly ecstatic after their perilous escape from the grimness of Hungary under communism. There were opportunities aplenty and he grabbed them, graduating with an English degree from Bristol University, funding his studies with work as a Hungarian interpreter and eventually finding his way into sports journalism. Which is how he ended up at the Tokyo Olympics in 1964 and meeting my mother.

2

YASUKO

I cling to Mum's legs, shy around strangers. She crouches at my level, gently coaxing me from anxiety. When she breaks into a smile, it's like gazing at a flower.

We sing nursery rhymes and pop songs from the radio. I love watching her, animated and kittenish, dancing and clapping along to the music – a petite, beautiful doll.

When the beam of her attention is on me, I bask in its warmth. But, when it's directed elsewhere, I feel a sting of jealousy. I am not special, I am like everyone else. She is not mine alone and I have to wait my turn.

Women find her sweet and charming and I see the look of protective, puppyish devotion in the eyes of some of the men.

I try to copy her, but I have none of her delicate sweetness. I long for some of her beauty and charm to rub off on me, but I see no evidence of it and I am awkward and inadequate by comparison.

I love her, but I feel like I love her more than she loves me.

My mother, Yasuko, was born in Manchuria, north-east China, which by the time of her birth, in 1943, was an established puppet state of the Japanese Empire. My grandfather, Sanji Oyamada, was himself born and raised there and, having qualified as a doctor, ministered to the medical needs of the Japanese army stationed in Shenyang, then later to the last emperor of the Qing dynasty, Pu Yi, who had been installed as a nominal ruler.* In later life, watching Bertolucci's *The Last Emperor*, Sanji wryly dismissed the film's romantic content, saying that Pu Yi was gay and that his wife and many concubines turned to opium to ameliorate their sexual frustration.

Tamiko, my grandmother, was from a privileged background, benefitting from a private education and graduating in domestic science from the Nihon Joshi Daigaku (Japan Women's University). When she moved to China to wed my grandfather via traditional arranged marriage, Sanji took his wife's Nagazumi surname, in recognition of her family's status and political connections (her cousin Torahiko Nagazumi was a close friend and chamberlain to Emperor Hirohito). As the Second World War raged around the globe, the couple raised their two children – Mum and her older brother Atsushi – in the protected environs of the Japanese-controlled Manchukuo state.

With Japan's surrender in 1945 and the dismantling of Manchukuo, many of the region's Japanese citizens ended up in refugee camps. Whether toughened by the childhood trauma of losing her own mother at the age of ten or merely galvanised by an entitlement born of her class (depending on your view),

---

* Musical family connection no. 1: Keigo Oyamada, known by the moniker Cornelius, is the grandson of Sanji's oldest brother Koichi, which makes him my second cousin.

Tamiko shifted into survival mode and shielded her family from the atrocities of the invading Red Army by striking a deal with the GPU (Soviet secret police), to whom she provided room and board in the family home.* Sanji always credited Tamiko's wits in securing the protection of the Russian officers and said that without her actions, they would have been dead for sure.

When the turbulent political landscape shifted once again, Sanji's medical skills were commandeered by Chiang Kai-shek, head of the National Government of China. Chiang, who had been educated in Tokyo and served a couple of years in the Imperial Japanese army, was protective of his resident doctor and, during the retreat from Mao Zedong's forces in 1949, offered to bring the family to Taiwan, promising safe harbour in Taipei and an education in America for Atsushi and Yasuko. But Tamiko, who had had her fill of living abroad, insisted on returning to Japan and the family fled, bargaining off most of their material goods to buy safe passage on the last cargo ship out of China.

Tamiko's father had passed away some years earlier and, as his sole heir, she inherited land in Yamaguchi province. Having gifted the main Shimonoseki house to her father's mistress (Tamiko disapproved of mistresses generally but appreciated that her father's had nursed him through his final years), she sold the remaining assets to settle the family in Kawaguchi, a

---

* Both branches of my family, at opposite ends of the globe, shared tales of terror regarding the notorious Red Army, recalling the soldiers sporting rows of watches up their arms as trophies of gunpoint pillaging ('*Davai chasy*' – 'Hand over the watch'). I realise that both the Berényis and the Nagazumis were on the wrong side of the conflict and many would justify the violence inflicted on their people, but the details are chilling and instilled in me a lifelong belief that, whatever shit life throws at you, war is surely the worst. Also, those with privilege tend to survive far better than those without.

provincial city in Saitama province on the northern outskirts of Tokyo. They bought a large two-storey house and built a doctor's clinic with adjoining accommodation for the staff. Sanji sold his Leica camera and lenses – one of the few treasures he had managed to carry in their escape from China – to a high-up at the US army base to fund the purchase of an X-ray machine and the family business was up and running.

The couple worked long hours. There were few doctors operating in the area and evening surgery and night-time callouts were standard. Tamiko managed the clinic's finances and controlled their investments, as well as running the home. But the war had devastated much of Japan and the Nagazumis' middle-class life contrasted sharply with the poverty suffered by most of their Saitama neighbours.

This was a point of pride for Tamiko, who had battled hard to keep the family financially stable, but Yasuko, bullied by her classmates for her privilege, would plead with her mother to clothe her in the cheap rubber flip-flops and utilitarian fabrics worn by her peers, rather than the leather shoes and fancy coat rescued from their previous life in cosmopolitan Shenyang. When a few years later, Mum attended the prestigious Aoyama private girls' school in Shibuya, she found herself at the opposite end of the social spectrum. Tamiko's home-sewn garments and decoratively crocheted gloves now felt twee and unsophisticated and Yasuko couldn't match the effortless elegance of her well-heeled classmates who had no idea where Kawaguchi even was – actually, a bit of a blessing since she now felt cripplingly aware of the small town's provincial limitations compared to wealthy Tokyo society.

I'm aware that Yasuko's social anxieties seem embarrassingly inconsequential against the background of Japan's post-war devastations. Indeed, Tamiko's response was to admonish her daughter for her ingratitude at the good fortune and opportunities afforded her. She was committed to arming her two children with lifelong financial security, insisting her son pursue a medical career and planning a suitable marriage to a doctor for her daughter. Atsushi was accused of laziness and harshly punished if he received anything less than top academic marks and Yasuko was under no less pressure to excel. At age seven, she was sent for lessons to a former concert pianist, who would sting Yasuko's hands with a conductor's baton if she hit a bum note or failed to keep perfect time. The hours of daily practice under Tamiko's praise-free surveillance extinguished any joy she might have felt in her musical talents and to this day, Mum will say that she never played for herself, only for her mother and teacher. Even in later life, when my stepfather furnished their Hollywood home with an ostentatious grand piano that had to be winched into the house at great expense through an upper-storey window, I rarely heard her play.

Outwardly, Yasuko complied with Tamiko's hard-line regime, but with increasing resentment, and, as marriageable age approached, she despaired at having no say in her future. Bored to distraction by Sanji's medical colleagues and the nightly dinner-table shop talk between father and son as Atsushi's studies progressed, she dreaded the prospect of being parcelled off as a doctor's wife – a life that to her seemed achingly dull. Rather, she dreamed of travelling to England – the birthplace of Shakespeare! – to experience the world on her own terms. But Tamiko was a formidable matriarch and it would take a revolutionary act to scupper her plans.

3

A CHANCE ROMANCE

The 1964 Olympics was a huge deal in Tokyo and Mum's English-speaking skills got her selected by her university as an official 'companion' – effectively a tourist information guide stationed at the reception desk of the Prince Hotel, which stood in the shadow of Tokyo Tower. She was proud to have been picked and the job provided officially sanctioned freedom from Tamiko's all-seeing eye, although having to wear full kimono regalia all day and fend off attempts to engage her as an escort were tiresome. One persistent guest wooed her with an enormous bottle of Vol de Nuit perfume, which would have cost a king's ransom at the time, in his efforts to ship her off to Monte Carlo as a bride for his elderly father.

Ivan had blagged himself an international press pass and reported on the Olympics as a freelancer, though he seems to have spent as much time on hedonistic pursuits as attending the Games and filing copy, prolonging his stay for several months and hooking up romantically with one of Yasuko's university friends, also on 'companion duty'. My parents hit it off as friends and when Ivan headed back to London, he promised to maintain contact with Yasuko through letters, primarily as a means for her to practise her English.

The stint in Japan had given Ivan a taste for international adventure and he immediately set off on an epic journey over land and sea to Australia, to track down his father, who he hadn't heard from in over twenty years. The resulting reunion was, ultimately, a disappointment and Dad never lost the edge of resentment when describing the man he had travelled many months and miles to reconnect with. He found Paul Berényi oafish and charmless, only interested in bragging about his new family and successful hairdressing business, all the while emphasising his happy severance with everything, including his long-lost son, that had preceded this second-chance paradise. As is often the case, it was the journey rather than its goal that was life-changing. While Ivan accumulated hair-raising adventures on his epic trek, hitch-hiking and stowing away and getting by on his wits, he conveyed the amusing details in letters to Yasuko. Her own responses would be waiting for him at pre-arranged post-office stops in Istanbul, Baghdad, Delhi and beyond.

As the correspondence progressed, the tone of the letters intensified. Yasuko had found a sympathetic listener for her dissatisfaction with her strict, traditional upbringing and expounded on her dreams of escape. Ivan, meanwhile, inching ever closer to the moment when he might reunite with his father, poured out his self-doubts and the details of his traumatic upbringing in Hungary. They shared their past and their present, discussed literature and cinema and art, confessed and empathised and fell in love.

Dad said Yasuko's missives – so open and heartfelt, read and re-read – kept him going on that long uncertain journey; Mum chimed that Ivan's letters – perceptive, sincere and full of hope – provided precious distraction from her gloomy destiny. By the time Ivan returned to London, their long-distance romance had solidified into an elaborate plan. One morning, Yasuko headed out the door, ostensibly attending an appointment at the hairdresser and said goodbye to her parents. The family was none the wiser until Mum's friend and confidante, having waited until an agreed hour, informed Tamiko of the truth – that Yasuko was already on a plane and bound for Heathrow, with no plans to return.

———

Ivan had a lifelong habit of being self-servingly economical with the truth, but he'd been honest enough with his future bride about the rocky state of his employment and finances. Yasuko was unconcerned, claiming that money was never particularly important to her, although I would argue that never having been without it makes you unqualified to make that statement with complete certainty. Less agreeable was the dawning realisation that Ivan's daily life, prior to her arrival, involved a relentless pursuit of casual bed-hopping affairs, many of them conducted with the various nubile singles occupying the hippie commune he lived in. Still, London in the Swinging Sixties was hard to beat – Yasuko was twenty-three years old, fulfilling her dream, romantically in love and surrounded by a convivial, bohemian party crowd, so there were plenty of positives. Their whirlwind wedding and the prospect of a family were bound to settle Ivan into the role of a responsible husband and father.

In April 1966, the magazine *London Life* ran a feature on international couples living in the capital and Yasuko's face ended up gracing the cover. The piece mentioned that she was a fluent English speaker (unusual at the time – English-speaking Japanese in the UK were mostly consulate employees) and on this basis and her photogenic beauty, she was contacted out of the blue by film producer Betty Box with an offer to appear in the film *Deadlier Than the Male*, starring Richard Johnson and Elke Sommer. Yasuko's protestations that she had never taken a drama class at school let alone acted in any professional capacity were batted aside by Betty ('Don't worry, we'll teach you'), who reassured her that all that was required was for her to source a traditional Japanese kimono for the role. Tamiko (who, despite the scandal of the elopement, remained supportive of her daughter) air-mailed the necessary items and Yasuko was whisked off to Italy where, despite her misgivings, the friendly crew and cast stepped her through her performance.

One opportunity led to another and, while Richard Johnson was chatting with his friend Albert Broccoli, who happened to be filming his latest James Bond movie (Johnson himself had originally been considered for the Bond role in *Dr No*), Yasuko's name came up.* Having lucked into one major film with only a kimono and a facility with English to make up for her complete lack of acting experience, she was now cast in another.

Most of *You Only Live Twice* had been shot on location in Japan, but, by the time Mum was on board, the production was filming

---

* Richard Johnson seems to have been very well connected and set Mum up with a modelling job for Antony Armstrong-Jones in a 'beautiful women of the world' photo shoot for British *Vogue*. Following the session, the bevy of exotic belles was invited for an evening at Kensington Palace, where Mum was met with the eye-popping spectacle of the Earl of Snowdon in full drag and guided into a dance with Princess Margaret, who had cross-dressed into a tail-coated male role for the soirée.

final footage at Pinewood. The iconic bath-house scene, where a bevy of bikini-clad handmaidens minister to the ablutions of Sean Connery, is often fondly remembered by male friends of my age who, brought up on a childhood of Christmas Bond screenings, recall it as a landmark moment for their nascent hormones. For Yasuko, the experience was made somewhat less 'sexiful' (to quote a particularly wince-inducing line of dialogue) by her recent realisation that she was by now three months pregnant. With her energy focused on sucking in her belly, Yasuko lacked the muscle to compete in the scrum of actresses keen to minister to Connery's lathering and you can spot her in the scene attending to Tetsuro Tamba (playing secret service agent Tiger Tanaka). Mum claims that she was in any case more impressed at meeting Tamba, who was a huge star in Japan – a fact that none of the other women were aware of since, as Mum pointedly mentions, they weren't actually Japanese (one had Burmese heritage and the other two were Chinese). But it was standard at the time for east Asians to be interchangeably cast. Mum herself went on to play Chinese, Vietnamese and Singaporean roles during her career – 'they thought we all looked the same, anyway'. However, being authentically Japanese did, by Yasuko's account, play a part in a call-back some months later to appear in the film's title sequences and provide overdubs for some of the scenes.

Excited as she was at the offer, not least because the Bond film paid phenomenally well, she expected the invitation to be rescinded when she sheepishly had to break the news that she was by now visibly on the verge of giving birth. But title designer Maurice Binder showed no signs of annoyance, accommodating her by nixing the planned silhouette body shots and instead propping her up on cushions with a parasol behind her while filming close-ups of her face and providing kindly reassurance that any obstetric stirrings could be instantly responded to by an on-hand doctor and swift passage to hospital.

As it happens, it was a close call. I was born four days later.

4

BEAUTIFUL TREE

I was born shortly after midnight on 18 March 1967. My name in the Japanese kanji writing system (美樹) means 'beautiful evergreen tree' and Mum was thinking specifically of the actress and model Miki Irie, who was herself mixed race – half Japanese and half Russian (she went on to marry the world-renowned conductor Seiji Ozawa). It's a popular name in Hungary, too, albeit as a shortening for a male name, Miklós (Nicholas). So there were resonances in her choice.

Dad came up with my middle name, Eleonóra, after his mother, but he wasn't around to gift me this blessing on my birth. According to Mum's account, when her waters broke, he'd been gone for days and she'd had to walk to the hospital alone. 'I suspected he was off sleeping with some woman. All the Hungarian friends came visiting and everyone was asking: "Where is Ivan?" The nurses, too: "Where is your husband?" It was so humiliating. I had no way of reaching him. He finally turned up the next day, but I lowered my expectations of him after that.'

Mum was brought up in a culture where wives were expected to tolerate their husbands' affairs, but her own mother would never have put up with such behaviour herself. When Tamiko arrived in London to coddle her first-born grandchild, she instantly took in the situation and tried to persuade Yasuko to return to Kawaguchi. But Yasuko had no desire to deal with the stigma of being a single mother raising a mixed-race daughter in Japan, which in respectable conservative society would make both of us outcasts.

To give Yasuko and Ivan a solid start to family life (and distance Dad from the temptations of the single girls inhabiting their Chelsea apartment block), my grandparents fund the deposit on a four-bedroom family home on Staverton Road, in Willesden Green. The move to London's north-west suburbs in no way means settling into a life of dull respectability and there are regular parties and gatherings with the lively Hungarian crowd, who are welcoming and protective of Ivan's young wife. But the convivial set-up is disrupted by visits from Dad's mother Nora, who dotes on me but is from the outset hostile towards her daughter-in-law. When Mum returns from food shopping, Nora grabs the bag off her and wails: 'Poor Ivan! He has to eat this? You don't care about him at all!' When Yasuko takes lessons in Hungarian from Ivan's friend Peter Pallai (he went on to work as a journalist for the BBC Hungarian service for almost forty years), the better to communicate with her mother-in-law, Nora puts the kybosh on their sessions with relentless anti-Semitic slurs against Peter and insinuations of ulterior sexual motives. She spits out Yasuko's meals and gasps in outrage at her parenting, sneering at her appearance and denigrating every attempt at friendship.

Ivan shrugs off all this as Nora's harmless possessiveness, a mother naturally wanting high standards of care for her son and grandchild. But however much he normalises Nora's behaviour, it's clear that she is jealous of anyone close to Dad and relentlessly, spitefully alienates them. Ivan is either too self-centred to see it or too lazy to do anything about it and sometimes actively plays up to it. When he gets sick with the flu, Mum walks in to find Nora spooning soup into his mouth, cooing and caressing while he smacks his lips and nuzzles like a baby. It's a bizarre and unsettling scene and Mum takes it as an indication that their relationship is far from normal.

Still, Yasuko dutifully accepts that as Ivan's wife she must try her best with his mother and makes every effort to please her, including visiting Hungary so Nora can spend the summer in the company of her grandchild. It's just me and Mum, because Ivan as a refugee feels unable to return himself and I'm impressed by Mum's spirit – a young woman far from home, driving across a continent to an unfamiliar country with her toddler in tow. And she loves Hungary – the culture, the architecture, the music and the people. Everyone in the local Balaton village knows about Nora's malignant personality, so they are sympathetic and hospitable to Yasuko. She is warmly welcomed into their company, which of course infuriates Nora even more.

Nora continues to bully Mum, but underestimates her resilience. Yasuko has had plenty of experience hiding her true feelings under a dutiful veneer and she isn't about to be crushed by Nora's passive-aggressive mind games. For her, the positives far outweigh the negatives: she has a family, chosen for herself rather than imposed by arrangement and a glamorous career she's only recently discovered she even wanted. Living in London, with a wide circle of cosmopolitan friends, she is regularly travelling and working in Europe. Life is full of excitement and adventure. The only insurmountable problem is Ivan.

Though they are very much in love, at least they were at the beginning, he never stops womanising. By 1970, when I am three, Ivan travels to Mexico to report on the World Cup and is gone for months. Any money he has earned when he finally returns has been blown on whatever woman he's been shacked up with. Mum is familiar with the pattern and has grown tired of wasting her energy on berating and cajoling, in the hopes that he might change. She has embarked on an affair of her own and is biding her time, preparing for an exit.

––––––––––

Dad always claimed that Mum's career was as much to blame for their split as his cheating (which he never denied) and implied that her arty acting crowd made him feel unwelcome. But Mum is adamant that far from being resentful of her career, Ivan was delighted by how well paid her work was, which suited him because he never managed to hold down a regular job himself. Moreover, Yasuko being away days or weeks at a time for filming allowed him the freedom to get up to all sorts of mischief.

Still, I have a fifteen-page letter, addressed to Tamiko but never sent, in which Ivan appeals to his mother-in-law to intervene and save their marriage. The typed sheets read like a diary, documenting their sad, end-of-relationship conversations and his desolation at losing her: 'I am dead inside. I have smoked 200 cigarettes in the last two days and slept virtually nothing in the last two weeks. I am not saying this for sympathy, just to explain why perhaps I am now willing to acquiesce to anything. You see, for me it was my destiny, that I marry Yasuko and that I keep beside her, whatever happens. The better things in life always come very hard and perhaps two people can only really love and appreciate each other if their love is purified in the blaze of selfishness and wantonness.'

Yet there is barely any acknowledgement of the humiliation and upset visited on Yasuko by his relentless infidelity and no promise to change. In fact everything is framed as though Dad is fighting to save his family from the temptations of her career and her lover. Even his description of Nora – 'Yasuko dislikes my mother, who spoils Miki and is always looking for sympathy and is full of old-girlish self-pity' – excuses Granny's behaviour as trivial and casts Yasuko as the aggressor – a view that literally no one else supports.

By my parents' account, I am a happy little kid, but even I know something is up. My earliest memory is sitting between them on their bed – Dad lying on his side, making smiley faces at me but blinking away tears; Mum, impassive and angry. Then as a toddler in our garden, running back and forth between them and stumbling on my fat little legs, laughing and shrieking but worried that either one might vanish while my back is turned. Dad's letter describes a visit to the zoo: 'Miki can feel that not everything is alright between us and keeps asking, "What is wrong with you two these days?" She is a very sensitive and perceptive child.' And there's the time I lie on the floor reading aloud to Mum and, sensing her distraction, say, 'You're always so sad. Is it because of Daddy?', to which she pauses and then says: 'Yes.' Which, according to Yasuko, is the moment she makes up her mind to leave.

5

NORA

Mum has left Dad for a photographer she met on a magazine shoot, who in turn has split up his own family to be with her. While I happily play with his two children, I dislike Michael intensely and am delighted when the relationship ends. But I am generally hostile to all my parents' lovers. In my mind, the pecking order for Mum and Dad's attention should be each other, then me, then last of all whoever this new stranger is. With Dad, this isn't a problem – he rarely commits to any of his girlfriends so they aren't a threat; but Mum, more conventionally, centres the men in her life, which means I am expected to do likewise. I treat them like interlopers, with suspicion and resentment, even into adulthood.

My time is split between Mum and Dad, depending on their work schedules. In some ways, it doesn't feel so different; I am used to both of them being away for long periods – Mum for acting gigs, Dad on his press jaunts – and am enjoying the daytime distraction of starting primary school, at New End in Hampstead, happy to move on from the nursery in Willesden where the enforced afternoon naps still evoke a stress memory. While Mum is juggling work and parenting on her own, Dad relies on a fleet of ex-girlfriends and friends' wives to help out when it is his turn to have me. When their goodwill runs dry, he solves the problem by permanently relocating Nora from Hungary to Willesden. This must have seemed like a splendid idea at the time – Nora has no other family and is always griping that she doesn't see enough of her son and granddaughter. She can provide free and reliable childcare, filling her days with the maternal joys of cooking, cleaning and doting on her progeny, allowing Dad to work and live as he pleases. There are, unfortunately, some snags to this apparent win–win situation. Firstly, Nora has none of the trappings of the houseproud matriarch. For half her life she was serviced by domestic staff and she regards menial tasks as below her status. Ivan's childcare, too, was carried out by a nanny, so she has little idea of the practicalities. And, even if she had the will to be an efficient housekeeper, she is by now in her seventies, overweight and unfit and incapable of keeping a four-bedroom home in habitable order.

Another downside is her inability/refusal to learn English, which makes it hard for her to form new relationships and increases her social isolation. Worse, she is also an irredeemable racist. Having come from an exclusively white, European environment where, in her opinion, much of the less desirable indigenous population had been conveniently murdered or dispersed by Hungary's collaboration with the Nazis, she finds north-west London a horrifying dystopia of jumbled-up ethnicities. She hisses her disgust at shopkeepers, passers-by, my schoolfriends – anyone, in fact, who doesn't appear to originate from a country on her approved list. I sometimes raise the point that her characterisation of the Japanese as 'bow-legged mongrels' must include me, but her answer is a clipped and dismissive 'that's different'.

But by far the biggest problem is a bitter, angry self-pity that threatens to overwhelm her at every moment. The slightest thing can set her off and, once triggered, there is no stopping her. She takes offence where there is none to be taken, responding to perceived slights with unbridled malice, brooding obsessively on grudges and poisoning the atmosphere. While Dad chooses to downplay these shortcomings, dismissing them as 'harmless', our friends, neighbours and visitors are either appalled or feel pity, excusing her behaviour as a symptom of her isolation and the difficult times she has lived through. But these adults have the luxury of being able to walk away. With Mum moved out and Dad now freed from the responsibility of having to care for me in her absence, I have little choice but to be in Granny's company. When the storm clouds come, there is nowhere for me to shelter.

———

Granny and I occupy what used to be my parents' bedroom, while Dad has moved himself downstairs to sleep in what was once the front parlour. Without Mum's acting and modelling money and the financial support of her parents, Ivan needs extra cash to pay the mortgage and the bills, so the remaining three bedrooms are populated by lodgers. He's held onto his upstairs study, though, not least because he's had to step up his workload. He frequently overpromises and is eternally behind on deadlines, hammering away on his typewriter through the night.

Granny takes every opportunity to put the blame for our financially constrained circumstances on my mother's dissolute behaviour. She refers to her as '*a Japán kurva*' ('the Japanese whore') and relishes recounting evermore sensational and melo-dramatic accounts of her ill treatment of me: how she once heartlessly threw me down the stairs as a baby, frustrated by my pitiful crying, loudly proclaiming that she hoped I would die; how she would sadistically jab me with nappy pins, resentful of my curbs on her freedom, while Nora begged her to hand me over so she could soothe the convulsing, distressed infant; how her neglect led me to develop bronchitis (cue vivid impersona-tions of my raspy breathing) and if it wasn't for Nora – my dear and loving grandmother – calling the ambulance while Mum was out gallivanting, I would have surely perished. There's no mention of where Dad was during these episodes when Mum was apparently trying to murder me, but even as a five-year-old, I know it's all bollocks. Any doubts I express of Nora's version of events are dismissed – I am too young to remember. But hearing Mum being trashed upsets me and I am traumatised by the violent images she plants in my imagination. When I beg her to stop, she snaps into cold admonishment, outraged by my betrayal. She is only telling me the truth to protect me from my mother's evil influence, but my response shows that I am unde-serving of Granny's bountiful, selfless love.

When faced with any hint of pushback, Nora resorts to invok-ing the Almighty. Clasping her hands in prayer and staring skyward, she implores Christ to observe and punish the terri-ble injustices committed against her: 'You see, Jesus? You see? Witness the ungrateful child's cruelty towards her poor defence-less grandmother.' Then to me, relaying the judgement from the Lord's side of the discussion: 'He will throw you into the fires of hell. It could happen any time. There is nothing I can do to rescue you.' I try to defy Nora, but it's hard when she has a deity batting for her side and, even though her version of the Messiah doesn't quite chime with the benevolent figure I've learned about in parables and carols, I am still some years from being able to hold my own in a theological debate. When I burst into Dad's study, pleading for him to intervene, he sighs with disappointment. She is a doting old woman who deserves a break. Yes, she can be hard work at times, but she completely adores me and spoils me rotten and I should be more tolerant.

It's difficult to refute this. Granny is ever-attentive, always ready to cook on demand, never too busy to cosset and fuss. We bake *pogácsa* pastries together and she patiently allows me to take over the fun elements, punching out the shapes with a shot glass and decorating the tops in a criss-cross pattern. She gives me pocket money from her pension to buy armfuls of comics from the newsagent, which I read in front of the telly while being serviced with an endless supply of fizzy drinks, enormous Galaxy chocolate bars broken into individual cubes and, rather oddly, chopped-up rashers of raw bacon. We play marathon sessions of card games – rummy, canasta, complicated versions of whist – which she indulgently allows me to win. When she performs dramatic, flourishing pieces on the piano and teaches me to play the scales with the proper fingering, I test her perfect pitch by hitting random keys and delight in her talent at identifying them correctly. She sews eiderdowns and pillows for my dolls, so they can sleep snug in the cardboard beds she has covered in soft fabrics and decorated with colourful buttons. And she marvels at every drawing and piece of writing I produce, every crappy plasticine model and *Blue Peter*-inspired craft project, cooing encouragement and lovingly storing my works for safekeeping.

But she suffocates me with her demand for constant, reciprocal affection and becomes vindictive if I fall short of unquestioning loyalty. She is jealously possessive of me and drives away anyone I show friendliness towards with hostile stares and grimly muttered curses. Only Dad is allowed into the fold. Otherwise, she wants me to herself, cut off from everyone else – 'You can't trust anyone, friends always betray you in the end. I am the only person who really loves you.' When visitors call round, she tells me they speak behind my back, that they say I am a terrible child and horrible to my poor, loving grandmother. So I feel ashamed and judged when they attempt to engage me in conversation. Even when we're alone, she constantly tests my devotion. Every mundane interaction requires me to bow low and kiss her hand, in recognition of her ladylike status and she'll suddenly grow cold if I fail to use the appropriately respectful form of address. As we walk to the shops, she withdraws her promise of treats, outraged that I have failed to observe the correct etiquette by walking on the road side, ready to chivalrously take the impact if a car goes out of control. In order to make up for these insolent missteps, I have to prostrate myself at her feet and beg forgiveness – literally.

I'm beginning to suspect that any love Nora seems capable of administering has to be earned through grovelling 'respect', unquestioning submission and constant affirmations of her unassailable virtues. But I am still too small and young to defend myself against her manipulations and come out worse if the situation escalates to physical confrontations, when she digs her nails into my flesh and claws the skin from the backs of my hands. I swallow down my rage, hoping my resentment can be soothed with another round of cards or some more chocolate treats if I play along with her wishes.

At bedtime, she fusses and fiddles at me. Granny imposes her own unusual hygiene standards, ignoring my feet, black from playing barefoot in the garden, and my teeth, coated from an all-day assault of sugar. Instead, she makes me lie still and naked so she can 'clean' me, paying meticulous and prolonged attention to my nether regions. Tucked up in our shared bed, she reads me Hungarian fairy tales from elaborate picture books, but tends to fall asleep mid-sentence, the book flopping on the cowpat spread of her breasts. Sometimes I stare at the toothless cavity of her mouth, fallen open as she snores, and want to stick my fist inside until she chokes.

6

AN ATHLETIC FELLOW

Mum moves into a two-bed flat in Little Venice, in a mansion block bordering a tree-lined stretch of the Regent's Canal. Her newly furnished apartment on Maida Avenue is bright, clean and welcoming and Yasuko is sociable with the other parents at school, so I get invited for playdates and birthday parties and have friends over to play in the open, uncluttered rooms and neat, communal garden. I spend most of the week in Willesden nevertheless and, though I miss being away from Mum, it's exciting to see her modelling in magazines and appearing on TV.

Looking back, Yasuko maintains she never took her career particularly seriously – it was fun and paid well, but she was only ever offered minor parts as au pairs (*Bless This House*) and housemaids (*The Protectors*, *It Ain't Half Hot Mum*). She enjoyed the kudos of landing a part in the RSC production of *Jingo*, performing alongside Anna Massey and Michael Williams as a twelve-year-old war orphan in Singapore (yet another stereotyped casting for a petite Japanese woman), but her biggest role came in *Decameron '73*, an *Oh! Calcutta!*-style 'erotic' rock musical directed by Peter Coe at the Roundhouse. I recall sitting in the darkened theatre, watching Mum as she walked across the stage, had her floor length robe ceremoniously removed and then gracefully wrapped her limbs around an actor, the two of them posed in naked, gymnastic glory. Mum is adamant that I never attended a performance, but the startling image of my mother cavorting before an audience in the altogether is seared into my mind's eye and I vividly recall the girl sitting next to me, whose mother was also in the cast, responding to my wide-eyed shock with amused sophistication.

The play attracts the attention of Victor Lownes, a charming roué who runs the Playboy enterprise with Hugh Hefner. No doubt impressed by Yasuko's acting, rather than the 360-degree eyeful he's just enjoyed, he drops by her dressing room to introduce himself. They date for a while, casually, and Yasuko brings me along to stay at his Georgian pile in Hertfordshire, Stocks House, a vast 42-room mansion with a disco and a swimming pool that houses a training camp for Playboy bunnies and is the site of ribald and extravagant celebrity parties.

Yasuko is busy and independent, making friends and travelling, wooed by interesting, cultured men. I note that while Ivan's infidelity was an eternal source of outrage during their marriage, Yasuko seems warmly tolerant of such behaviour from the men she is now dating. I imagine that their wealth and status outweigh such indiscretions. But she is in her twenties, enjoying her life, and it's exciting to be invited along for the ride.

I am six now and my parents have been separated for more than two years, but I continue to harbour fantasies that they might eventually reunite, despite the parade of boyfriends who waft through Mum's flat. But none of these nameless, fleeting men threaten to become a permanent fixture, so I tolerate their presence, content to conduct relations on the mutual acknowledgement that our lives and interests only converge on a shared appreciation of my charming and beautiful mother.

At some point, however, the liberated '70s frolicking loses its sheen. Though Mum continues to make good money from acting and modelling, the advent of her thirtieth birthday brings worries about our long-term future and she seeks reassurance by consulting a psychic, based in Sloane Square, whose illustrious client list includes Peter Sellers. The session reveals that she will eventually marry 'an athletic fellow' and live in Los Angeles, 'surrounded by thousands of photographs'. The fortune teller's insights into little Miki's destiny are limited to a recommendation that I have my tonsils removed. Personally, I am sceptical of the supernatural and am willing to bet that any direct hits were lucky guesses among the numerous false possibles that were likely offered in the two-hour session, but Mum immediately books me in for a consultation at Paddington Green Children's Hospital, where I am shortly afterwards admitted to undergo surgery and resolves to welcome her fate with open arms, confident of any choices she makes that chime with the prophecy. The 'athletic fellow' turns out to be stuntman-turned-director Ray Austin, who she had first met in 1971 while filming two episodes of *Shirley's World*, a comedy series starring Shirley MacLaine as a globe-trotting photojournalist. Whatever interest had been sparked during their initial brief encounter now develops into a full-blown relationship and Ray quickly becomes a regular fixture in our lives.

At the start, I am as charmed as Yasuko. Ray is energetic and entertaining, forever cracking jokes, playing pranks and performing impersonations of comedy heroes and film stars. He treats me to exciting, child-friendly excursions: once to the home of the Chipperfield family, the circus-owning dynasty, where I get to play with a chimpanzee; another time to the set of *Space: 1999*, which he is currently filming, where I run around the vast soundstage and play in the moondust. I am thrilled that he's directed episodes of *The Adventures of Black Beauty* and brandish signed photos of Judi Bowker and Stacy Dorning at school; and I sit entranced as he re-enacts the kung fu moves he'd taught Diana Rigg while working as stunt coordinator on *The Avengers*. His two daughters – Araminta (Min), who is almost exactly the same age as me and her little sister, Johanna (Jo) – often come and stay at the flat and I revel in having them as playmates for entire weekends, sharing splashy baths and pre-bedtime pyjama romps.

But the speed with which Ray has muscled into every corner of our daily lives is unsettling. Mum's attention and affection now revolve around him and I feel pressured to be similarly deferential. I bristle when he rearranges the flat to his own tastes, chucking out the comfy corduroy scoop chairs and installing his own fussy antique furniture, repainting the fresh, white walls with dark reds and sombre greens. And he seems needlessly picky about my table manners and scattered toys, insisting on setting me an earlier bedtime and gently scolding Mum if she indulges my delay tactics.

Still, Ray is demonstrably making an effort to create a stable, family environment. Whatever my misgivings, his feet are firmly under the table – his table, actually. So I grudgingly accept that my parents' split is irreversible and shelve any fantasies of their romantic reunion.

––––––––––

Back in Willesden, Dad is usually barricaded in his study, hammering away two-fingered on an electric typewriter in an impenetrable fog of tobacco smoke. Occasionally, a lung-busting bellow summons Granny to serve him with coffee and morsels of salami and smoked cheese. I am always half listening for a pause in the typing and the creak of his office chair, anything that might signal that he's ready for a break and I can be in his company, nestled on the sofa in front of the TV to enjoy a major sporting event, American cop show or blockbuster movie.

These evenings around the telly represent Staverton Road at its most content. Dad chain-smokes and cuts clippings from a daily delivery of publications from all over the world. He has expanded his usual freelance work – writing about athletics and boxing – to capitalise on his ability to speak several languages and recycles the magazines' contents for articles on shipping, computers, cars, whatever – subjects on which he has barely a layman's grasp. Every available inch of floorspace is used as an elaborate filing system for his paperwork. Clippings are cut and collated, stapled to other sheets of paper and spread around the house, spilling from his study across the landing, balanced on every step of the staircase, then snaking along the corridor and finally exploding into full crazy-paving chaos over the living-room floor.

Dad has a very selective view of mess. Blind to the riot of paper that surrounds us, along with the overflowing ashtray, crumbs from his snacking and proliferation of drained, stained coffee cups piling up around him, the wet ring mark from my Coke bottle on the scarred wooden coffee table elicits a yelp of disapproval. As does my wiping sticky fingers on the balding leatherette sofa. I might find such criticism more acceptable if the rest of the house didn't look like it had been ransacked by rioters and his own manners weren't so questionable. Instead I laugh out loud at the hypocrisy, which Dad gamely accepts by letting loose a window-rattling burp.

The many half-typed sheets of Dad's journalism are repurposed, either as a home-made supply of snot-rags for him to loudly blow his nose into and then crumple into a black bin bag at his feet or for me to use for drawing projects that consist of: endless re-imaginings of an idealised family comprising Daddy, Mummy, me and two imaginary siblings (no Granny); dolls'-house cross-sections of a meticulously decorated family home; gymnastic routines rendered frame by frame; and impossibly pinch-waisted, long-legged, wavy-haired princesses. Art is my wish-fulfilment therapy and I am emotionally attached to stationery: there is a drawer upstairs I call Pen Heaven, full of used-up felt-tips that I feel too guilty to throw away. I arrange my favourite colours together so they can make friends.

Granny, meanwhile, works her way through a bottle of Warninks advocaat, nodding off in her wingback armchair and occasionally startled awake by Dad letting rip a deafeningly loud and gleefully executed fart, to which she responds with sniffy disgust – a reaction that merely increases Dad's delight and sends him into wheezing hysterics culminating in a heavy smoker's coughing fit. Among the many downsides of rousing Granny from slumber is that she will suddenly notice if we happen to be watching anything that references the Second World War (almost unavoidable in British 1970s TV programming), prompting her to spend the rest of the evening heckling the telly with brooding snarls of 'Lies . . . stinking, rotten lies!' When her comments threaten to drown out the TV dialogue, Dad shuts her down with a sharp bark. 'Shut the fuck up, you dried-up old cunt' is a commonly uttered phrase in our home and I barely recognise it as bad language. In fact, exposed to Dad's constant and casual use of swearwords and Nora's elaborate and vindictive cursing, I have acquired an impressive range of filthy expressions myself, in both English and Hungarian.

Once the convivial viewing is over, Dad will either return to his study to tackle a long-elapsed deadline or scrub up for a night out on the pull. Wired on my standard evening diet of Coca-Cola and chocolate, I am wide awake and loudly reluctant to be lumbered with only Granny for company. Occasionally, if I play my wheedling cards right, he agrees to take me along. With a celebratory shriek, I am dressed in a party frock and ready to go in minutes, delighted to be included in Dad's nocturnal adventures. We head off in the car to a house party or local nightclub where the host or proprietor is willing to ignore the inappropriate parenting and turns a blind eye to the orange-squash-and-vodka cocktail that Dad deems appropriate sustenance for an eight-year-old. I am thrilled to be out in the grown-up world, chatting excitedly with Dad as we hit the dancefloor, but I know the drill and at some point the primary purpose of our night out – snaring an appropriately attractive woman – must be addressed.

Dad scans the room for a likely specimen and gives me instructions to engage with her – a shy hello from a lost-looking little girl is highly effective bait. Having sent me ahead for first contact, Dad can retrieve his daughter and use the opportunity to chat up the target in earnest. While I'm pleased to have been an accomplice – part of Dad's dynamic duo – it's a self-defeating skill because I am from that moment sidelined. No longer the centre of Dad's attention, I become bored and begin yawning and he has the perfect excuse to usher his catch home, back for drinks chez Berényi, so I can be put to bed.

There are times when Dad's plans backfire on him; times when the women are sweet and maternal and, back in our shabby living room, are happy to look at my drawings and indulge my chatter. Then it is Dad who is sidelined and I get malicious enjoyment from watching his frantic behind-the-back gesticulations for me to fuck off to bed. He can't be too blunt or he'll blow his 'can't say no to my little girl' cover and I milk it for all it's worth – threatening to crack out the Monopoly or inviting them to style my Girls' World doll. Eventually, however, I am forced to leave – scooped up and carried away, sulking at the injustice.

7

THE BEST OF BOTH WORLDS

Ray has moved in and we have to follow his rules. Dad doesn't follow anybody's rules, but Mum is growing increasingly intolerant and critical of his unreliable habits. A major moan is his persistent lateness and last-minute rearrangements of my pickups and drop-offs, both at school and at the flat. And Mum has started to notice signs that I'm picking up bad habits.

When Dad is lounging about at home, he wears the same slouchy clothes for days on end. I am equally indifferent and barely bother to get dressed, running about in vest and knickers and barefoot outdoors. Dad's manners are non-existent when he isn't in social company. He eats with his hands and licks the plate, burping and farting and picking his nose. Granny mutters and tuts at his behaviour, always drinks tea from a cup and saucer and eats meticulously, cutting her food into tiny morsels and dabbing at the corners of her mouth with a handkerchief after every swallow. But I love Dad and I hate Granny, so who am I more likely to copy?

Dad is equally tolerant about me throwing myself around the room, turning cartwheels and using the knackered living-room furniture as a gym prop. I copy Olga Korbut's chin stand, throwing my legs over my head and lowering my feet into my eyeline. Dad thinks this is amazing and insists we should find a coach to make me an Olympic champion (never happens, obviously). When I do the gymnastics in front of Dad's friends, they look at me oddly. They don't see Olga Korbut, they see the lack of clothing. And they seem uncomfortable with my feral behaviour. I overhear a conversation with Dad in the kitchen: 'You're bringing up the child all wrong.'

I am less able than Dad to recognise the boundaries between public and private etiquette. He can scrub up and behave himself when needed, whereas I struggle to maintain the façade when reintroduced to the stricter discipline of Maida Avenue. On one occasion, I calmly tell Ray to fuck off, which sparks a spectacular row as Mum flailingly defends me from his crimson-faced outrage. Embarrassed by the slip of his normally affable demeanour and, in an effort to regain Mum's sympathy, Ray instantly stages a rather unconvincing heart attack, clutching his chest with a frozen grimace and knocking over half the dining-room furniture before eventually falling to the floor in hyperventilating spasms and croakily pleading for one of the tiny tablets of questionable origin that he keeps in an ostentatious antique gold pillbox by their bedside. All is forgiven once Mum has made the requisite tearful fuss, coaxing me to apologise and please, just for once, call him 'Daddy'. I comply, through gritted teeth, to make Mum happy.

There are other, less dramatic examples that something is awry with the parenting in Willesden. During a standard dental check-up, two brown and rotting milk teeth are plucked from my mouth with little difficulty or anaesthetic. Yasuko is baffled and embarrassed, insisting to the disapproving dentist that she makes me brush my teeth without fail, but she has no knowledge of the sugar-saturated diet and lax standards of hygiene I enjoy at Dad's. At a panto matinée of *Gulliver's Travels*, she asks me whether I can read and understand the words in the scrolling narrative projected on the stage backdrop and is horrified at my response: 'What words?' A visit to the optician reveals that I am chronically short-sighted, a condition no doubt exacerbated by my habit of sitting inches close to our Staverton Road TV – so close that I can make out individual pixels – in my efforts to block out Nora's interfering presence.

On previous occasions, when I have divulged details of what constitutes normal behaviour in Willesden, Mum is understandably outraged and tasks me with the responsibility of universally practising the regime and discipline of Maida Avenue – which is precisely the opposite response I am after. So I now keep any pertinent explanations a secret from her, playing innocent on the bad language (picked up at school, don't even know what it means) and shrugging off the health issues as inexplicable and probably inherited. I don't want to give her any excuse to cut my time with Dad. The tonsillectomy, however, brings everything to a head.

───────

The operation itself is fine. Mum and Ray visit and, even though I wish I could see her on my own, Ray entertains the entire ward with Norman Wisdom-style comic stunts and impersonations of Eric Morecambe, which are genuinely funny and make me popular, by association, with the nurses and other children.

Dad is not around, sadly – off on some foreign jaunt, I think – but Granny's visits are mercifully short, restricted to hospital visiting hours.

Post op, Dad's latest girlfriend picks me up and drops me home to Willesden with aftercare instructions from the hospital, which I dutifully translate into Hungarian for Granny. My throat is raw and painful and I want nothing more than to lie in bed and read in peace. But Granny, who has been starved of company for several days, is determined to air the maelstrom of disturbing paranoid fantasies that have been trapped and swirling in her crazy, deluded head. She runs her familiar gamut of fuming about the low-class neighbours (distracted nods from me) and the sinister black men who follow her in the street (mm-hmm), then veers into the past – saintly Nora, wooed by suitors, betrayed by jealous friends (sure, whatever). I am nodding off by now, which is not at all the fulfilment that Granny craves, so she ups the ante – the Japanese Whore, Jesus is Watching, the whole nine yards. This provokes the desired attention and I am fully awake, screaming at the top of my lungs to drown out her incessant, repetitive incantations. There is a sudden rush of pain and vomit gushes from my mouth. At least the shock of this silences Nora, but I am not finished. Dashing to the toilet, I start spewing blood – thick, dark brown clots in the red stream.

Back in hospital, I am now on another ward. My second internment is less pleasant and I am tethered to a drip and frequently examined. To facilitate these regular checks, I am naked under a flimsy paper gown, which makes me feel vulnerable and embarrassed. And there are daily injections when I am made to lie prone with my bottom exposed while a nurse administers the shot. This, however, evokes disturbing echoes of Granny's bed and I wriggle and cringe, ignoring the nurse's frustrated instructions to relax and keep still, however much she warns that, if I keep moving and don't unclench my muscles, the needle will snap off inside me. In the end, it takes four of them to hold me down, while I thrash and resist, panicked into rage and calling them every fucking cunting swearword under the sun. Their shock is palpable. I am a pariah, a bad seed, an abhorrence. Meanwhile, no one has seen fit to inform Mum that I am back in hospital, so my only visitor is Granny, whose presence makes me glower with hate. This only confirms everyone's conviction that I am a terrible child and Granny is treated with commiserating sympathy, which she laps up with hammy, whimpering thanks, smiling triumphantly when their backs are turned.

If I'd had the confidence to express myself properly, I would have simply asked to have the injections in my arm. I have no problem with the drip that is threaded into my vein – can't they see that? But I have burned my bridges with my appalling behaviour and am too ashamed to try to break through the staff's brisk dealings with me, noting the secret exchange of looks that pass between them. Better to be silent and impassive, clenching my fist so the needle of my drip shoots a distracting jab of pain into my hand.

When Yasuko turns up to collect me from school, my teacher informs her that I've been readmitted to hospital – 'Didn't you know?' Furious at the humiliation and appalled at Ivan's failure to ensure my welfare while he is off indulging his own selfish needs, Mum is now openly and angrily critical of Dad's failures

47

as a parent and grows tight-lipped at any mention of him. Dad, meanwhile, has become fully aware of Ray's influence over Mum since he inserted himself into the fray to give Ivan a piece of Yasuko's mind. Ivan refers to him as 'The Ray', uttering frequent withering references to his working-class origins and tattoos, while declaring my mother a weak-minded fool and making crude, sexual assumptions about Ray's hold over her.

I refuse to legitimise the vilification of either parent, leaping separately to their defence, which leads each one to believe that I have taken sides against them – Yasuko with a piqued frown, Ivan with a disappointed sigh. In an effort to shield them from criticism, I speak about them both only in glowing terms and focus all my complaints on the secondary players – Nora and Ray. But, while Mum enjoys chiming in with her own experiences when I slag off Granny, accounts of her lunacy fail to raise much concern and are simply mined for comic potential. Ray coins the moniker 'Noracula', which playfully references her Transylvanian birthplace but falls some way short of capturing the full extent of Granny's monstrous nature. I stop mentioning her since it just gives Mum and Ray fuel to bond over a common disdain for Dad's circumstances. Any issues I have with Ray are brushed off by Mum via scoffing comparisons with Dad's failings. Admittedly, he is hardly on a par with Nora, although I find his let-it-all-hang-out embrace of nudism disquieting when faced with him strolling about the flat, dangly bits level with my eyeline. And the comedy antics and Tommy Cooper impersonations have also begun to grate. I sense the edge of competitiveness at the core of this entertaining horseplay – Ray needs to be centre stage, hogging the limelight and the lion's share of Mum's attention, of which I am getting less and less. They are so wrapped up in each other and their work and friends and lifestyle – correction, *his* work and *his* friends and *his* lifestyle – that I feel left out in the cold. Requests for some unadulterated me-time – 'Will it be just us or is Ray coming?' – are received by Mum with exasperated complaints about the demands on her attention and rhetorical 'Don't you want me to be happy?' pleas.

I concede defeat and focus on the positives. Two homes mean two birthdays and two Christmases. After all, I still get Mum to myself at bedtimes – for cosy chats when she tucks me up – and the respite from Nora is a relief. Sure, I have to abide by Ray's boundaries, but at Dad's there are no boundaries at all. In Willesden, I can do what I like – stay up late, watch TV, eat as many sweets as I want and run about half-undressed, throwing myself around the furniture in gymnastic abandon. Making the switch from one to the other can be challenging, but I decide I am lucky to have such contrasting experiences and cherry-pick the best of both worlds.

Mum lands a regular part in *Space: 1999*, but this presents an unforeseen risk since many of the crew are fully aware of Ray's chequered past. On one occasion, a guest star on the series draws Yasuko aside and comments: 'I hear you are dating Ray Austin. You're a *very* brave woman.' It transpires that Ray's idealised family-man image belies a trail of wrecked marriages and five (*five!*) abandoned offspring.* Far from heeding the klaxon warning of a potential character flaw, Mum remains buoyant and forgiving, accepting Ray's explanations that the

---

* Six, actually. Decades later, another is discovered, the result of an affair conducted shortly before Mum.

serial abandonment of his progeny is the fault of mad, bad and ill-suited ex-wives. So what if he has a reputation as a woman-iser? Everyone deserves a second (or even fifth or sixth) chance. She indulgently flips the negatives to positives, arranging social meet-and-greets with the various exes, extending invitations to the kids and sending birthday, Christmas and wedding gifts. Before this outreach programme has the chance to collapse from his indifference, or his children get to tell their side of the story, Ray proposes marriage.

With Yasuko fully on board, Ray is given free rein to take over our future as well as our present. He makes barbed half-jokes about the Maida Avenue flat's perceived shortcomings and wistfully pontificates on the idylls of a joint move to the coun-tryside. Apparently the 45-minute commute to film *Space: 1999* is absolutely killing him. Such a shame we don't live closer to Pinewood, outside London.

Mum, however, is fondly attached to her home and has no interest in timber-framed cottages and pony paddocks. A compromise is hit upon following a dinner party at the charming mews house of Keith Wilson, production designer on *Space: 1999* and several other Gerry Anderson projects, who lives with his partner Ian on a quaint Georgian terrace near Windsor Great Park. Mum puts down a deposit on 15 Adelaide Square, once again aided by the Nagazumi coffers.

I am swept along with their plans, seduced by visits to Windsor Castle and the safari park and enticed by the prospect of being able to walk to school and have local schoolfriends and playmates living close by. Dad, though no fan of Ray, perceives he has little say in the matter, given that he pays Yasuko no alimony or child support and she has made no claim on the Staverton Road house, despite being fully entitled to half its value. The deal is agreed and my time is parcelled off: weekdays in Windsor, for school; week-ends and holidays in Willesden. Thus, we swim in the current of Ray's plans. The genius is that he somehow convinced everyone it was as much our idea as his.

8

DEMONS

For all the parties and gatherings I've heard about when Dad and Mum were together, we rarely host company in Willesden these days. The house is sliding into grimy decline, Nora is too mad and I am annoyingly intrusive when grown-ups come to visit Dad. He therefore enjoys most of his social life outside our home and abandons my demands on his company if a better offer arises. After all, the whole point of having Nora around is so he can come and go as he pleases.

When his friends turn up, jolly and conversational, in anticipation of a night out on the tiles, my mood is unpredictable and often unstable: hyperactive and loud, milking attention while I have it; whiny and clingy, wanting to delay their departure; or silent and scowling at the prospect of being left behind with Nora. Dad faffs about as he always does (he never has any qualms about leaving people waiting for him), off to make a last-minute phonecall or search for his keys or demand a quick snack from Nora. Left in my company, these men fidget and pace, alert to the sound of Dad's movements and an imminent escape.

The one exception is Sam. A short, stocky man with bryl-creemed black hair, Sam always welcomes me with a beaming smile, engaging in conversation and giving me his full atten-tion. He is similarly charming and attentive to Nora, enquiring into her welfare and complimenting her on her youthful vigour, which makes her simper and smile to his face, despite making anti-Semitic comments behind his back. And Sam doesn't mind being left alone with me. He'll sit on the sofa and smile and chat and when Dad reappears – 'Come on, let's go!' – he doesn't instantly switch his attention away but says something nice: 'Sorry I have to drag your Daddy away. Hope the sports day goes well. Can I have one of your lovely drawings to take home?' And offers a proper goodbye: 'Give your Uncle Sam a kiss.'

On one occasion, when we are alone together, he crouches down to my level and suggests we play a game. My mind spins with the possibilities: a marathon session of estimation whist? The new Downfall game I got for Christmas? Or we could just watch TV together and I could show him my favourite comics. Instead, he slides his hand down the back of my knickers and strokes my bottom. Then suddenly Dad is calling and he is up and away, waving cheerily and out the door. And I am left on my own wondering what just happened.

———

Sam turns up one evening bearing a huge doll and a faceful of smiles. He seems surprised that Dad is out, but graciously accepts Granny's offer of coffee. As she potters around in the kitchen, I fuss over his present and chatter excitedly. I haven't forgot-ten his previous offer to play games and am ready to set up the

Scrabble board. Sam, however, wants to play 'postman's knock', which I have never heard of but apparently it involves kissing. I sit astride his lap, like I do with Dad and plant little kisses on his face. But instead of pointing at his eyes or nose or chin, like Dad does, he slides his fingers into my knickers. I feel shocked and a little scared, but I am flattered that he is giving me his undivided attention and shows no signs of wanting to leave. So when the door creaks ajar, signalling Granny's approach with the coffee, I scream at her to fuck off and she retreats.

Sam is a regular visitor at our home for a period, so there may have been other similar incidents, but I don't recollect. Maybe there weren't – perhaps the experience was less satisfying than he'd hoped; or maybe it was me that stopped playing along, savvy that he couldn't be trusted to keep his side of the bargain and let me have my turn at picking a more conventional game for us to play. What I do recall is answering the front door one day, aged around twelve or so, to find Sam, grinning from ear to ear – 'Hel-lo Miki, it's your Uncle Sam!' – and being hit with a gut-punch memory of his face up close to mine, rolling his fingers around his leering, wet mouth to make them slippy, while sing-songing 'knock-knock, who's there, postman, postman's knock'.

Many years later, during a late-night confessional with a friend, I said that I'd slammed the door in his face, that I'd told Dad what he'd done to me, that he went after Sam and beat him to a pulp and that we never saw the bastard again. But that's not actually true. In fact, I just looked away, embarrassed and ashamed and mumbled, 'I'll get Dad.' Then Dad came to the door and they went off to wherever the fuck it was they were going.

I've been somewhat selective in describing what went on with Nora. It's been easier to discuss the occasions when I merely allowed things to happen; harder to stomach the flash memories where I was an active participant, when I stood on our shared bed and glued my open mouth to hers, mimicking the French kisses and caresses from movie love scenes while she giggled coquettishly. There are other, more graphic examples of what went on between us, but I can't bring myself to share the visceral descriptions. Suffice to say that Granny was always up for re-enactments of anything I'd witnessed on screen or picked up from Dad's inappropriate anecdotes. And, unless you are turned on by that kind of thing, the detailed account of a small child doing what I did really isn't an image you want to dwell on.

It's also difficult to construct a coherent narrative from snapshot memories. I end up filling in the gaps, trying to make sense of the timeline. Nora's overattentive 'lie still, I'm cleaning you' sessions were certainly the starting point. But whether the episodes with Sam emboldened me to experiment more with Nora or whether Nora alone groomed me and Sam was merely lucky to have stumbled across a willing participant, I'll never know. But the normalisation of intimate sexual activity means I fail to recognise the boundaries of acceptable behaviour and I occasionally jump on male visitors to the house, kissing them on the mouth and guiding their hands on me, believing that this is what they want, that this will make them like me. If they are shocked, they don't show it. Most are tolerant but gently, firmly dissuasive; some not. I have a vivid recollection of a man distractedly stroking my skin while we watch *The Yearling* on TV. Gregory Peck – I love Gregory Peck, who looks a bit like Dad – is playing the loving father of a boy who befriends a deer. It's a classic weepie.

When the film is over, the man offers me a biology lesson, peeling back his wrinkled foreskin to reveal the round, pink surprise of the glans and making visible the fragile testes nestling within his scrotum. Later, I find his pony-tail holder on the table, fine blond hairs trapped in the elastic and use it to tie up my own hair.

The bath in Willesden is enormous and I often jump in with Dad, to splash and chat. When I gigglingly enquire about the hidden surprises in his own genitals, his face darkens with concern and, after a pause, he jumps from the water and quietly suggests that it is probably no longer appropriate for us to share baths together. This saddens me and I realise I must have done something wrong. I'm just not sure what.

Child sexual abuse is more widely discussed these days, but for much of my life I thought victims could only be children who were cornered by threats or snatched by strangers. So I have struggled to accept – to *believe* – that I was a victim, because I feel like I acted as the instigator. Of course, when I see other children, including my own, at the age I was when all this took place, I recognise that this is a shockingly twisted way to frame it. But it's really, really hard to shake that feeling of complicity.

And it took me a very long time to learn that sex is not something that you offer up to people as a way to appease them or make them like you or stop them from being nasty to you. That you can stop when you want to stop and that your own feelings of discomfort or objection are not signs of inadequacy, but are valid personal boundaries that should be heeded. I was angry for a while with my parents, that they hadn't spotted the signs – the obsessive tics, the abnormal shyness, the indications that something was awry. But there were so many things this could be put down to – their divorce, Mum moving away, changing schools – and it was easy for each one to blame the other for whatever weird personality traits I might have shown.

I did tell Mum, decades later, about Granny. She went very quiet, then restated her observations about Nora's twisted nature. It wasn't the cathartic experience I'd hoped for but she is from a different generation and background and I don't blame her for not having the words to explore my predicament. I told Dad, too, long after Nora had died. I tested the waters by first revealing Sam's abuse and he chimed that Sam was a sleazy bastard who, on their nights out, was forever wanting to drag him to strip shows and brothels (Dad always sneered at the idea of paying for sex, which was for losers). While this wasn't quite the outpouring of sympathy I was after, I felt emboldened that he'd believed me and dropped the Nora bombshell. He took it on board and looked at me levelly, saying: 'Please. This is my mother you are talking about.' And I accepted that, understanding how uncomfortable it was for him to hear. At least I'd said it, so he knew not to bang on about Nora like she was some kind of saint.

I probably should have sought professional help at some point to deal with it all, but, when I was recommended psychiatric treatment after a particularly bad self-harming episode, I worried that I might be locked up as a lunatic, so I threw away the paperwork. And I've been put off by my subsequent brushes with therapy. The first guy I saw charged me an eye-watering sum to sit in his enormous house for an hour and tell me that I seemed to be coping fine and lots of people simply 'get over' this kind of thing. I might have trusted his diagnosis more if I hadn't later discovered that he and his wife had an open relationship in which he was very much an unwilling participant, which rather undermined my faith in his ability to confront difficult issues.

As for the block of NHS appointments I got when I had some struggles after the birth of my first baby, I didn't even bring it up. I'm not sure what kind of therapy requires you to stare impassively when a patient compliments you on your new hair colour or says hello when you walk past them in the supermarket car park, but rebuffing my ice-breakers with a look you might normally reserve for someone taking a shit on your shoes didn't engender the atmosphere of trust I was hoping for in order to grapple with the darker reaches of my psyche. So I've reached my own conclusions and handled it as best I can.

Children do crazy things, innocently. A normal adult doesn't exploit that behaviour and might actually speculate where on earth they learned it. I was unlucky enough to meet some very abnormal people in my childhood, one of whom had unfettered access. As an adult, I flared with anger for a while and withdrew from Mum and Dad, blaming them for not protecting me. But they are all the family I had and cutting off from them felt like I was letting my abusers wreak further harm, so I forgave, though I wasn't able to forget.

You can get mired in blame and excuses trying to figure out which bit of your past makes you behave in certain unacceptable and self-defeating ways. These things need to be confronted and explored and I've done that – in conversations, in my diaries and in lyrics. But, at some point, I had to accept the damage and move on. Otherwise, you're just letting the fuckers win.

9

A CHAOTIC JOURNEY

It's summer 1976 and me, Dad and Granny are loading up the car for our annual holiday in Hungary. Much of the boot space is taken up with binbags stuffed with Dad's work-related newspaper clippings, which means the largest suitcases are piled on the back seat next to me. Balanced precariously on top and blocking any view of the rear window, is a large cardboard box with a selection of on-the-road snacks – tubes of Primula squeezy cheese, pungent salamis, jars of pickled cucumbers, loaves of Slimcea bread, apples, boiled eggs and tubs of cottage cheese emptied of their contents, mixed with spring onions and paprika and then repackaged into their containers. This larder of perishables grows warmer and softer as the heatwave sun beats down on the roof of the car and it is my job to construct snacks on demand as we head towards our destination. In the back seat, where the windows don't open, the smell of garlicky meat and decomposing fruit mingles with Dad's chain-smoked Rothmans cigarettes. I have just enough space – and gymnastic flexibility – to manoeuvre into a variety of positions to relieve the pins and needles that plague me throughout the journey.

This is Dad's third Ford Capri of the decade. Its aerodynamic lines draw envious looks from the Trabant- and Lada-driving locals on the dusty roads around our holiday villa in Balatonbog-lár, a small resort town on the southern shore of Lake Balaton. But Dad's complete lack of motor maintenance skills (and refusal to pay for anyone else's) mean that the vehicle's every minor malfunction and cosmetic scrape has deteriorated to its extreme – seats collapse, doors fail to lock, the dashboard's meters and gauges display wildly inaccurate readings and the exhaust farts and belches clouds of filthy smoke. While the men in neighbouring houses spend Sundays on their front patios lovingly attending to their cars with Turtle Wax and Dustbusters, Dad's idea of vehicle care consists of hastily brushing fag-ash and crumbs from the seats, hanging a Feu Orange freshener from the rear-view mirror and tipping the overflowing contents of the ashtray out of the window when a red light offers a convenient pause in the traffic. Whatever sportscar glamour the ailing, neglected Capri once had is erased by packing its confines with a cantankerous old lady, a nine-year-old child and half the portable contents of our home.

Despite the compromised state of our transport, Dad insists that the 1,000-mile drive can easily be accomplished in under two days and pooh-poohs the expense of a hotel in favour of breakneck overnight motoring. If it was just me and Dad in the car – in my imagination, fellow swashbucklers on the open road – this would be a thrilling proposition. However, most of the cramped car's remaining airspace is permeated by the malevolent presence of Granny, who throughout the stifling journey sits grim-faced, buttoned up in a winter coat with a leopardskin-print fez perched on her home-styled bowl cut, muttering sour criticisms of our friends and neighbours and mining her memory for historic grudges to justify her default mood of bitter injustice.

As she sips from a collection of miniature 'medicinal' bottles concealed in the handbag clutched in her lap, her mood grows increasingly belligerent and her complaints become louder and more personal, zoning in on a general critique of Dad's lifestyle ('I thank God that my poor saintly mother isn't alive to see what you have become') and reserving particular venom for his current crop of girlfriends. I wonder in retrospect whether Dad deliberately selected his conquests from a variety of ethnic origins to more easily differentiate between them: the Irish one, the Indian one, the East German one, the Brazilian one. Certainly, this global spread affords Granny plenty of ammunition with which to launch into a stream of racist invective, eventually settling into tirades against her well-worn favourites: Jews and Gypsies.

Dad does his best to raise the mood, drowning her out with a singalong of X-rated renditions of Hungarian ditties ('*Köszönöm hogy ügyvözlettek, nyalyátok ki a seggemet*' – roughly translated: 'Thank you all for your courteous greeting, lick out my arsehole') and his customised version of 'This Old Man' ('With a ding-dong bloody-hell give a dog a bonk'), and we play alphabet list games that, after several rounds of animals, edibles and geographical locations, switch to a more unconventional focus on rude words and insulting phrases in any language. Dad always wins but I pick up some useful rarities – 'quim', in particular, I retain for future Scrabble games.

Such road-trip jollity fails to dissuade Granny from pursuing her downward mood to its bitter conclusion and, realising that her barbs are failing to land with Dad, she sets her sights on me instead and resorts to her usual mantra of loudly castigating my mother with obscene relish. I begin shrieking from the back seat, demanding that she be silenced. Dad's efforts to calm the situation with the kind of reasoning tones you'd attempt on a sulky toddler ('Come on, Nórika, don't be so unkind') rather than an embittered old woman in full schnapps-induced rant merely escalates the barrage of slurs. Aware that he is now having to mediate two increasingly volatile factions, Dad tries to reframe Granny's vile outbursts as playful banter by bursting into donkey-braying laughter while prodding at her, pinching her cheeks and tickling at her ribs. I've seen this work occasionally, where the physical horseplay sends her into giggles, but just as often, like now, she slaps at his hands furiously and begins screaming '*SEGITSÉG! GYILKOSSÁG!*' ('HELP! MURDER!') in an ear-splitting operatic howl. As Granny's screeching grows more frantic, I join in the fray, grabbing for objects to toss at her – empty cigarette cartons, sandwich crusts and apple cores – while Dad snatches away items of clothing – her hat, her scarf – and threatens to throw her possessions out of the window.

None of this preoccupying hysteria encourages Dad to slow down and, distracted from the road ahead, he swerves the car into the path of oncoming traffic, at which point angry car-horn blasts alert us to the near-death scenario, jolting us from the in-car insanity. Dad sighs and expresses his exasperation with some colourful Hungarian, I sulk quietly in the back seat and Granny, exhausted by the exertions, falls into a snoring slumber. We know she's awake again when the muttering resumes.

Much of the drive time is crushingly boring and I occupy myself with books, puzzles and drawing, made-up stories enacted in Fuzzy Felt scenarios and whispered conversations with Sindy dolls. When the reading eventually leads to carsickness and the pens and toys have scattered into unreachable areas of the foot-wells, I mine the vehicle's confines for other ways to pass the time. Creating elaborate drawings with a saliva-tipped finger on my window offers limited distraction since the rear-passenger pane of a Capri is a frustratingly small canvas. However, the detritus from Dad's chain-smoking allows me to strip the foil from inside the empty fag packets, carefully peel away the backing paper and fashion tiny sculptures of gymnasts and ballerinas from the fragile silver sheets. Even the process of eating an apple is elevated to fairy-tale significance in an effort to provide a mental escape – a princess and a prince live at either pole of a tiny planet and each bite represents an encroaching ocean. I walk my fingers around the remaining 'land', chattering their drama until only a slender bridge remains to facilitate their nightly trysts. With one last bite, they are doomed to pine away for lost love.

Night-time drives offer even fewer diversions, though I learn to read fast in the intermittent moments when motorway lamps provide a brief flood of light. I play at guessing the number of kilometres left to reach the turnings for Brussels or Stuttgart or Linz, but the road signs are too infrequent to maintain interest. Mostly, I call on an arsenal of obsessive tics I have developed to occupy the monotonous hours. My go-to time killer involves quietly humming a rise and fall of notes – less of a tune and more of a sentence, where top-note squeaks provide a physical sense of strangulation and I get a pleasurable chest rumble from the low ones. However, Granny is quick to weaponise this against Dad: 'You see? Listen to her. She isn't normal. This is your fault.' So I resort to biting my finger- and toenails down to the quick; experiment with how long I can endure resting the pad of my finger on my eyeball; gently stroke the skin of my inner forearm, which feels so unbearably soft on my fingertips that I mouth-breathe in concentration; and tear strands of hair from my head and roll them into a sausage shape. When a roadside toilet stop affords the opportunity, I surreptitiously set fire to this hairball with Dad's lighter and rub the embers between my fingers because I like the smell. This is long before the invention of personal stereos and smartphones, so I have to make my own fun.

Occasionally, Dad pulls off the autobahn into one or other *en route* city – Bonn, Frankfurt, Munich or Vienna – to replenish our fetid comestibles with a trip to the supermarket. I marvel at the alien snacks and unfamiliar sugary drinks, then bask in the sunshine and sophistication of a street café to gorge on a pastry treat *à la terrasse*. As we cruise through the city, I scour shopping parades for stationers and toy shops, which, when spotted, provoke insistent whining until I am treated to a fresh supply of felt-tip pens, colouring books and dress-up outfits for my dolls. Such perks, however, come with strings attached. Sure, we've avoided the cost of hotels and, with the car's petrol gauge stuck on Empty, have preserved some fuel by spending a disquieting night coasting with the engine off along B-roads in the pitch darkness. But still, a 1,000-mile drive requires funds and, thankfully, we have come prepared. Weeks before setting off on our expedition, Dad went on a spree in Willesden High Road's finest bargain shops, loading up with an eclectic supply of goods. It now falls to me to sell them on the city's streets, with Granny in tow offering prices in German and guarding any earnings by stuffing the cash into the depths of her brassiere.

I should point out here that at nine years old, I am generally cripplingly shy with strangers and not ideally suited to the self-confident banter required for an impromptu market stall. Thus it is that I find myself at a busy intersection, modelling the top half of a ladies' safari suit (I am tall for my age but still, it hangs off me) and waving a set of walkie-talkies in a bid to catch the attention of passers-by. Unbelievably, the shower fittings are a hit, as are the make-up sets and *Top of the Pops* cassettes (I put this down to the sexy girls in hot-pants featured on their covers and the buyers are none the wiser that the compilation tapes consist of cover versions rather than original recordings). But despite my best efforts, we fail to offload the 'I Heart Disco' placemats or the orange melamine boiled-egg cooker (wrong voltage, for fuck's sake). Dad, having circled the city's one-way system several times, eventually scoops up his sales team, ready to continue our journey east.

Just one more diversion. Pulling up at the kerb on a residential side street, he announces that we just so happen to be right outside the apartment block of a 'pussy' from his past. With false promises that it will just be a 'quickie', he hot-tails it into the building, while Granny and I are left pavement-side for several hours with orders to deal with any traffic wardens. I do wish he could have at least found a legal parking spot – it is dispiriting enough to know that our journey will now be at least a day longer due to his shenanigans, but the prospect of an altercation with a figure of authority and the possibility of a fine ramps up my anxiety. When a traffic cop does finally knock on the window, Granny launches into a stream of plaintive German and I am so terrified that we might be arrested that I burst into tears. This turns out to be an effective tactic and the official retreats, clocking from the number plates that we're likely to be moving on and will cease to trouble his beat for much longer.

The break from his imprisoned family has at least put Dad in an upbeat mood. Back on the road, he regales us with a blow-by-blow description of his seduction technique and eventual vigorous coupling, along with observations on the looseness of his conquest's waist (and vagina) in the wake of pushing out the last of her three children and a backstory on the tragic waste of space she married, fortuitously out at work, who is woefully under-equipped to meet her carnal needs. Granny, ever jealous of any female Dad pays the remotest attention to, begins to bawl: 'Open the window! I can smell her cunt on you!' But Dad, drained of seminal fluid, doesn't have the energy to indulge in the usual full-blown cycle of baiting and bickering. Falling asleep at the wheel and woken only by our screams as the car drifts across the lanes toward the autobahn's central reservation, he eventually pulls up on the hard shoulder for a nap. Nora and I sit in silence and darkness while the car rocks in the tailwind of heavy-goods vehicles hurtling past at motorway speed, inches close.

———

Dad has tasked me with smuggling our western currency into Hungary, since I am the least likely to be searched. I play my innocence to maximum effect, clutching a teddy bear and sucking my thumb, but the sizeable roll of notes stuffed into my knickers and Dad's frequent eye signals to keep still and stop squirming, are making me anxious. I experience a *Midnight Express*-style panic attack and vomit a chocolate-and-Fanta cocktail all over the floor. One of the guards takes pity on my plight and after a muttered pow-wow, we are released without further delay.

It strikes me as I write this that, despite Dad's apparent swagger as a ducker and a diver, he missed the more obvious tricks for getting away with breaking the rules. Maybe don't drive a car so riddled with defects that one glance tells you it is unfit for the road. Or pack your vehicle to suspension-busting extremity – the red alert for every customs officer, anywhere. Or travel to the very country you are meant to be a refugee from – your status given away by carrying 'travel documents' rather than a passport. As a child, I admire Dad's ability to get away with hoodwinking authority, but frequently come a cropper when volunteered as an accomplice.

Still, Hungary under the Soviets requires a certain subterfuge and vigilance, so perhaps it is just as well that I've had practice in such matters. I am under strict instructions to keep quiet about our UK living arrangements since communist law only allows home ownership under constant occupancy and second homes are forbidden. Government informers are everywhere and any whiff of suspicion that Nora is now resident in London could result in her (our) property being confiscated. Even prior to her Willesden resettlement, keeping a hold of both the Budapest flat and the Balaton villa required permanently installing an old family friend to act as a placeholder.

Like much of Budapest, our *fin-de-siècle* apartment – located on the wide boulevard of Krisztina Körút on the Buda side of the Danube – emits a haunted echo of more affluent times, its original grandeur still evident from the huge windows, high ceilings and tall, wooden double doors of the large street-facing rooms. On arrival, we unpack ourselves in the larger of these two rooms – vast enough to house two double beds, a three-seater sofa, a heavy, ornately carved dining table, two wardrobes, a sideboard, a wall of books and an enormous tiled stove. The other is occupied by Iluska (pronounced *Ilushka*), a soft-spoken, delicate divorcée who serves me tea from a fine porcelain set, allowing me to sprawl on her floor and draw pictures while we listen to classical music on her mahogany radiogram. One of the things I love about our holidays in Hungary is the many hospitable friends and families who offer me respite from Nora's claustrophobic presence.

After several days in Budapest, we head down to Balaton. The three-bedroom bungalow is crumbling with disrepair, but I love its old-country charm and its unimpeded view of the lake and the simple homely kitchen with its curtained pantry where baskets of plums and peaches, picked from trees, are left to ripen. Lizards skitter across the walls, frogs flop about on the rocky edge of the lake and the garden teems with a friendly ecosystem of grasshoppers, ladybirds, glow-worms and beetles. I even grow to appreciate the huge black spiders populating the villa's chalky ceilings, since they harvest the hordes of mosquitoes that feast on me, leaving large hard swellings that have to be sprinkled with vinegar to soothe the itching.

When the sun shines, crowds of friends pass through our garden to access the lake, stopping for a coffee and chit-chat. I am free to roam the neighbourhood, visiting local families to play with other children, puppyishly devoted to big-sister figures who indulge me by playing cards (with the traditional Hungarian 32-card pack), board games and badminton.

The lake itself is a wonder. Nearly 50 miles from end to end, from our Balatonboglár vantage point you can see across its width to the opposite shoreline where the Bakony hills fade blue into the distance. The water is warm and so shallow that it takes a ten-minute walk to reach a decent swimming depth and locals treat a dip in the lake as an opportunity for a leisurely stroll and a catch-up with neighbours. Us children leap about with frisbees and plastic balls, free to play with little supervision in the vast extent of safe shallows, jumping from the raised platforms used by lake fishermen and squealing and ducking underwater to avoid wasps that, stranded from the shore, are looking for a head to settle on.

Storm warnings are issued by the low boom of a distant cannon, prompting everyone to empty from the lake and hastily gather up blankets and picnic baskets from the tree-lined shore. As the weather rushes towards us across the water, I help shutter the windows against the imminent pummelling with joyful urgency, then dash back out to run along the grassy shoreline with my hair flying and excited shrieks snatched away by the wind.

Dusk is a spectator event, as we gather to watch the sun dip down behind Badacsony (the 'coffin hill') and prepare for cookouts of *szalonnasütés* barbecues or a bubbling cauldron of *gulyás*. During night storms, I watch lightning dance on the hills opposite, like a distant firework display; on clear nights, I marvel at the constellations, spotting shooting stars, lying on my back and lost in the shimmering miracle of the Milky Way stretched across the heavens.

My memories of Hungary are bathed in a nostalgic gauze of warm sunlight, but even as a child I picked up that the political situation cast a noticeable pall of dissatisfaction and paranoia over its citizens. From what I observed, Soviet communism for most Hungarians engendered a wilful rejection of all its ideals – our local friends refused to speak more than a few words of Russian, despite years of lessons at school and their enforced reading and study of the entirety of *Das Kapital* failed to engender any appreciation of Marxist philosophy and instead provided the tools with which to condemn communist ideology all the more eloquently. Dad himself remained darkly distrustful of any whiff of left-wing sympathies and throughout my childhood fanatically affirmed his support for Heath, Thatcher and Reagan. He despaired at my own adult political leanings – a common moan among many of his Hungarian crowd on their children's baffling views. I once asked, in a bid to justify my anti-Tory stance, whether they believed in affordable housing, a state-funded health service and free university education. 'Absolutely!' came the answer. 'Well,' I said triumphantly, 'in Britain that makes you left-wing.'

And yet it was also true that, despite the direction of travel in British politics, these things were all still available in Thatcher's Britain, whereas in Hungary they were not. Housing was unaffordable to most of the population, certainly in the major cities, while medical treatment required cash bribes at every level of the hierarchy, from consultants to nursing staff – a practice that continued decades after the fall of the Berlin Wall. Even education, while free and of a high standard, required backhanders, political connections and complete adherence to the party line for the best schools and universities. Under the surface of its communist ideology, all interaction with state-run systems required capitalist-level exchanges of money – just hidden and unregulated.

So, while I voted Labour, joined in the support for the striking miners and passionately loathed the Tory government, I was never in total agreement with the left-wingers in my own circle who extolled the goals and ideologies of the Soviet Union, claiming they would much rather live in Russia than America. It struck me that, if they'd been citizens in the east, none of these firebrands would have had the liberty to take part in nuclear-disarmament demos and gay-rights parades, producing their anti-establishment fanzines, signing on the dole and playing in bands. Their eulogising over the superior culture and architecture of Russia overlooked the fact that, unless they secured high-up party positions, they were more likely to be grafting for a pittance on a collective farm than enjoying leisurely strolls around Red Square and taking in performances by the Kirov Ballet.

10

MIKI AUSTIN

The terraced Georgian house in Adelaide Square is converted and renovated by a fleet of carpenters and electricians from Pinewood as a pre-wedding gift from the *Space: 1999* team. The work is of such an impressively high standard that, one Saturday, Mum answers the door to find Prince Charles on the doorstep, Range Rover parked outside and a bodyguard in tow, requesting if he could possibly be indulged with a tour. Ray practically shits himself with excitement and breathlessly points out the craftsmanship and antique furnishings, lapping up His Royal Highness's gracious praise.

The house is, indeed, beautifully fitted out and immaculately clean and tidy. Ray and his most recent ex-wife, during their brief marriage, ran an antique shop in Bedfordshire and it appears he has moved its contents wholesale into our new home. The knocked-through living room is crowded with several centuries of ornate furniture, their surfaces artfully cluttered with snuffboxes, crystalware, miniature portraits and collectible knick-knacks. Every available inch of wall space, from cornice to skirting board, is covered in a patchwork of paintings and prints and I have to be constantly vigilant not to knock over any priceless artefacts as even an accidental nudge has Ray tutting and realigning his meticulously positioned treasures. As an act of rebellion, I slide down the bannisters when he isn't around.

Settling into her new home, Mum immerses herself in fostering an idyllic domestic environment – cooking, gardening, sewing patchwork quilts and getting to know the neighbours. Despite the outward glamour of Ray's directing jobs, he doesn't earn sufficient funds to cover the cost of the new life he has walked us into, so Mum continues to take on acting and modelling jobs, though it is now she who has to endure the long commute to London for her theatre work. Ray, meanwhile, basks and blossoms in her loving care, quitting the Gauloises cigarettes and shedding weight at an anorexic rate via the 'orange diet'. His old friends and acquaintances marvel at Yasuko's good influence, privately congratulating her for working miracles. She is a terrific cook and a friendly, conversational hostess, so we have frequent guests for dinner. We get two cats, Kuro and Chako and a golden Labrador that Ray names Bruce, after Bruce Forsyth.

Best of all, I get my own bedroom. Back in Maida Avenue, my tiny frame was marooned in a vast double bed in a designated guest room, so any possessions I didn't want swept into the bin from Ray's obsessive tidying had to be ferried back to Willesden at the end of my stay. Here, I finally have my own space where I can read and write and draw and play without interference – although Ray complains if I sprawl on the floor rather than sit at my desk and any giveaway thump of me practising gymnastics has him thundering up the stairs.

I am enrolled at the Royal Free School, a Church of England middle school, ten minutes' walk from our new home. Ray's plans wait for no man, woman or child, so I have been plucked from my Hampstead primary halfway through the term and thrown into the new environment.

Royal Free has many, many rules that dictate when and where you can sit, stand, walk and speak and blatant incursions are met with corporal punishment. The building dates from 1705 and, as we file past the headmaster's office on stone steps worn shiny and bowed with centuries of tread, appointed school monitors shush any chatter to and from assemblies and break times. In my first-year classroom, we sit at old-fashioned wooden double desks with lift-up lids and parrot thankful mantras at the beginning and end of the day. The ink wells are unused though we all write with fountain pens, fingers stained with blue Quink.

Whereas New End comprised a mix of children and teachers from a range of ethnic backgrounds, Royal Free is almost exclusively white English. Everyone struggles with my name – Miki, I am repeatedly informed, is a boys' name and I am subjected to taunts of Mickey Mouse and Mickey Finn. One bright spark comes up with the nickname Holly Holly Hong Kong, which I actually don't mind since at least Holly is universally accepted as a girls' name. No one can get their head (or mouth) around Berenyi, since Hungary is a country outside of any familiarity ('Hungry?'). The nearest they get is Biryani, which brings with it Indian impersonations consisting of hands in prayer and wobbly-headed 'bud-bud' noises. There is a playground chant that goes 'Chinese, Japanese, Dirty knees and What are these?' to which the accompanying gestures are pulling your eyes into slants upward, then downward, then hands on your knees and then, finally, squeezing imaginary tits. The punchline is followed by Sid James 'phwoarr' guffaws from the boys and saucy squeals from the girls, but my ethnicity now provides an extra layer of fun with toothy-overbite 'Ah so!' exclamations.

I'd never given much thought to my 'foreignness' before, but the burden of having an immutable characteristic become a source of ridicule is par for the course in an environment where everyone suffers similar indignities. Unless you're blessed with a bulletproof saints' name (Stephen, John, Michael, David, Christopher) or are one of the multitude of girls called Nicola, Tracey, Catherine or Sarah, you stand to be mocked and all surnames are mangled and mined for derision. Being too short (Titch/Midget), too tall (Lurch/Beanpole), too fat (Fatty/Hippo), too poor (Gyppo), not academic enough (Dur-brain/Thicko) or crap at sports (Spaz) singles you out for taunts. Boys who display the merest hint of vulnerability are derided (Homo/Poof), as are girls who hang out in close, impenetrable friendship groups of two (Lesbo).

For all the casual cruelty among the children, my parents' divorce ('Ray's my *step*-dad; my real dad lives in London') elicits empathetic concern, which comes as a surprise since no one has ever asked me about my personal feelings on the matter. Even my Japanese ethnicity eventually becomes a point of fascination when parcels from Tamiko bring stylish clothes that are a cut above the generic C&A polyester worn by my classmates; stationery and hair accessories emblazoned with Hello Kitty and Snoopy characters; and packets of nori and osembe, which I describe as 'Japanese crisps' and everyone delights in sampling, shrieking 'uuuurrg-ghhh!' when I reveal the killer ingredient: seaweed.

Yasuko is widely admired as being stunningly beautiful and glamorous. She is cast in a film called *Wombling Free*, playing a

Japanese housewife who for whatever reason spends much of the screen time wearing a kimono, despite the suburban London setting. Having an actress as a mum brings star quality and my friends are wowed that I got to meet Bernard Cribbins. Ray is filming *The New Avengers* and drops me off one morning in Purdey's yellow TR7, which makes everyone want to be my friend for at least half a day. When he begins work on *The Professionals*, I arrive home to find Lewis Collins sitting in our living room and am surrounded the next day by a clamour of children at school demanding I recount every detail of my encounter.

I'm eventually accepted and find a friendship group. While my ten-minute walk to school had initially been plagued by a thuggish boy to whom I had to pay a daily fee of 2p or he would 'smash my face in', I am now regularly part of a walking bus of schoolchildren, invited to drop by friends' houses and stay for tea. One of this group, a fellow Four-Eyes, becomes my first 'boyfriend'. We play darts and Mousetrap and I teach him how to kiss. He leaves a box of Milk Tray on my doorstep for Valentine's Day.

————

Now that Mum and Ray are married, he wants me to take his surname. Apparently this will 'make things easier'. Dad is understandably stung by the encroachment and puts his foot down at any official change, but a compromise is reached and I become Miki Austin only for the purposes of school. He sometimes fixes me with a disapproving look, deriding my new name in heavily accented Hungarian: Miki *Awe-styn*. I roll my eyes and tell him not to make a fuss – it's just a name and Ray is not and never will be my real dad.

Truth be told, I am slightly relieved. Miki continues to be a difficult name to carry off (I fantasise about changing it to a more assimilated 'Michelle') and at least now I have a surname that the teachers and other children can actually pronounce. Though I am frequently referred to as 'Bionic', in reference to *The Six Million Dollar Man*'s Steve Austin. It's a hugely popular show and I am more flattered than insulted by the slow-motion running and 'Der-ner-ner-ner' theme tune enacted on my behalf in the playground.

Dad picks me up from school on Friday afternoons and I proudly point him out to my friends, running to the beat-up old car, elated to see him and chatter my news. The weekend restriction makes our time together all the more precious and he is happy to indulge me, aware that the newlywed household in Windsor represents a competitive threat. I have been campaigning for my own bedroom for some time, away from the cloying abuses of Nora and when the turnstile of lodgers in Staverton Road leaves an upstairs room vacant, Dad willingly concedes me the space, pointing out that it is twice the size of my room in Adelaide Square.

We spend almost all our time together – watching TV, playing cards, going to the cinema, enjoying regular trips to the local swimming pool and sampling the global cuisine of London's varied eateries. (This includes Middle Eastern mezze on the Edgware Road, borscht at Bloom's in Golders Green, dim sum on Gerrard Street, curry at the local Indian – Dad insisting I try everything and refusing to take no for an answer, despite my grimacing at grainy couscous or too-spicy curry.) He is reluctant to abandon me, even when work demands it and I am bundled along to an amateur boxing night, entrusted to the care of coach Kevin Hickey, watching the weights from fly to heavy battering each other while Dad sits ringside reporting on the action. Sunday comes around all too soon and I am caught between wanting to delay our departure to spend more time with Dad, but anxious that we return so I can prepare for school on Monday. We drive up the M4 with false cheer and he drops me off at Adelaide Square, with a happy-sad tilt of his head before he kisses me goodbye.

My 9 p.m. bedtime at Mum's is generously late compared with my classmates, but after two nights of being up well past midnight, my body clock is thrown off kilter. Lying in the dark brings all my anxieties crowding in. I fret about school and worry whether the friends who were my friends on Friday will still be my friends on Monday. A lot can change over a weekend. Mum and Ray have a telly at the end of their bed and I can hear the dramatic music or canned laughter or the bang and crash of car chases and gunfire, depending on what they are watching. If I was with Dad in Staverton Road, we would be watching together. When I close my eyes, I can picture the scene so clearly it hurts: me lounging on the sofa with Dad, the two of us making bantering comments and sloppily eating snacks. I am overwhelmed by the need to wrap my arms around his neck and feel his big bear-like head resting against mine. I miss him so much it makes me choke.

I have a talisman that gets me through these difficult nights. If the very last voice I hear before bedtime is Mum's, then I will be able to sleep. I say goodnight several times, but Ray has a habit of speaking right after Mum's sing-song reply. I should probably tell them my superstition, so it works out right every time, but even I can see that asking Ray to only whisper after I've gone to bed is a bit much. And, in any case, revealing the trick could mean it loses its power.

Mum lets me keep the bedside light on so I can read, which is an effective distraction. I can lose myself in *Harriet the Spy*, *The Phoenix and the Carpet*, *Stig of the Dump*, *The Secret Garden*, *Polly and the Wolf* or *The Chronicles of Narnia* – worlds where parents are mostly absent and children come through challenging adventures unscathed. I am smitten by the oddball, outcast characters in the Moomin books, who are loved and welcomed, however obnoxious, cowardly, vain or strange, by the loving family at the heart of the stories. But falling asleep on my book with the light on all night annoys Ray and when he angrily snaps off my bedside lamp it wakes me up again. Sometimes I creep on to the landing and watch TV through the crack in their door – *The Sweeney* or *Fawlty Towers* or repeats of *Monty Python's Flying Circus*. If Mum laughs or makes a comment, I stuff my fingers in my ears and rush back to bed, cloaked in the comforting spell of her voice.

It would be simpler to just tell Mum what I am going through, missing Dad so much. I'm sure she'd understand. But I know this will hurt Ray's feelings. He has accepted that I refer to him as my stepdad or occasionally 'my other Dad', which is the best I can honestly muster, but I know this is not the star billing he craves.

On the whole, this period represents the most settled chapter of my childhood. I sing in the school choir and am picked for the netball team, join the local Brownies and am signed up to tap-and-ballet classes at the local Scout hut. I get a purple Raleigh bike for my birthday and Ray teaches me to ride it, ditching the trainer wheels and flying me down the hill of the Long Walk. Best of all, I eventually get access to a local gymnastics club after spending a year on the waiting list and learn to execute perfect walkovers – forward and backward – which I practise at every opportunity. When friends come over, we run around Windsor Great Park, chasing through the trees, collecting conkers, roller-skating and riding bikes or having snowball fights, depending on the season.

As the year passes, my sense of home shifts toward Windsor. I want nothing more than to fit in, but this is difficult to achieve when I am away every weekend. Many of the social aspects to my numerous pastimes occur while I am away and returning to school after a half-term holiday is a minefield that involves evaluating shifting allegiances and inveigling my way back into friendships that have developed in my absence. Meanwhile, there is a noticeable drop-off in Dad's initial commitment to our fun-packed weekend quality time. He increasingly farms out responsibility to mini-cabs and cash-strapped friends for the Friday and Sunday drives to ferry me to and from Staverton Road and what was once a cosy opportunity for chatty catch-up is now a lonely chore endured in silence. When I am dropped off in Willesden, Dad is often nowhere to be seen and there is no indication of when – or even if – he will return. I hole myself up in my bedroom, marking time until he reappears, but Nora, who has been waiting all week for my company, does not take kindly to being abandoned and paces the landing, wailing her complaints. I slide my bedside cabinet in front of the door to bar entry.

Left in my own company and actively trying to avoid Granny's, I am obsessively industrious – reading, drawing, creating a sprawling world for my Sindy dolls by constructing items of furniture from empty cereal packets and origami paper, modelling tiny telephones from Play-Doh and fashioning miniature home-made magazines for the dolls to browse. I play my Abba cassette on Dad's portable tape machine, singing along and acting out elaborate performances, complete with costume changes, to an imagined audience. The sad, resigned break-up lyrics of 'Knowing Me, Knowing You' are my melodramatic crescendo and my voice breaks with emotion on the line 'In these old familiar rooms, children would play; now there's only emptiness, nothing to say'. Outwardly, I must seem an admirably self-sufficient and imaginative child, but my playing is no mere pastime – it is a compulsion that must provide enough engrossing distraction and imaginative escape to block out Nora's mad rantings and quash my loneliness and resentment.

All such anxieties dissolve when Dad is around. Even when he is busy working in his study, it's enough for me to know he is one room away. But I worry about him breaking his promise of evenings together and make pathetic attempts at securing his attendance: flagging up must-see highlights in the TV magazines and setting up board games and score sheets for card tournaments, ready for his participation. One evening his friend Gabi drops by with news of an enticing party that promises 'wall-to-wall pussy'. As Dad races off to scrub up, I burst into tears. From his glance alone, I can tell that Gabi thinks I am crazy and spoilt. But the only reason for me to be in Willesden is to spend time with Dad and I resent every moment I am there and not in his company. When I am stuck with Nora and Dad is out working or gallivanting, I brood on the events and gatherings I am missing out on in Windsor.

But, whether Dad is there or not, he insists that I stick to the agreed timetable. I beg him to let me stay in Windsor for my best friend's birthday party or when my stepsisters Min and Jo are coming for the weekend, but he is insistent – he says Nora misses me terribly. Mum commiserates with me and castigates Ivan's selfishness; Dad points out that I don't like Ray, so why on earth would I want to spend more time with him? Both are true, but also miss the point – I want the best of both worlds and don't want to lose either, but being caught in the middle is hard.

11

A MOVE TOO FAR

I'm not sure when the sexual abuse ended, but it did. No longer sharing a bedroom with Nora and living away in Windsor diminishes her influence. And being around 'normal' families means I have a better idea of the boundaries of acceptable behaviour. That said, Ray's uninhibited attitude to nudity continues to make me uncomfortable. At home, he is invariably bollock naked beneath his white towelling dressing gown and nonchalant about the loosely tied garment flopping open as he lounges about relaxing. At age eleven, he deems me ready for a video screening of his 1970 London Film Festival award-winning short *The Perfumed Garden*, an arty soft-core realisation of a sixteenth-century Islamic sex manual culminating in an orgasmic encounter in the shrubbery.

Ray is rebelling against the sexual repression of buttoned-up attitudes by stripping body parts of smutty innuendo and parading them without embarrassment. Personally, I'm unconvinced by these lofty claims and see it as yet more justification for him to act exactly as he pleases, however ill-at-ease it makes anyone else. And it also has a gaslighting effect of normalising my own abuse. Sex is natural – I shouldn't be having uptight feelings about it.

But sex is now becoming a minefield at school. The age range at Royal Free goes up to thirteen and our playground is shared with the older boys. Having outgrown the dry-peck thrills of kiss-chase, they circulate naked centrefolds of heavy-breasted, slack-mouthed, suspender-strapped women, snarling 'this one looks like you' at the girls. It's an early taste of having my self-image hijacked – whatever view I have of myself, I am cast as an obscene heap of trussed-up flesh. Some of the girls take the baiting as a compliment and join snogging and groping sessions around the back of the toilet block, deriding those deemed too ugly to be invited or too chicken to take part. Other girls label them 'slags', though the incessant discussion of them belies their jealousy. The rest of us navigate an ever-narrowing isthmus of wriggle room between being labelled either a slut or a prude. But even this territory is becoming increasingly fraught as the girls turn on each other.

My friendship groups become fractured and fractious. Deanna, my best friend, has become popular and competing for her attention becomes exhausting, not least because a wan worm of a girl in our expanded group plots to cause a rift between us. I make friends with Anthea, but am accused of 'stealing her' from another girl, who retaliates by regularly thieving my possessions from my desk and sneering unapologetically when I retrieve them from her bag. Julie is a new arrival who takes an instant and aggressive dislike to me. She follows me in the park, threatening to set her Alsatian on me and at school stares daggers while penning poisonous notes that she passes around the class. We get dragged to the head's office after a playground tussle, where Julie acts the victim and triumphantly flourishes a wad of ineptly forged notes full of four-letter insults. I present my own evidence of her 'foreign bitch' and 'spastic eyes' scribbles that have, via friends, ended up in my hands. Though I've managed to convince the head of my innocence, Julie is a fucking psychopath and I am fully scared of what she might do next.

During a gym lesson where the class are maniacally tearing around the room, I suddenly find one boy's efforts at leaping dance moves so hysterically funny that I double up on the floor and piss myself. As an impressively huge puddle spreads across the floor, the class falls still and silent. The teacher excuses me and I head to the toilets, contemplating the option that I simply keep walking, out of the school, down the street, past the town's borders and into the countryside, never to return. But no one ever taunts me with this incident. Not even Julie.

Mum and Ray are called into the head's office. The school has no strategies for dealing with my anxieties and it's felt I would be best off moving. I am enrolled at Brigidine Convent, a fee-paying girls' school, also walking distance from my home but in the opposite direction. Though I am once again dropped in mid-term, fitting in is less of an ordeal since many of the girls are themselves only recently arrived. There's even a fellow refugee from Royal Free, who also left due to bullying, so I don't feel like a complete loser.

Sister Catherine encourages me to find solace in the Bible, so I read the Good Book from cover to cover. I'm eager to please, but Nora has rather soured my expectations of Catholicism. Despite my best efforts, Jesus fails to materialise in any miraculous manifestation, while Nora continues to enjoy his regular support and conversation, which I find dejecting. I'd love to be part of the ceremony of Communion – which, frankly, is the only distraction during the marathon boredom of Mass – but my efforts to find faith are fruitless and I take it as proof that I'm beyond redemption.

Still, Brigidine is a happy haven. I make close friends and my school report is a string of A grades. We read *The Hobbit* for English and wear lab coats for domestic science and are allowed to learn without the threat of corporal punishment or the fear of being bullied. One girl, Siobhan, belts out an impressive rendition of 'Tomorrow' from the musical *Annie* in front of the class and I see no sniggering from the room, just rapt applause.* There is of course occasional bitchiness and fall-outs, but nothing compared to the relentless aggression of Royal Free. When I leave, less than a year later in the summer of 1979, I am almost hysterical with grief. Even Dad pauses with a sad look when he recalls collecting me that last day of the summer term, acknowledging it was a lovely school and I was heartbroken at having to move.

———

Mum and Ray take a holiday to the US, staying at the Palm Springs home of his decades-long friend, Patrick Macnee (the actor, most famous for portraying Steed throughout the *Avengers* TV series). During poolside discussions, Ray bemoans the class snobbery within his profession, claiming he doesn't get the respect he deserves and misses out on well-paid work. Patrick assures him that Hollywood is in dire need of able TV directors and sets him

---

* A decade later, I catch up with Siobhan in the company of Lawrence Hayward, when she becomes a member of his post-Felt project, Denim.

Top left: Dad, 1940s – the haircut and lederhosen are a bit of a giveaway.

Top right: The Nagazumi family with newborn Mum – 1943, Manchuria.

Nora: *left*, enjoying the Budapest café society; *below*, when I knew her, all love and joy long gone.

Mum and Dad's whirlwind romance: after meeting at the 1964 Tokyo Olympics, they eloped a year later to London and married in 1966.

Miki Eleonora Berenyi, born 18 March 1967. Mum looking remarkably happy and hopeful that my arrival might tame Dad's wayward behaviour.

Above: Dad and I were regular patrons of the photo booth at Willesden Green station.

Below: Sun-lounging in the garden of Staverton Road, in my standard garb when staying at Dad's.

Top left: Aged four, on my trike in Japan.

Top right: Birthday in the Maida Avenue flat. Mum was always great at throwing a party.

Right: Technically my first proper photo session, in traditional Japanese get-up.

Above: Christmas in Los Angeles. Peking duck prepared by Mum and Tamiko; Ray in obligatory towelling dressing gown.

Below: With my stepsisters, Araminta and Johanna, on the set of *Hart to Hart* (a rare pic with my glasses on as, understandably, I usually whipped them off for photos).

The Vidal Sassoon School haircut, properly primped and styled.

Left to my slapdash care, it looked like a mangled animal, so I cut it all off.

Schoolmates posing as Duran Duran. *Left to right*: Emma (Roger Taylor); me (John Taylor), Alice (Simon Le Bon); Maxine (Nick Rhodes); Bunny (Andy Taylor).

Ray didn't approve of my new look and said he could no longer be seen with me in public, which suited me just fine.

The girls behind Alphabet Soup.

Johnny and Chris at my flat on the Caledonian Road.

Top: More haircut experiments – red tips, then finally going for the full bleach to blonde, ready to slap on the red.

Right: Me and Chris in the Lake District, taking in the splendid views and looking to the future.

up with an agent who finds him a gig there and then. One job leads instantly to the next and, awed by earning ten times his usual fee, Ray envisions a dazzling future.

He is undaunted by the prospect of relocating to Los Angeles, having spent his twenties in Hollywood, hobnobbing with the stars during his years as Cary Grant's driver, bodyguard and protégé. He takes Yasuko on a tour of his old haunts, treating her to dinner at Chasens, a favourite with major movie players in its heyday. As they settle themselves in a booth, heads turn and there are whispers of recognition. Mum watches bemused as Ray mingles with Barbara Stanwyck, Olivia de Havilland and various other veteran stars dotted around the room. From the coy looks and knowing smiles, she is left in no doubt that he must have had affairs with several of them.

With the backing of a studio, Ray gets his green card in record time and, within months, he and Yasuko have picked out a luxurious rental property in a remote arm of Mandeville Canyon, a meandering 5-mile stretch that winds from the Brentwood end of Sunset Boulevard towards Mulholland Drive. Min and Jo accompany me on a holiday visit, glamorous beyond belief: Mum zipping about in a flashy silver Pontiac Trans Am, treating us to hot dogs at Carneys; Ray cruising us down palm-tree-lined boulevards in a Chrysler Cordoba, its rear seat the size of a bed. We visit him on set filming *Salvage 1* and *Hart to Hart* and collect autographs from Andy Griffith, Robert Wagner and Stefanie Powers. The house has a pool and jacuzzi and we go on day trips to Disneyland and Universal Studios. At the end of the visit, we head home to our respective drab lives, leaving Ray and Yasuko to live the dream.

But, within the month, a raging brush fire tears through the area. Mum is only alerted to her imminent cremation by the arrival of two policemen at her door. The driveway is already aflame and the house and its contents are only saved by firefighters dousing the property with water from the swimming pool. Days later, when Yasuko is able to return to the charred hillside, she finds the bottom of the empty pool packed with dead animals, who had been desperate to escape the inferno.

So much of my childhood feels vivid and present, perhaps because the years were distinctly marked by disruptions that serve as markers in the timeline. But here my memory is fuzzy. I can remember the details, but struggle with the order. If the fire happened in October '78, with Mum and Ray already living in LA, how and why was I living in Windsor, having only just started at Brigidine? Mum is clear about when her cats were moved to LA but can't explain where I was. She says she must have been intermittently travelling between Los Angeles and Windsor to sort the sale of the house in Adelaide Square. But my many recollections of my friends' homes and routines – sitting up with a schoolmate's parents watching TV because the kids' 6 p.m. bedtime was too early for me and my wakefulness would keep them up; the mother doing my school needlework project herself because I was so hopeless at it; Dad becoming friendly with another classmate's father following repeated weekend pick-ups from their Maidenhead house – suggest I was babysat in Windsor for extended periods.

Dad said he didn't want me moving to LA, convinced he might never see me again. According to his side of the story, he hired a lawyer who interviewed me, asking whether I'd rather go to America with Mum or stay in the UK with Dad. I have no memory of this incident myself, but it's a stretch to believe he made the whole thing up. And he never crowed in triumph at my decision – that I didn't want to leave the UK and, if forced to choose, would rather live with Dad. He had the good grace at least to apologise for putting me in such a difficult situation, admitting it was a desperate act and he felt terrible about it.

In this light, my sudden decline at Royal Free makes sense. I'd always believed it was my awkward character that led me to being picked on by classmates, but, working backwards, the stress of having to choose between being whisked off to an unfamiliar country, away from Dad, and staying in England, an ocean and a continent away from Mum – and, in both cases, losing the Windsor community I had grown so settled in – must have been debilitating. No wonder I was too derailed by anxiety to tough it out in the playground.

Ray – the only winner in my lose–lose situation – made efforts to appease Mum's concerns over leaving me in the exclusive care of Ivan. I recall perusing shiny brochures for boarding schools, spread across the living-room floor, with Ray marvelling at the stately-home grandeur of numerous select institutions. Apparently, I can get in on a performing-arts scholarship for the one he is enthusiastically waving under my nose. I am despondent and glum, because it is laughably ridiculous to think I am confident enough to pass an audition. And, in any case, how does parking me in a school where I'll be separated from *both* my parents in any way solve the problem? I can hear him in the kitchen, hissing at Mum: 'What's the point if she's not even going to *try*?'

Mum must have felt both guilty at leaving me and rejected by my choosing Ivan. But it was Ray I was rejecting, not Mum.

Despite her rebellion against her upbringing, Yasuko was a good Japanese girl and that meant centring your man and accommodating his wishes. I'd noted with resentment that Ray had moved us from London to Windsor and now to LA at his whim. What were the chances he'd grow bored again and drag us to some other corner of the globe at a moment's notice? And, with Dad 6,000 miles away and Mum unable to stand up to Ray's control, what leverage would I have if he decided (as he had with his own children) that my presence interfered with his plans for the next incarnation of a perfect life?

It would have been nice if Dad could have given his blessing for my move to America with reassurances of continuing closeness; or if Mum could have put her foot down and insisted on staying in the UK. But ultimately, I'm at peace with my decision, however unqualified I was to make it. It's a human habit to justify past actions with retrospective logic, but moving to the US and being at the mercy of Yasuko's misguided choice in men would have been a worse outcome than the crap I eventually had to weather with Dad, where I at least had some independent agency and a better crack at carving my own path into adulthood.

12

COMING APART AT THE SEAMS

The devastating fire, which stripped Mandeville Canyon's surroundings of vegetation, is followed by heavy rainfall that sends
the unanchored earth pouring down the hillsides. The elderly
couple at the bottom of Mum and Ray's drive are buried alive
in their home. Packs of hungry coyotes, their prey decimated by
the run of natural disasters, prowl the area's properties in search
of food and one of Mum's beloved pet cats is snatched away
before her eyes. Despite being offered a knockdown price to buy
the house, Yasuko insists they relocate to the Hollywood Hills –
less isolated but still reassuringly high above the LA smog.

Ray wastes no time stuffing the place with his antiques shipped
over from the UK and paints the walls in regal reds and greens.
Though the floor-to-ceiling windows offer breathtaking views
across the urban sprawl, all light is sucked up by the sedate décor
and the house feels perpetually dim. The extra wall space accom-
modates huge portraits of unidentified aristocrats acquired at
auction, which Ray tells visitors depict his ancestors. Though he
signals to us that he is joking with a secret wink, Yasuko winces at

the lie. I note that Ray's hammy Cary Grant impersonation has become an almost permanent affectation when he is in company.

Mum makes continued efforts to woo me with the LA life. I go body-surfing in Malibu and to a ski camp in Big Bear and enjoy hangouts and sleepovers with her friends' families. But the more glittering temptations Yasuko dangles before me, the more I dig in my heels. I get that life as a Hollywood rich kid has benefits aplenty, but I want community, not luxuries and I see no evidence of it here. I don't like being chauffeured everywhere, however nice the car. There's no independence and no way of escaping Ray. And the years of upheaval and relocation have made me *less* resilient and open to change – aware of how difficult and exhausting assimilation can be. And I refuse to be separated from Dad, who I miss when I am in LA. But the reverse is no less upsetting and my diary records daily how much I pine for Mum. Once I am home, jetlag and anxiety play chaos with my sleep patterns and I cry myself to sleep nightly. It's only when Dad reappears that I can handle the separation. (*14 Jan – Dad is home!!! I slept in his bed tonight and guess what? I slept the whole night! Now that he is back, I don't miss mum so much.*)

Dad manages to wangle me a place out of borough, at a single-sex state school in west London.* I am instantly renamed 'Metal Mickey' (a robot from a popular kids' TV show) and my designated guide, Maria, walks me through Ladbroke School's daily routines, offering helpful tips on how to avoid getting beaten up. Despite the mix of children from multiple ethnic backgrounds, closer friendship groups seem drawn along racial lines. Since no

---

* Like many of London's public assets, the Victorian building was sold off and has since been repurposed as a Virgin Active health club.

one else is Japanese or Hungarian, I fall in with the closest adjacent approximation: Maria and Sonia (Spanish and therefore fellow Europeans), Corinne (like me, 'half-caste') and Rosemary (Chinese, which is near enough to Japanese for everyone to consider us a good match). Though many of the school staff are able and dedicated, their job is to teach and they only call out behaviour that might disrupt that end, so bullying is tolerated if it can be ignored. My bus fare is stolen on a weekly basis and there are frequent fights during break times.

I don't alert Dad to any problems, knowing he'd expect me to deal with them on my own. His parenting style is to treat me like a diminutive adult, coopting me into his adventures and expecting me to keep up and I don't like to disappoint him. Mum does her best to parent from abroad, sending parcels of clothes and letters with practical advice on booking optician and orthodontist appointments, how to use a coin-op launderette and, following a disastrous home haircut, instructions on what to ask for at a hairdresser's. But I never go. I'm starting to find interactions with strangers daunting and obsessively collect change so I can keep communication with bus conductors and shopkeepers entirely silent by handing over the precise money. Mum is concerned by my school report, which reveals deteriorating behaviour and weeks of absenteeism and sends a £20 cheque to cover entrance examinations for a list of London private schools, where she feels I will be better served. She is frustrated by Dad's failure to care for me properly, but I defend him, aware of the chasm of difference between their financial circumstances.

Union strikes have led to lost work and Dad is struggling to pay the bills. In need of extra funds, he stuffs the house with lodgers who are willing to overlook the chaotic shabbiness of our home and turn a blind eye to my regular screaming rows with Granny. Ganesh is a Malaysian accountancy student whose deep-rooted respect for elders makes him unerringly polite and willing to make time for Nora's relentless stream of self-pity, even when he can't understand a word she says. Another is the delicate, doe-eyed Raji, similarly brought up to treat the elderly with patient respect. She is doted on by Nora until she makes the unforgivable mistake of being seduced by Dad (I witness this event, unnoticed, when I unwittingly walk into the living room and find them coupling on the sofa), after which Granny paces up and down outside her room, muttering malignant insults in Hungarian and torturing the poor girl with abusive mind games.

Tan is a diminutive Filipino who walks around the upstairs landing in his Y-fronts and shows me topless Polaroids of his girl-friend. He pushes a porn mag under my bedroom door, which I peruse with curiosity.

I'm left wondering whether Tan's gift is an attempt at seduc-tion, but I've already been sufficiently disgusted by his daily ablutions – long sessions of loud catarrh-clearing that initially made me wonder whether he was drowning in the bath – to be immune to any efforts at grooming. I fold a sarcastic 'thank you' note within the pages and quietly slide the magazine back under his door. Meanwhile, Dad's relentless pick-ups furnish further inappropriate examples of adult sexual relations and my diary entries provide graphic details: *When I came home, Dad had gone to pick up a bird. I heard them come home and she was reluctant to have it off so she locked herself in the loo. 5 June – At 4 a.m., Dad got a call from Mary. She is grovelling for Dad to come over and fuck her. She is really ugly though.*

On my way home from school one day, an older boy falls into step with me and puts his arm around my shoulders, pulling my top away with his other hand and taking a look at the view. I instinctively push him away and tell him to bugger off, but am left with a nagging doubt that this may be normal courtship and I have acted inappropriately. At home, I continue to run around in vest and knickers and even Dad is growing uncomfortable at the sight of my developing body. When I sit sprawled across Ganesh's lap as he patiently guides me through my maths project, Dad half-jokingly comments that I may be provoking some unintended excitement. It's the closest he comes to any direct guidance on how to handle my sexuality as I undergo puberty. Thank God I start my period during a visit to Mum's (*Imagine if I get raped, I might become pregnant*), having her on hand to instruct me on sanitary towels and tampons. Dad's response when I break the news is to let out a surprised whoop, then look at me sadly and comment, 'You're not my baby any more.' Coming into my room and waving the pack of Regular Tampax he's found in the bathroom, he quizzes me with a concerned look: 'Why aren't they small?' I hurl a pair of shoes at his head, along with a string of swearwords.

My twelve-year-old self's diary is swollen with stickers, drawings, magazine clippings and letters. The tone throughout is defiantly cheerful and tough, more a reflection of who I want to be than who I am. But being distanced from my mother – and missing her – saps a lot of energy and any further stress tips me over the edge. I become thin-skinned and easily triggered, unable to handle the least disappointment. And Dad is always disappointing me. He forgets to leave me money so I miss out on going swimming with my friends, then chastises me for lack of resourcefulness, saying I should have just bunked in. He complains when I outgrow my uniform and shoes, calling me 'Too Tall Miki' as he grudgingly hands over the cash. His promised return dates from trips abroad are never honoured and, though I appreciate he has to travel for work, I know full well he habitually pads out these excursions with sexual conquests.

On one occasion, I have a complete meltdown over the evening's TV viewing. Ray has been directing regular episodes of *Hart to Hart* and when the series is screened in the UK, I savour every moment, feeling the connection to Mum. This evening, fifteen minutes before air time, Dad insists on watching something on the other channel. I fully lose my shit and end up kicking in a glass panel of the kitchen door, lacerating my leg in the process. The fit of violence and hysteria gets me what I want – I watch the show in determined concentration with my bloody leg wrapped in a tea towel, ignoring Dad's pensive glances and eventual outburst: 'You were such a sweet little girl, Miki. What happened?!' He's right, though. I am awkward, surly, bespectacled and demonstrably unhinged, transitioning from his adoring little buddy into a dispiriting version of pre-womanhood, with my stupid haircut, wonky teeth, smattering of acne and, apparently, too-large tampons. This is not the daughter he'd planned for or wanted.

---

22 April – Today in maths Joanne tried to nick my purse. I think I better go to the doc on Thurs because my leg has not really got that much better. Amazingly, I didn't cry myself to sleep tonight thinking about Mum. I think I am getting used to all this travelling now! Dad is coming back in four days!! I wish he'd hurry up!

I eventually accept that there is simply no point in sitting around and feeling sorry for myself. Falling apart isn't an option – I'd be betraying Dad by proving him an unfit parent to Mum and causing her untold stress, as she is buoyed by my reassurances that I am coping well. I am so *tired* of being a loser and resolve to get a grip. The GP surgery is next door to our house and after weeks of hoping the weeping, blackening wound on my leg will simply get better on its own, I overcome my muteness with strangers and eventually get it seen to. The doctor admonishes me for failing to visit earlier and prescribes me a month's worth of disinfectant creams and gauzes. But it feels like an achievement on my part – step one on the ladder to self-sufficiency.

I resolve to improve my diet by turning to the freezer section of the local Budgens, eschewing Nora's dinners which are increasingly swimming in grease. I work my way through an O-level maths book gifted to me by a teacher and hijack Dad's dusty collection of Linguaphone French cassettes, in an effort to make up for a year of non-existent lessons. I find a Lyn Marshall yoga book in the charity shop, which I use for daily exercise and busy myself with cleaning tasks, to make the bathroom and kitchen less revolting to visiting friends. Timetabling my life becomes a reassuring coping strategy, each tick on the list providing evidence of self-improvement and ordered achievement.

The bullying at school is tackled via a two-pronged strategy – bargaining my skills and toughening up my image. For the former, I freely share my homework for copying and offer to decorate pencil cases and bags with band logos: the Madness 'M', the Beat's dancing girl, the Specials' ska man. For the latter, I talk back at the less experienced teachers in class, get banned from the local grocer's for shoplifting and learn to blow smoke rings and 'French inhale', though a night of perfecting the techniques with a pilfered pack of Dad's Mores leaves me doubled up on the sofa in an agony of stomach cramps. I instigate a playground fight that ends up in a huge scrap involving half the class and am hauled before the head. (*14 March – All in all a good day. I was very popular with everybody.*)

Dad takes this positivity in good spirit. He joins me in my health drive – we split grapefruits for breakfast and go jogging together. He even hooks up with a regular Hungarian girlfriend called Zsuzsa, who, in the absence of my mother, provides the caring feminine influence I crave. She attends to me through an alarming bout of thrush and offers make-up and styling tips to deal with my spots and greasy hair. My approval is noted and Dad makes a genuine effort to make the relationship work.*

I dutifully sit the various entrance exams for private schools and receive news that I have been accepted at Queen's College in Harley Street. Mum is delighted and the head at Ladbroke School is visibly relieved when I break the news. I don't consider how, in our cash-strapped circumstances, Dad will be able to afford his half of the fees, but I am less concerned about his welfare now that I am fully managing my own and he seems enthusiastic about the change, his disillusionment with my current school complete since I've started speaking in exaggerated cockney peppered with Jamaican patois. I steel myself, yet again, for a new environment.

---

* They marry a year later, but it doesn't last. Dad claims she showed her true colours once the ring was on her finger, but it's just as likely she experienced a similar revelation and realised that marriage to Ivan promised little more than taking over responsibility for his mother and child.

13

ASSIMILATION

Queen's College sits among the private medical clinics and legal practices ranged along Marylebone's Harley Street. The school has no uniform, but imposes a no-trousers policy, which is unfortunate, since the only vaguely fashionable items in my wardrobe consist of jeans and T-shirts. I pray that my cobbled-together outfit of unbranded leftovers from Ladbroke School's uniform and donations from Dad's girlfriend will pass muster. Though I am, yet again, thrown into a pool of established classmates, the girls are mostly friendly and welcoming, no one takes the piss out of my name and only Camilla snorts at my dorky outfit and hoots: 'Where the *hell* is Willesden Green?!'

I am initially coopted by the self-appointed Alpha set, a braying cabal of Sloaney girls which includes the neighing Camilla, whose own lack of any discernible academic ability belies the school's entrance-exam selection process. This is more down to the group's grabby entitlement of having first dibs on any new toys, rather than any glittering impression I might have made and my novelty wears off as my increasingly bizarre fashion choices – a mix of Zsuzsa's cast-offs and a selection of far-out samples from Mum's fashion-designer friend Michiko – provoke side-eyed sniggers. When I unwisely accept an invite to a party peopled by intimidating poshos, my snazzy pink parachute suit is openly ridiculed and the torture is prolonged when Dad fails to collect me at the appointed time and I pale at the proposed taxi fare required to swiftly vacate the premises.

Mum sends me a cheque for clothes and I buy an outfit copied exactly from the mannequin display at Miss Selfridge (powder-blue sweater dress, cream tights, ankle-bunched leg warmers and gold ballet pumps). I make efforts to fit in by tempering my speech, though my maths teacher, Mrs Brass, is unimpressed and warns me: 'You're developing that awful Queen's College accent.' But she has no idea that the way I speak has already undergone a multitude of fluctuations over the years.* I spend a month getting used to the gas-permeable contact lenses I've been sent from Japan, increasing my tolerance in half-hour increments. The agony and involuntary weeping eventually subsides and I triumphantly ditch the bottle-thick glasses that have plagued me for half my life.

My diligent efforts to catch up in class are noted by our impos-ing and eccentric head, Mrs Fierz (so posh she pronounces 'off' as 'orf'), who hails me with encouraging jollity as we mingle our way past her to morning assembly and eventually I get the wolf-whistle approval of our history teacher, once I adopt the rah-rah skirt favoured by many of the pupils and receive the same

---

* My accent was often commented on during the Lush years, the mix of cockney swearing and RP apparently revealing me as a fake. But, as a bilingual child of immi-grants, I found switching accents a normal part of assimilation and, even now, the way I speak can vary depending on the situation (and how much I've had to drink).

lingering, leering stares from our physics teacher tolerated by the other girls. It's creepy, but it feels like acceptance.*

Some of the girls spend their holidays visiting second homes in exotic-sounding places I've never heard of and I big up my global exploits in Los Angeles, Tokyo and Hungary to give the impression of parity. I lie to sidestep awkward questions and join in the bitchy bullying of a geeky classmate, ensuring I'm not bottom of the pecking order. At Christmas, I plunder the parcels sent from Japan and America to buy my way into the affections of each and every classmate, making up any short-fall in my blanket Yuletide gift giving via shoplifting trips down Oxford Street.

Meanwhile, I remain guardedly vague about details of Staverton Road, particularly after visiting various well-appointed properties in Kensington, Highbury and Hampstead. In the face of concerned enquiries about my mother living so far away, I am maniacally upbeat. ('It's great having a mum in LA! I get brilliant holidays!! I'm fine living with Dad, we're so close!') My mantra is to show no weakness and the strategy seems to work. In short, I end up fitting in. Not seamlessly, of course: at Ladbroke, I was considered suspiciously wealthy (the first time Maria came over, she was staggered by the comparison to her own council flat: 'Is this *whole house* yours?!'); at Queen's, I'm regarded as being 'a bit rough' (one girl's reported assessment from her parents). And I am not a good enough actor to erase entirely my misfit, mixed-up baggage, but all I crave is enough acceptance to avoid being a complete outcast.

---

* Queen's College recently removed its portrait of Mrs Fierz, hung on the wall to commemorate her headship, reputedly because of her tolerance of the inappropriate sexual behaviour of certain male teachers.

While I am honing my identity in London, Ray has embarked on a similar project in Los Angeles. Eschewing the casual work-wear favoured by TV studio crew, he crams his wardrobe with a showy rainbow of identically cut bespoke suits from Rodeo Drive and accessorises his perma-tan with a safe-load of bling. Mum is showered with diamond-encrusted jewellery from Cartier, which she finds gaudy and not to her taste. She bridles at being used as a prop to brag about his financial success and fears his next purchase will be a tiara.

But Ray's gone full method actor for his role of successful English gentleman, refining his mannerisms and accent and loudly signalling his superior class by making snobby observations of the hoi polloi. On a lavish trip to Hawaii, when Mum and I join him during filming for *Magnum, PI*, he bristles with embarrassment as we hoick our luggage through the hotel, ushering us to leave the grunt work to 'the staff' and muttering 'We're better than that'. When a stuntman friend from Ray's Pinewood days comes to holiday with his family, he derides their East End accents and lack of sophistication, vowing never to invite them again.

I'd never chimed with Dad's sneering at Ray's working-class background, which is the least problematic thing about him. The opposite, in fact – I stand in admiration at his hard-won achievements. Born into poverty, raised on a council estate and with little formal education, he became embroiled in local gang activity, destined for a criminal career. Being conscripted at eighteen to serve in the Korean War was an experience so traumatic that he only ever spoke about it once to Yasuko, on the understanding that it would never be mentioned again. On the plus side, however, his athletic ability was recognised and developed during army training.

After returning to civilian life, his future was turned around by an offer to move to Hollywood (reputedly arranged by the Krays, but this may be an embellishment) to work as Cary Grant's chauffeur, bodyguard and all-round Man Friday. He went on to become his stuntman stand-in in *North by Northwest*, which in turn led to a successful career as a stunt coordinator (*Saturday Night and Sunday Morning, The Loneliness of the Long Distance Runner, Cleopatra, Tom Jones*). Being a stuntman in those pre-insurance days of filming was in itself a lethally dangerous profession, so I appreciate that Ray has had a tough and precarious climb to get to where he is. And to then make the leap from one successful career to another, by becoming a director, was no mean feat either.

But their extravagant lifestyle draws some unwelcome attention. During a trip to Las Vegas, the house is burgled and Ray's collection of Rolex timepieces is swiped. Though the goods are recovered, Ray is stung by the violation and pays close attention to the investigating LAPD cop's advice – arm yourself with a gun and, if faced with an intruder, aim at the heart. Also, fire a shot in the ceiling *after* you've dispatched the trespasser, so you can claim you gave fair warning. He installs a high-security alarm system and, ignoring Yasuko's objections, secretes a number of weapons around the house, one of which I discover with a shock under his pillow when I help make the beds. Rather than being reassured by this arsenal of protection, the expectation of threat leaves me in a state of panic whenever I am alone in the house. Every passing car and outside noise sends my heart racing and on nights when Mum and Ray are out hobnobbing, I watch TV with a cocked pistol cradled in my lap.

My visits to LA are more enjoyable when I have my stepsisters for company, but maintaining outward good cheer while suffering constant separation anxiety from all the transatlantic to-ing and fro-ing is hard on all three of us and adolescence has made us more argumentative. Min bullies her sister and is fiercely competitive with me, which leads to bickering spats, where Ray invariably takes Min's side, blaming me and scolding Jo for disloyalty. During one row, he flies into a rage, chasing me through the house, then thrashing my arse repeatedly. Mum is furious and starts packing a suitcase, threatening to spend the rest of the holiday booked into a hotel with me. Realising she is serious, Ray deploys his go-to scene stealer and fakes a heart attack. I mischievously suggest that we call an ambulance, keen to see how Ray improvises his apparent proximity to death when faced with qualified medics, but he croakily insists he will manfully weather the storm and I am left to coolly observe the handmaidens showering him with concern as he milks the situation for maximum sympathy.

For the rest of the holiday, Min and Ray increasingly withdraw into each other's company, leaving Jo and me spending most of our time with Yasuko. From my perspective, this is a marvellous outcome and I suspect it's what Min, too, has craved all along. She wants nothing more than to be with her daddy and to have him to herself all the time. I know just how she feels. But the stress has been trying for Ray (the 'heart attack' is invoked as evidence) and it's agreed that in future Min and I will have to be separated, our holiday visits alternated: I will come for Christmas; Jo and Min at Easter – which means, from January '82, I won't see Mum for six long months.

14

THANK YOU FOR THE MUSIC

Most of the music I listened to during my childhood came via the telly: back in the 1970s, Shirley Bassey, Cilla Black, Marc Bolan, Nana Mouskouri, Lulu and more hosted light-entertainment shows and I found the cosy evening-in-the-company-of style comforting, with chit-chat, some mild humour and then a big finish featuring an influx of dancers, like the party's really taken off now. I loved the kid-friendly antics of *The Monkees*, but the glam acts on *Supersonic* terrified me – Gary Glitter and Alvin Stardust with their stary eyes and the bizarre heavily made-up blokes who looked like brickies in drag. A bit too much of a challenge. I was more familiar with Judy Garland and Carmen Miranda than the landmark rock acts of the era and was better versed in theme tunes and adverts, which often featured catchy melodies and well-crafted orchestrations. Many years later, when I was in a band, I'd often soundcheck my vocals by singing commercials for Richard Shops, C&A and Smarties.

I loved the lush fantasies of film musicals and my favourite was *My Fair Lady*. The story of Eliza Doolittle, made to conform to be recognised as worthwhile, held a particular appeal and I knew every word of 'Just You Wait', where she fantasised with relish about her mentor and tormentor meeting his death in a variety of vivid scenarios. But I loved *Oliver!*, *Singin' in the Rain*, *Fiddler on the Roof*, *Top Hat* and all the rest and would flail around the living room copying the dance moves, although the only one I really nailed was Laurel & Hardy's routine in *Way Out West*.

Dad wasn't much into music himself, though he would often sing Elvis's 'Heartbreak Hotel' and Adam Faith's 'What Do You Want' in a comically exaggerated Hungarian accent, while the soundtrack to our pan-European drives included Donna Summer, Michael Jackson and *Saturday Night Fever* – he did, after all, enjoy the occasional bop at discotheques when scanning the dancefloor for conquests. In Hungary, Nora would often tune the crackly radio to the woozy violin and lively percussive cimbalom of Gypsy music (despite being wholly intolerant of the ethnic group who performed it); and, in Japan, my grandfather Sanji would play me English-speaking solo artists from Nat King Cole and Frank Sinatra to Dusty Springfield and Julie Andrews – gesticulating at the album covers and exclaiming in delight: 'Very famous in Japan!'

Mum had played the piano as a child and I'd pester her to perform Chopin's 'Minute Waltz', marvelling as her fingers flitted up and down the keys. We'd blast the radio when driving around in her Mini Clubman, singing along to top-forty hits. Even though Mum was grudgingly allowed to play her Carly Simon and Roberta Flack tapes at home, Ray's only concession to contemporary music was the Carpenters and Manhattan Transfer. I'd have to watch *Top of the Pops* on a tiny black-and-white portable in the bathroom to avoid him snapping off the telly in disgust or else surreptitiously phone Dial-a-Disc for daily access to popular hits.*

I'd listen to tapes (Abba, ELO, Blondie – I'd developed a torch-bearing devotion to Debbie Harry ever since the band performed 'Denis' on *TotP* and was beside myself with rapt excitement watching her appearance on *The Muppet Show*) on Dad's portable cassette player but he needed it to use for interviews so access was intermittent and playing the few singles I'd bought from Spin It Records on Willesden High Road (a cosy little shop most notable for the beautiful collie dog who lay sleeping in the display window) on the ancient valve-powered radiogram in our Staverton Road living room wasn't much fun with Nora patrolling the area. Mostly, I just listened to Radio 1 on a tiny transistor radio in my bedroom, until the happy day when Sanji gifted me with a Sony Walkman during one of my Japanese visits. One of the few contemporary English-language pop choices available in the music catalogue he ordered from was a cassette of Madness's *Absolutely*, which to this day I associate with the cultural dissonance of singing along to 'On the Beat Pete' while lounging on a futon atop a tatami floor, surrounded by rice-paper screens. But I was a fan of Madness already, because at Ladbroke ska was universally loved. The music spoke of urban working-class life and several of the bands reflected the ethnic mix of our school, which made it relatable to all the girls. I wasn't working-class myself, but I was in that environment and trying to fit in with it. I especially loved the Specials – there was a vulnerable sadness to Terry

---

* Dial-a-Disc: a service run by the Post Office where you could listen to current chart singles.

Hall's vocals and their lyrics were my first introduction to a political thinking separate from parental influence.

My Walkman became an isolation tank, providing complete sensory escape. While books, films and TV programmes had long offered absorbing distraction, this remarkable bit of kit shut out the rest of the world entirely. I could close my eyes and immerse myself in other worlds – the cool spaciness of the Human League's *Dare!*, the off-beat rabble-rousing of the Clash's *Combat Rock*, the colourful dreamscapes of The Teardrop Explodes' *Kilimanjaro*. But it hadn't occurred to me that music could be an 'interest' – like a hobby, to be explored, analysed and discussed – until I became friends at Queen's with Maxine, who lived one stop away from me on the Jubilee line in Kilburn (and who remains my closest friend to this day). It was a revelation to sit in her bedroom, the walls covered in band posters and a collage of images cut from music magazines and discover that talking about music could be a bonding experience and a route into friendship, intimacy and easy conversation.

15

EMMA

Emma Anderson's arrival at Queen's is pre-empted by some malicious bad-mouthing from one of the Alpha mob, who remembers her from an exclusive Kensington prep school called Lady Eden's. To me, this serves as a glowing recommendation and I feel an instant connection since we are wearing the exact same gold-and-black-weave flats. Emma, too, is an only child and she bemoans being plucked from her much-loved boarding school, Rosemead in Littlehampton, because her parents were no longer either willing or able to pay the fees. I myself have recently been informed by the school office that Dad has failed, from the very beginning, to pay his half of my education and I am in danger of being slung out unless the finances are rectified. So Emma's admission, along with her experience of reluctant uprooting, makes me feel we share common ground.

But unlike me, Emma seems unassailably self-assured. When she discovers the slanderous gossip circulated about her, she is outraged – 'Bloody charming!' – but shows no signs of vulnerability. When subjected to pointed questions about country houses and skiing trips, she is frank and upfront – no searching for the least-worst response or offering muttered admissions braced for humiliation. And, when one unguarded answer prompts shrieks from Kim of 'Oh my *God*! Everyone – Emma's daddy doesn't have a *car*!', she is unfazed, commenting that Kim is a moron and ridiculing her cut-glass howl. 'Emma's daddy doesn't have a *car*!' becomes our shorthand for mocking witless snobs.

She is also very, very funny. Her laugh – sometimes so debilitating that she has to yelp and gasp for air – is infectious and her humour is outrageous and inventive. She makes up insane, filthy stories about an imaginary character called 'Old Mary', revelling in their shock value.* And, when we bond over music (Emma has been to see Japan play live, which is exciting and impressive), she initiates a pop chart of smutty band names and songs – 'Hairless Mammaries' by Durex Durex, 'Tin Bum' by Crapan, 'Let's Bang On' by Hairy Fannylow, 'Oh Goolie' by Breaking Heavings – the hilarity increased by the tortuousness of the puns.†

There are five in our group – Maxine, Bunny, Alice, Emma and me – and we develop gang confidence. While the moneyed mob brag loudly about their encounters with Westminster boys at parties and balls, we obsess over the latest top-forty entries, combing *Smash Hits* for pop facts and song lyrics, diplomatically selecting separate band members to develop crushes on and poring over the handwritten gig lists issued by Our Price

---

* 'Old Mary sat in her rocking chair, wiry pubic hair stuffed into an old pair of Y-fronts, holding the severed penis of her dead husband.' I can't recall the rest but there was something about 'deflowering virgins with a rusty spike' and toasting Christmas with a goblet of blood.

† 'Careless Memories' by Duran Duran, 'Tin Drum' by Japan, 'Let's Hang On' by Barry Manilow, 'Oh Julie' by Shakin' Stevens.

(the Oxford Street branch has a ticket booth) for future gigs to attend. Emma lives within walking distance of the school and her home becomes our unofficial HQ.

———————

Emma's family lives in a private apartment within the grand premises of the Naval and Military Club (known informally as the In & Out) on Half Moon Street, Piccadilly, where her father, William – in semi-retirement following an illustrious military career – is the club secretary. Polite and personable, he is most often absorbed in a book or newspaper, puffing away quietly on a pipe. Emma's mother, Dilys, is larger than life and bears all the trappings of the lady of leisure – always fully made up and flamboyantly accessorised, tinkling a cocktail tumbler and wafting a vapour trail of perfume and cigarette smoke. Compared to Mum and Dad, they seem old – more like grandparents than parents. Dilys proudly shows us a framed photograph of Emma dolled up in frills and ribbons, curtseying to the Queen Mother and addresses her daughter as 'Emmy darling', which makes Emma's jaw tighten.[*]

We are encouraged to confine ourselves to Emma's bedroom, which is equipped with a fancy hi-fi, telly *and* a Betamax VCR (uncommon at that time even in living rooms, never mind kids' bedrooms) and spend our after-school sessions watching hours of bands' TV performances that Emma has compiled to videotapes and with which we become so obsessively familiar that every hand gesture and facial expression is delighted in and commented on,

———————

[*] 'Emmy' becomes her early nickname among our group, embellished to 'Emmy-woo', then truncated to 'Ewoo'.

every flicker of interference noise that occasionally sizzles across the screen pre-empted with a rehearsed groan. The club's kitchens provide dinners of scampi and chips to order, delivered via a dumb waiter and Dilys offers us the choice of Woodpecker cider or ginger beer from a well-stocked mini-bar of mixers. The two seem interchangeable and I have no idea at this age that cider contains alcohol, which goes some way to explaining why our evenings round at Emma's often crescendo into riotous lunacy.

Our shrieking laughter brings Dilys to the door, pleading that we 'do please keep the noise down' as 'Daddy needs his peace', to which Emma responds with rising impatience, 'Yes ALRIGHT! Just GET OUT!', inviting a calm and jolly 'No need to shout, dear'. In all their interactions, Emma seems prickly and ready to snap, which Dilys blithely ignores. The apartment has no outside space and the rest of the club is verboten, so when the confines of her bedroom become claustrophobic, we decamp to the steps of All Souls' Church opposite Broadcasting House, on the lookout for band members appearing on David 'Kid' Jensen's evening show; or head out to the busy streets of Piccadilly to giggle at the tourists. On one occasion, Emma dresses for the promenade, grabbing her father's shooting hat and mother's mink fur, trailing a loaf of Hovis in their tiny Yorkshire terrier's dog lead and parading around Berkeley Square doing mocking impersonations of Dilys.

It's not uncommon for teenagers to feel embarrassed about – even hostile towards – their parents, but I've never witnessed another child be so casually and habitually rude to one. Apart from myself. It's the first time I've met someone of my own age whose relationship with an adult family member even glancingly matches my own intolerant anger and Emma's behaviour makes me wonder whether I've discovered a kindred spirit.

16

MADHOUSE

After some lawyer-backed efforts to force Dad to pay his half of my school fees, Yasuko accepts that, if she refuses to cover the costs, it's me that will lose out. Dad's not bothered either way. Uppermost in his mind these days is a sour-faced bleached blonde called Lynn, who he chaperones around nightclubs and on trips to Torremolinos. Closer to me in age than to Dad, she regards me with hostile, competitive contempt. But Dad is enamoured and doesn't seek my approval. I'd call it a mid-life crisis, but really that applies to his entire adult existence.

Meanwhile, conditions in Staverton Road are in free-fall. Dad, who like Nora grew up expecting invisible hands to carry out the donkey work, has no practical skills whatsoever. He is baffled by non-functioning items and passively observes the deterioration as carpets grow threadbare and damp patches spread across the walls. Occasionally, a friend or lodger is commandeered into tackling odd jobs, but since Dad is unwilling to pay a professional, abandoned repairs and renovations are everywhere – a light switch dangling from a hole in the dining-room wall, a half-smashed cistern lid trailing plastic string for operating the broken flush mechanism, plastic tubs positioned to catch radiator leakages, bathroom fittings caked in lime, doors that don't close, windows that don't open, peeling paint, missing doorknobs, broken appliances littering every room . . . the neglect is overwhelming. On one particularly blustery day, a 4-foot section of my rotting bedroom window sails free of the surrounding brickwork and smashes to pieces in the front garden. I cover the hole in black binbags, which is how it stays for the next six months.

Nora's contribution to this chaos is to fill the house with clutter from her only remaining pastime – spending her pension money on daily shopping trips to Willesden High Road. Not satisfied with packing her bedroom with crockery, glassware and decorative tat from the local pound shops, she hoards an apocalypse-ready pantry of dry goods, jars and canned foods and regularly empties the kitchen of equipment, hiding half-drunk mugs of tea in the stereogram speakers, a frying pan of oil in the piano stool, dirty cutlery down the side of her TV-viewing armchair and plates of leftover meals under the sofa. The mice love it and their droppings are everywhere. On one heart-stopping occasion, I investigate a scratching noise emanating from a chest and, yanking open a drawer, snap the backs of two rodents gorging on a rotting loaf of bread.

Paranoid that her precious trinkets will be thieved by the lodgers, Nora has an armoury of locks fitted to her bedroom door. She keeps the keys – and those of the rest of the house's internal doors – on a kilt pin attached to her undergarments, her approach signalled by their jangling as she patrols the house like a prison guard. Rather than securing her haul, this gives the impression that there is something in there worth protecting and on a rare occasion when we are all out together, the house gets broken into. The intruder clearly had some insider knowledge because nothing has been touched bar Nora's door, which is hanging off its hinges. One can only imagine the burglar's frustration, having breached the vault, at finding nothing more valuable than the contents of a charity-shop sorting room. As the police dust their way around the surfaces of the house, one officer takes in the scattered papers, broken furniture and general disorder and commiserates over the wanton destruction perpetrated by the intruder. My rather downbeat reply is: 'Ah no, it's always like this.'

My obsessively ordered bedroom offers an oasis of respite from the decay, but efforts to defend its borders are no match for Nora, who repeatedly throws open my door and bursts into the room, accusing me of stealing her curtains (or some other random item) or locks it from the outside to establish the upper hand. Unable to find peace, she disrupts mine. It's impossible to even make a cup of tea without starting a fight with Granny because she has hoarded away everything – cups, spoons, kettle, pans, tea, sugar – claiming they have all been 'stolen'. Restocking the kitchen involves breaking into her fortress bedroom, which in turn requires my fumbling in her underwear to access the fiercely protected keys. This provokes fruity giggles among her howling protests of violation, then a call to 999 emergency services. This move was effective the first time – I was terrified by the two officers rushing into our home, comforting the sobbing Nora and shooting me suspicious looks, despite my reassurances that there had been no robbery. Now I just wait out the drama as she wails our address down the phone, then positions herself in my doorway smiling with malevolent triumph.

I have grown inured to Granny's tears and howls, unmoved by her age and her declining mobility. I watch her struggling bulk descending the stairs and coolly imagine planting my foot on her back and booting her into oblivion. It would be so easy to rid myself of her, to finally be free of her poisonous presence. Just one quick kick and she'd be on the floor, irreparably broken. It's not guilt at committing murder that stops me, but the knowledge that I would be caught and jailed. Hold it together, Miki, bide your time. No point in letting her ruin the rest of your life. One day you can leave and be rid of her for ever.

———————

Unbelievably, Dad has kept his promise and I get a hi-fi system for my fifteenth birthday. I spend every moment listening to records borrowed from the local library, recording songs off the radio and making mix-tapes for my Walkman and to send to Mum, who now has her car stereo permanently tuned to the alternative music station KROQ – a musical bond that bridges the vast distance that separates us. On the downside, I get caught thieving singles from HMV in Oxford Street. Dad collects me from the police station, where he gives me a conspiratorial wink and fakes a bit of fury, then chides me: 'If you're going to shoplift, the trick is not to get caught.' But he is, despite repeated reminders from me, absent for the at-home interview to discuss the charges and court date. The social worker waits with me for an hour, noting my increasing agitation and, when it becomes clear that Ivan is a no-show, casts his eyes around the squalor of our surroundings and sighs: 'I think you've got enough problems as it is.' I get let off with a caution.

At weekends I spend as much time as possible with my friends. We do Saturday circuits of Carnaby Street, Kensington Market, Portobello Road and King's Road – perusing the clothes and accessories, checking out the youth tribes and thrilled when we spot musicians out shopping. One particularly fruitful afternoon nets us Mike Nolan of Bucks Fizz, Malcolm Ross and David McClymont from Orange Juice and Big John of the Exploited. We kit ourselves out with army-surplus and workman gear from Laurence Corner, which we cover in sew-on badges and marker-penned band names and dye the rest of our clothes black. The Vidal Sassoon School on South Molton Street offers free hair-cuts from students, which we spike up with egg white and sugar.

At school, Mrs Fierz jovially refers to us as the Funeral Brigade, barking that my Siouxsie-style eye make-up is 'marvellous! You must show me how to apply it sometime!' The rest of the staff are tolerant – despite outward appearances, we are well behaved compared to disruptive girls who feel that paying fees entitles them to throw their weight around in class. But, while some of our peers find our peacocking fun, others sneer at our uniform identity and ridicule us for trying to look 'hard'. It baffles me that they even care, given that we are in no position to compete with their trendy designer clothes from expensive boutiques on New Bond Street. But I realise now that those who rule the roost don't like having their values rejected. You're meant to slavishly follow their lead, always falling just short of their standards – not carve out your own space and pursue an alternative. This mixed reception is replicated in the outside world. Some tourists ask to pose for photos while others back away in terror; we get stopped to chat by friendly punks, but are also chased by skinheads. On one Tube journey, I am trapped and shoved about by a group of Mohicans who only relent when they spot a Damned badge on my clothing.

While it's great to be part of a gang, my desperation to escape Nora, along with the emotional hole left by months of separation from Mum and my increasingly distant relationship with Dad, make me pathetically needy. I fish for invites on Fridays after school and overstay my welcome. After inveigling myself into dinner, then overnight, then much of the next day at Maxine's, she informs me that the family are visiting a relative suffering from a brain tumour in hospital. 'Can I come?' I ask brightly, leaving Maxine to conduct urgent, whispered discussions with her mother: 'I don't know what to do, she won't leave!' My ploy is less successful with Alice, whose parents insist on a 9 p.m. bedtime for the whole family and any late pick-ups mean waiting alone in the chilly library; while Bunny has a huge family of distant cousins that she cycles through, claiming imminent gatherings, when she needs an excuse to get rid of me. Emma is less circumspect and when my presence has worn thin, she simply moans: 'Look, can you just GO?'

It's a shame that I can't be more honest and simply confess that I'm not coping with life at home, but I am more used to rejecting help than asking for it and cheerful denial has become my survival tactic for staying halfway sane. To my friends, my clinginess seems like a tiresome character flaw with no reasonable justification and I can sense them drawing away from me as occasional slips in their rehearsed stories give away weekend meet-ups that I've not been party to.

17

HAIRCUTS AND HORRORS

When I went for my student haircut at the Vidal Sassoon School, my shrugging 'do whatever you like' instruction prompted excited discussion among the teaching staff. I sit in the chair now, as Ricky perms, cuts and bleaches, talking the attentive students through his creation. It's more of a sculpture than a haircut, the lower half of my head cropped to an inch, topped with intermittent hanging strands and a ponytail of bleached corkscrew perm, which he backcombs into an explosion above one ear. Left to my poor maintenance skills, the careful construction usually ends up shoved into an elastic band, not dissimilar to your standard modern 'undercut ponytail'. But Ricky is delighted with his creation and arranges for me to appear at a hair show and have professional photos taken.

Thrilled to have found a new social group, I begin hanging out with the twenty-something crowd of students and teachers. I am invited along to regular evening get-togethers in the Running Horse, where I am talked out of my fandom of chart-toppers and directed towards Echo & the Bunnymen and Joy

Division. I tentatively try my first joint and end up sick as a dog slumped over the toilet for several hours, but Ricky looks after me and pays for a cab to take me home. This activity is treated with suspicion by my friends at school, who find my gushing descriptions of pub-night shenanigans with the Sassoon crowd tiresome. There are murmurs behind my back that I am getting above myself and my callousness is disapprovingly noted when their phonecalls to Staverton Road are met with howling entreaties from Nora, who has no idea where I am.

It's true – I never bother to explain my movements and sometimes return alarmingly late due to the unannounced transport strikes that plague this period. On just such a night, after being treated to dinner by the Vidal crew at the trendy Coconut Grove, I embark on the long trek home. Fast-walking up a deserted Lisson Grove, I abstractedly observe a couple far behind me and clock that they are still following as I navigate through the drunks and nightcrawlers populating the 24-hour knees-up of Kilburn High Road, then turn into the silent, winding stretch of Willesden Lane.

The sound of quickening footsteps makes me look over my shoulder and realise my mistake – not a bloke and his girlfriend, but two men, one of whom is running at me full tilt. My screams seem muted and small. Within seconds, I am hooked by the neck, stumbling towards a mass of shrubbery in the corner of my vision. I've dropped to the ground, forcing my attacker to drag my full weight and am grabbing at the bushes, arms scratched and bleeding. Then, suddenly, he's gone. I sprint up the road, desperately flagging passing vehicles. The third car stops and I throw myself in the passenger seat, sobbing with relief. I know nothing about my rescuer, only that he was kind and concerned and drove me home.

Dad is thankfully present and immediately rushes us to the police station. The uniform at the desk dutifully fills out a report, but, in response to Dad's demands that the massed forces of the Metropolitan Police rally to comb the area for the culprits, the policeman shrugs and admits that it's unlikely that anyone will be caught. My description is scant and his unsympathetic demeanour conveys a palpable vibe of 'What do you expect, dressed like that, girl of your age out at this time of night?' Dad is bristling with rage and we spend the next half-hour driving around the darkened streets. He's desperate to find someone to beat to a pulp, but I am not going to identify a random stranger just so he can offload his upset. Still, his concern is touching and I am grateful that he never once implied that I might have been 'asking for it' in any way.

I tell my schoolfriends about the assault and, though they seem shocked, they say little. It might help if I could cry or show my distress, but I am so unused to emotional honesty that I probably come across like I'm outlining the plot of a thriller. I'm later told of their muttering that it's typical that nothing *really* bad happened to me – if it had been anyone else, they'd have been murdered. It seems a little twisted to imply that surviving a sex attack is somehow proof of undeserved good fortune, but I get that presenting a relentlessly bulletproof exterior to the world can grate on those around you and sap their sympathy.

The Sassoon crowd, who are older, see through my veneer of cheery toughness. Their comforting hugs open the floodgates and I end up sobbing in the toilets with the girls. Two days later, I am back in the pub with one of the hairdressers, on whom I have a massive and undisguised crush. He is also feeling emotional – about to leave London for a new position within the Sassoon organisation – and, as we part at the station, he wraps me in an embrace. I am snapped out of bliss by a tap on the shoulder – a girl from their group is getting the Jubilee line and firmly insists that she will accompany me. My crush hastily pulls his hand out of my pants and I stagger off with my chaperone.

Any daydreams of an ongoing romance are dashed when my crush completely ignores me at his leaving do the following night. I exit early and decide to steer clear of the crowd for a while, aware that I have humiliated myself. Meanwhile, I obsessively replay the sexual assault, catastrophising my narrow escape. Thank God the second man did nothing. Had he grabbed my feet, I'd have easily been carried into darkness. And what if my assailant had punched me in the face? I might have been cowed into submission. I berate myself for not hammering on a door for help. But which door? What if the house I chose had been empty for the night? If I'd been listening to my Walkman, I'd have been oblivious to the running footsteps and instant, easy prey. On journeys to and from school, I scan passers-by and panic that I might be walking in step with my attacker. He could be standing next to me in the newsagent or sat across from me on the Tube.

———

Dad heads off abroad and is gone for months. He's immersed in a working friendship with a tech millionaire, convinced that ghost-writing his biography could finally be the big break he is after. Left alone with Nora's madness, obsessing about the attack and cut off from my social groups, I am spiralling, unravelling. Music isn't helping – it either jars with or exacerbates my volatile mood. Even writing in my diary seems futile and dry. So I burn my legs with cigarettes and rake my arms with a badge pin. Actively administering my pain, rather than being passively devoured by it, gives me the illusion of control. But the effect doesn't last long and hiding the scars, lying about them and lying to myself that no one has spotted them just makes me feel even more alienated and pathetic.

I recall the confusing sensation of uncontrolled tears with no apparent trigger; skipping lessons and swigging vodka in a toilet cubicle at school, cutting myself with a glass shard from the smashed quarter-bottle. I must have reached out to Mum because I stayed at the family home of one of her friends. Yasuko was always a fixer – good at calling in favours – though I wish she'd come herself. There's a clear memory of Mrs Fierz setting me up with a camp bed in a room at the top of the school. I don't know how long I lived there, but packing away my belongings and vacating the space by 8.30 a.m. for music tutorials became an established routine.

These serial upheavals are prelude to me becoming a boarder at Queen's College's hostel, where I get to cohabit with friendly girls and sane adults and am fed regular meals in a clean and ordered environment. Dad frames this move as a betrayal, but I suspect he is a little relieved and, in any case, Mum is paying for everything. But the hostel is only available during term-time weekdays and it doesn't erase my feelings of abandonment. I want love. Proper love. With me at the centre.

18

TEENAGE KICKS

Emma's dad retires from his post at the club and the family moves to a terraced Georgian house in leafy St John's Wood. In retaliation against the tastefully conservative décor, Emma plasters her ceiling with posters of bands and buys in a load of spray paints, sample pots and indelible markers, inviting our gang over to graffiti her bedroom walls, one of which bears the legend TOILETS ARE DIRTY in huge green letters. Dilys disapproves, of course, but Emma seems to revel in provoking her mother and concocts bizarre scenarios with which to string her along. She proclaims that she is going to see a band called the Wafting Farts at the Marquee, purely to bait her mother into repeating the name and pretends Satanic possession by lying on the floor, glassy eyed and chanting Latin declensions.

But Dilys is just as prone to pushing Emma's buttons, pulling her up on every dropped 't' in her speech and upbraiding her for unladylike behaviour: 'You'll never meet any nice young men if you act like that!' Much of the conflict between them springs from Dilys's determined hope that Emma will, like herself, marry well and become a housewife. It infuriates Emma that her mother dismisses her own ambitions – education, independence, a career – as adolescent whimsy. And I'm aware that Dilys can't stand me, not least because Emma's said as much. The feeling is mutual. But despite branding me a bad influence, her parents continue to allow me into their home, which I have to admit is remarkably tolerant of them.

On one of our Saturday excursions, we spot Tom Bailey of the Thompson Twins outside the trendy vintage American clothing store Flip in Covent Garden and rush to claim an autograph. He reveals that the band are about to take a new direction (we saw their last gig as a seven-piece back in April) and will be mixing at RAK Studios the following day. This just happens to be almost directly opposite Emma's new address and we spend the Sunday mucking about outside the studio, squealing every time we spot Tom in an upstairs window. When the front door opens, we hide on the steps to the basement, only to see his rather puzzled face staring down at us from street level. 'Would you like to come in?'

Thus it is that Emma and I sit on a couch in the mixing room, shyly munching on cheese sandwiches, exchanging OMG glances and nodding along enthusiastically to 'Love on Your Side'. This adolescent brush with a bona fide pop star provides us with a separate bond from the rest of our group and we spend hours together reliving every detail of the thrilling encounter. Tom's label – Arista – has its offices on Cavendish Square, a stone's throw from our school and it's a buzz to stop and chat when our paths cross. We get treated to free records and guest-list gigs and, when the Thompson Twins tour America, they invite Mum to their LA gig and she ends up taking them for meals and driving them out to Malibu for a day at the beach. I'm proud, if not a little jealous, that she is now friends with them, but Emma feels that the balance is now tipped in my favour and makes frequent comments that 'He likes you more than me'. Our other friends wonder if we're making the whole thing up.

As is often the case with close-knit groups of adolescent girls, the dynamic is forever shifting and fracturing, at the mercy of hormonal mood swings. Maxine and Bunny are the longest-established unit and I envy their unassailable closeness. Alice is often sidelined because her parents are so strict that she is ferried to and from school every day and allowed barely any freedom, so Emma and I, both sibling free and with zero family life, are often thrown into each other's company by default. But, while Emma seems happy enough barricading herself in her bedroom or winding up her mother for entertainment, I am needy for friendship and disproportionately insecure about any disagreements between us. On one occasion when we fall out, I write Emma a long letter of apology and buy her a Eurythmics single as a peace offering. While Maxine notes the generosity of the gift, Emma responds drily: 'I should upset her more often.'

———

There is a well-worn adage that being desperate for love makes you far less likely to find it and I am absolutely desperate for love. My recent Tube-station fumble is just the latest in a series of ill-judged efforts to lose myself in a romantic affair. Holidays with Nora and Dad in Spain, where I was free to roam unsupervised, offered promising opportunities with local boys, but I was scared off by the brusque speed at which these streetwise Romeos operated. It seems safer to take the more traditional route of pursuing romance at school discos and parties, where the boys are my age and there is at least some chance of conversation and mutual interests. But their tentatively paced efforts at a relationship aren't calibrated to my need for immediate, overwhelming passion and I abandon them in frustration. One promising encounter, on a school-trip cross-Channel ferry, sparks several months of exciting, yearning correspondence. However, the relationship reaches a humiliating conclusion when Dad, in a bid to find out where the hell I am, reads my diary and discovers I am spending the weekend at his parents' pub in Plymouth. The police track me down and promptly apprehend me as a runaway.

Frustrated that things move either too slow or too fast for me, I convince myself that the only thing holding me back from a proper full-blown relationship is my virginity, which I resolve to rid myself of at the first opportunity. Sex becomes an imagined portal to a mature self-knowledge and I convince myself that everything will fall into place once I achieve this initiation into the adult world. Mum had warned me, during a rare birds-and-bees heart-to-heart, that I should be wary of falling in love with the first person I sleep with and I take her advice literally, resolving to ensure I don't become clingy and demanding by meticulously profiling an ideal candidate: someone I fancy enough to fuck, but have no interest in pursuing a relationship with and who in turn seems nice enough to not cause me harm, but equally won't be hurt by my using them solely for the purposes of a one-night stand.

I meet my target during a Christmas visit to LA. Mum has introduced me to the daughter of a work acquaintance, whose Beverly Hills bedroom contains a waterbed, private phone line and walk-in wardrobe of off-the-peg trends ('I'm wearing Culture

Club tonight'). She introduces me to Quaaludes and Southern Comfort and brings me along to an all-ages nightclub called the Odyssey, where I'm trancing and dancing when a bloke hoves into my space, tilts my chin up with his hand and says: 'I could have picked any one of a hundred girls here but I picked you.' Bingo! He's the perfect candidate: vain, asinine and inept at trying to appear cool and sexy – in other words, harmless.

I nod and smile as he tells me about his imminent photo shoot for *GQ*, make appreciative noises while he details the cost and provenance of his wardrobe and feign enthusiasm when he suggests a weekend trip to the beach, where I am invited to watch him surf. But I need to get things moving before his airhead personality puts me off entirely, so I stem the stream of tiresome self-promotion by sticking my tongue in his mouth.

Back at his flat, I am introduced to his brother, apparently naked beneath a bathrobe, who eyes me wolfishly while patting the sofa seat next to him. He is devastatingly handsome, but has trouble written all over him and I'm not going to complicate the evening by getting sidetracked by an extreme case of sibling rivalry, however tempting. So I decamp to the bedroom, strip naked, smoke a cigarette and wait for my chosen deflowerer to join me.

I head off at first light, silently dressing to a soundtrack of gentle snoring. There's no point waking him or leaving an address or a number – my work here is done. I take one last glance at the blood-smeared sheets and thighs of my naked, nameless lover and slip on to the LA streets, the blush of dawn matching my glow at the physical memory of a genuinely pleasurable night and the satisfaction of a perfectly executed plan. Of course, it's not quite as simple as that. I spend the next weeks panicking that I might be pregnant and worry that the bruising around my nether regions is an early sign of a fatal STD. Even more annoyingly, I haven't miraculously become the confident mature woman of the world that I'd hoped.

There's a valid argument that loverboy got exactly what he wanted – a no-strings one-night stand – and I merely played into his hands. And yet I do feel empowered, however devalued that word has become. I did what I set out to do and I made a discovery: sex without love can be enormous fun when liberated from the hope that it's the beginning of something bigger. In other words, if you approach it like a man.

19

SWEET SIXTEEN

Throughout 1983, my calendar is stuffed with gigs. I latch on to every friendly encounter and capitalise on any opportunity for socialising. Panuddha, a half-Thai girl who greets me in the queue for Bauhaus with '*You're* the girl people keep mistaking me for!', coopts me into her Richmond crowd and I regularly join Nick and Dieter, who I get chatting to after a Simple Minds gig, at the bar of the Penta Hotel in Gloucester Road, where you can buy one cup of coffee and have it refilled all night ('like they do in America') and play free table-top games of Space Invaders.

As I approach my sixteenth birthday, the very last thing on my mind is the upcoming O-level exams. I flit between Willesden and my room at Queen's, as and when it pleases me – breaking curfew rules in the former while treating the latter as a doss house. The revolting squalor of Staverton Road is no longer a shameful barrier to inviting friends over, now that it's balanced against the tempting freedom from parental supervision. One Sunday get-together begins with some duty-free vodka snatched from Dad's wardrobe and ends with me, Maxine, Emma and

Bunny frantically trying to sober up a slurring and semi-comatose Alice, who has polished off most of the bottle's contents without the rest of us noticing. When Emma's father arrives for pick-up duties, he instantly clocks that Alice is pass-out drunk and alerts her parents to the situation before marching from the house in disgust. Alice's parents arrive shortly after, armed with torches – like the FBI entering a serial killer's den – and, ignoring our plaintive reassurances that there were no drugs involved, drag her off to get her stomach pumped.

The school is pressured into expelling the four of us, but Alice heroically takes the hit, insisting that she alone was responsible for getting blind drunk. Mrs Fierz accepts that we did our best to nurse Alice back to sobriety, albeit our methods consisted of clichéd film tropes – coffee, cold shower, fresh air, walking her around the block, chips to soak up the alcohol, making her vomit up the chips – everything, in fact, except risk getting found out by calling a responsible adult or an ambulance. We dutifully write letters of apology to Alice's aggrieved parents and are let off the hook, though Alice herself is disappeared off to a boarding school in Buckinghamshire the following term.

The head warns me that, if I don't curb the behaviour, I'll be thrown out of the hostel. I feel bad about disappointing Mrs Fierz, who has done so much to help me, but am terrified that missing out on even one social event will have me backsliding into desertion and loneliness, so I feign submission while already plotting how to bend the rules. I finally have some control over my environment, no longer at the mercy of my feckless parents and I'm not about to give up my newly discovered pleasures of gigs and a social life for a bunch of tiresome exams. Especially now that I have started going out with Dieter and have become a regular overnight visitor at his welcoming family home, a stone's throw from Parliament Hill Fields.

Our developing romance is, however, kept casual by Dieter's unspoken conviction that I am two-timing him with Nick. I never discover whether this complete misapprehension is down to Dieter's insecurity or some Iago-level shit-stirring from Nick, but the effect is that my boyfriend blows hot and cold and I am frequently left hurt and baffled by his behaviour. But on the good days, we drink endless cups of tea and listen to his records (Young Marble Giants, the Fall, the Cherry Red *Pillows and Prayers* compilation) and I tag along to gigs with his crowd. Moving away from big shows at the Hammersmith Palais and Lyceum to smaller gigs at colleges and arts centres has been a revelation. I am no longer plagued by the frequent gropings and threats of violence that a wide-eyed teenage girl pressed in among a crowd of mostly men is subjected to. With the protection of a crowd of male friends, I can throw myself into the moshpit – losing myself in music and energy, overwhelmed by the adrenalin and shared euphoria – and have allies to pick me up off the floor or defend me from unwelcome interference.

The frantic socialising leaves little time for schoolwork, though I do my best to revise on bus and Tube journeys and sit up until dawn on hostel nights, dosed up on Pro-Plus, cramming for my exams. But burning the candle at both ends takes its toll and I am frequently tired and ill. I worry that the boredom-fuelled rounds of toast at the hostel and late-night takeaway binges on after-gig traipses home to Willesden are making me fat – in my addled mind, another possible explanation for Dieter's occasional hostility. But I don't have the discipline to stick to a healthy-eating regime, so I solve the problem by throwing up meals, thereby adding an eating disorder to my arsenal of self-destructive habits.

Panuddha has been complaining that living with her parents is intolerable and talks me into finding a flatshare. Mum, ever the optimist, weighs the potential for disaster against finally breaking free from Staverton Road and agrees to pay my rent. She is already funding my accommodation at the hostel, so there will be little difference financially.

Number 8 Clanricarde Gardens, Notting Hill Gate, is part of a terraced row of five-floor Victorian houses clumsily subdivided into flats and bedsits. My new home is at the back of the property, on the raised ground floor and judging by the ceiling cornicing, must once have been a single room. Now, it is segmented by flimsy partition walls into five: a living room, two bedrooms, a hall space/dining area and a kitchen equipped with the requisite sink, fridge and cooker but with the quirky addition of a bath. This is covered with a wooden lid that doubles as a counter top and, when you need a scrub, can be propped against the doorless access to the rest of the flat for privacy. The communal toilet, shared with two other bedsits on our floor, is just outside our front door.

It's shabbily furnished but the ceilings are high. And, although the property's only two windows right-angle each other over a cell-sized basement yard, enough light pours in from a skylight at the back (originally part of a 'garden room'?) to keep the living room feeling bright. We sign the six-month lease and I sub Panuddha the deposit and first month's rent, then nip home to pack up my belongings. But there are immediate setbacks: the doorbell doesn't work, the phone seems to have been disconnected and I have run out of change for the electricity meter. Then Panuddha arrives with some bad news: her mother 'absolutely hates the flat' and refuses to help her with the rent. 'And, to be honest, I've realised I'll be loads better off living at home.'

Disaster is averted when Dieter heroically steps into the breach, moving into the flat to help me out with the expenses. We'd cleared the air over my imagined infidelities during a drunken and dramatic bust-up at a Higsons gig and our relationship is now steady enough to merit cohabiting. His friend Rob, also in need of accommodation, settles into the tiny windowless box at the rear of the flat, which has just enough space for a bed and a chest of drawers. It's a revelation to be living with people with practical skills and I am in awe as they set about fixing the flat's faults and redecorating. Our flat becomes a social hub: my friends drop by to hang out or to meet up with boyfriends away from parents and our parties spill out into the street − which sounds obnoxious but really the worst that happens is having to mop up some vomit on the stairs and the kettle getting filled with tomato soup.

Dieter and I share the larger of the two bedrooms, chuckling at its kinky wall of mirror tiles and speculating on the room's historic use − Clanricarde Gardens reputedly contains several brothels and we receive daily phonecalls from rasping men demanding, 'Have you got big tits?' Mum pays a flying visit and gives the flat a nod of approval, but, noticing that I am clearly sexually active, she rushes me to the GP to get put on the pill. I am delighted at how everything has worked out for the best and even a TV news report showing the firetrap slums of London, illustrated by a shot of what we dawningly recognise as our own address, doesn't dampen my enthusiasm for our new home.

But, while cohabiting sates my need for companionship and intimacy, it also exposes my more worrying traits to scrutiny and, when I return cheerfully from the toilet after what has become a regular post-meal vomit, Dieter hugs me, gazing at the scratches on my arms and soothes, concerned: 'You never relax.' I'm not used to having my breezy dismissals of dysfunctional behaviour challenged, so rather than open up I shut down, embarrassed at the focus on my weaknesses. Why dwell on the sad stuff when the best medicine is to seize every opportunity to have a laugh?

20

OBAACHAN, OKAASAN

Within the month, I am off on holiday to spend time with the Nagazumi clan. I'd visited Japan regularly throughout my childhood and, though the unfamiliar customs and my failure to learn Japanese always made me feel a bit of an alien, I loved being in an environment where family came first, with children at its heart.

Sanji and Tamiko's home is the bustling hub of the tight-knit Kawaguchi community. It's as eccentric and cluttered as Willesden, but with none of the neglect and malevolence. Evidence of my grandfather's many hobbies and obsessive collecting is everywhere: the hallways and landings are lined with a vast library of photo albums and a meticulously labelled archive of music cassettes and the living room is crammed with a crowded display of wind-up toys, marionettes and timepieces that burst into life on the hour, ringing out a chaotic symphony of whistling notes and synthesised tunes, while model trains clatter over a complex network of tracks winding around the furniture.

Tamiko obsessively dusts these trinkets with long-suffering exasperation at the extra housework, though she herself is no less

of a hoarder – the kitchen is a packed grotto of cooking imple-
ments, crockery (both Japanese and English style), tins, jars and
Tupperware and the house's many wardrobes and cupboards are
neatly stacked to bursting with carefully stored items, any single
element of which Tamiko is able to locate at a moment's notice.
In between managing the surgery and filing the office paperwork,
she is cooking, sewing and running errands, chivvying those
around her, reminding them of appointments and offering to
organise their lives – welcome or not. On my arrival, she talks me
through a fastidiously timetabled calendar of activities mapped
out in anticipation of my visit. I want nothing more than to lie in
my bedroom, listening to my Walkman and writing self-pitying
monologues in my diary. But Tamiko's having none of it and
railroads me out of surly inactivity, tackling my low standards of
personal hygiene by insisting I shampoo my spiked-up hair and
secretly laundering and darning my artfully destroyed clothing.

I begin to understand Yasuko's rebellion against her mother's
restless fussing and control and baulk when she puts the kybosh
on any social excursions of my own choosing. And her habit of
instantly grabbing a coat and accompanying me when, in need
of some head space, I might venture to step outside for a walk,
is suffocating. For God's sake – I drink and smoke! I've had
sex! I live with my boyfriend in my own flat! Can't she see I'm
an adult?!

And yet it is likely all too clear to Tamiko that I am, in fact,
far from able to handle being an adult. Alarmed by my under-
weight frame and wan complexion, she interns herself in the tiny
kitchen, cooking from scratch my favourite dim sum dishes and
Japanese delicacies. I vomit up the first few meals, but she per-
sists and I eventually abandon the habit – partly out of guilt that

it's a hurtful and rude response to her brilliant cookery, but also because Tamiko is sixth-sense alert to every movement in the house and my actions prompt agitated phonecalls to Mum. My self-destructiveness isn't just harmful to me, it's causing untold stress to my loved ones.

By the time we head off on a trip to the resort town of Karuizawa, with branches of extended family packed into the Nagazumis' woodland villa, I am noticeably happier and healthier.* Daytime forest treks and swimming pool visits are rounded off with a communally cooked feast and cheerfully noisy card games. At bedtime, the futons are unrolled and laid sardine-style on the tatami floor behind a sliding partition and I fall into peaceful sleep with the other youngsters, lulled by the clicking sound of mah-jong tiles as the grown-ups play and chat quietly into the night.

When Tamiko occasionally catches me looking spaced out or sad, she will sit down beside me, smiling inquisitively while gently stroking the self-harming scars on my arms. My instinct is to pull away, but I know that any effort to resist will be seen as a challenge to her persistent and unremitting love, which survives every test I throw at her. When, at the end of the holiday, the family sees me off at the airport Tamiko crushes me to her skinny frame in a tight, tearful embrace.† I don't realise it at the

---

* Musical family connection no. 2: Takashi, my cousin, is now a stadium-filling singer-songwriter in Japan, known by the moniker Hanaregumi.

† Tamiko died at the ripe old age of ninety-six, during one of our family visits to Japan. I stop short of crediting the timing with the sentimental belief that she 'hung on' until we got there, but I like to think that she received some comfort from knowing that the lost girl she had helped to raise had finally managed to settle, happily, with a family of her own.

time, but these trips to Japan, where I am surrounded by people who love me in a stable and happy environment, did me the world of good.

———

Mum calls one night, sobbing that she has left Ray. She has a new boyfriend, Gene – a model she met on one of her photo shoots – who is keen to say hello. I listen to him drone on that my mother loves me very, very much, but the sentiment might come across as more sincere if it wasn't punctuated by deep drags on a joint, delivered in the croaky non-sequiturs of a stoner. They have shacked up together in a rental house near the Pacific Design Center in West Hollywood.

Mum feels guilty about leaving Ray, who is – apparently – heartbroken. However, the break-up turns nasty when Ray tries to fob Mum off with a paltry divorce settlement and she learns, through mutual friends, that he has for over a year been deeply embroiled in an affair and was on the verge of abandoning their marriage himself. By jumping the gun and stealing his thunder, Mum has hurt Ray's pride and he freezes her out of their joint assets, hiring a formidable divorce lawyer who spins out every minuscule exchange for maximum cost. It is, however, unwise to under-estimate Yasuko, who is herself now fired by outrage that everyone but her knew about his infidelity.

On an occasion when Ray is out of town filming in Las Vegas, Mum squats the Hollywood house, assisted by a locksmith and armed with a file of legal papers, which she presents to the police who have shown up in response to the alarm system. Ray is apoplectic, but there is nothing he can do, as Yasuko reasonably offers to buy him out of his share. He dispatches an army of studio crew to empty the property of everything of value, with his new squeeze overseeing the proceedings. It's a humiliating experience for Mum, though she gains some grim satisfaction watching the looters spend several frustrating hours failing to remove an enormous chandelier hanging over the dining-room table. When the divorce papers are finally signed at an office in Beverly Hills, Ray completes the ceremony with a last dramatic faked heart attack, for old time's sake.

While life after Ray brings Mum many benefits – she will carve out a successful career running her own location company, representing photographers and continuing with production work for high-status clients – my visits eventually drop off, partly because I am busy with my own life, but mainly due to my undisguised loathing of Gene. He is something of a trophy – undeniably good looking and fourteen years her junior – and Mum claims his support was invaluable in battling Ray for the house, but he is boorishly obsessed with wealth and status and money is the only subject of conversation that animates him. His main talent lies in pissing off everyone around him with his moronic comments and opinions.

During one particularly stressful holiday visit, I grit my teeth as he throws a tantrum over Mum cooking 'the wrong pasta' for his own mother's Bolognese recipe, repeatedly screams from the upper deck of the house to have his drinks replenished while he sunbathes and berates her for her stupidity over every minor disobedience. It is infuriating to watch her cower before this obnoxious dickhead, who seems to believe that his good looks make up for a complete absence of intelligence or charisma. I can't control my anger when Gene bullies Mum and our rows cause her unwelcome drama. Her blame-on-both-sides efforts to keep the peace feel too dejecting, so I resolve to only visit when he is out of town. I spend the next sixteen years – and beyond – listening to Mum's accounts of Gene's many repugnant escapades, which cover drugs, affairs and an endless sapping of her finances and her energy, while he jealously denigrates her work and friends and blames her for his own failures. As I write, seventeen years after they finally split, he is pestering her to fund a $3,000-a-month defibrillator vest for a fabricated heart condition and wants her to co-sign a property deal so he can get back in the saddle with yet another get-rich-quick scheme. It's taken almost thirty years for her to finally and unequivocally say no, which is progress at least.*

I love my mother, but she has chosen to share her life with some insufferable men. On the plus side, putting up with their rampant selfishness gave her valuable practice in dealing with the monumental egos, hissy-fit prima donnas and self-obsessed wankers she had to mollycoddle during her career in the world of fashion and photography. But the men's demands meant our relationship had to fit into the tiny spaces in between. I feel guilty for abandoning her – first by being closer to Dad, then by not going to live with her in Los Angeles and finally by giving up on fighting her corner with Gene. But I am belligerent with people I can't stomach. Mum is altogether more accommodating – it takes an awful lot to push her over the edge, which I envy. I'd be a nicer person if I didn't give up on others so easily – and angrily. I just wish her judgement had been better.

---

* My favourite Gene anecdote is when he starts putting it about that he has carried out a paternity test proving that he fathered Ashton Kutcher during an affair. When I point out that Kutcher is, in fact, a twin, Gene doubles down on the lie, only claiming responsibility for 'Ashton's side of the womb'.

21

ALPHABET SOUP

Emma is feeling increasingly isolated and unhappy at home. Dilys, fixated on the fantasy of a society wedding featured in *Tatler*, tried to strong-arm her into developing some wifely skills by forcing her to sign up for a domestic science course. In defiance, Emma has taken matters into her own hands and is doing A levels at Paddington College. It's frustrating having to fight her mother for what any other parent would be proud and supportive of and the constant battles are grinding her down. Meanwhile, our original school group has become less close knit, pursuing new friends and love lives and Emma bemoans not having either. My proposed solution is that we expand our social circle by producing a fanzine. These DIY mags are as prevalent at gigs as flyers and their writers comprise a community of their own. 'D'you wanna buy a fanzine?' seems like an appealing icebreaker for entry into a new scene.

Issue A of *Alphabet Soup* features filthy versions of Peanuts cartoons, the perils of gig toilets, an extended moan about moshpit etiquette and a self-righteous rant against the music press's lack of distinction between Positive Punk and Goth. We interview a band called Geschlekt Akt who are playing at the Marquee, supporting Furyo. Unfortunately, the singer and guitarist don't get round to talking to us until the venue is about to close, by which time Emma and I are many ciders the worse for wear and the pause button on our recording device is left on throughout our chat. But we are undaunted by our ineptitude and bonded by the shared experience, spending much of our time producing the fanzine in uncontrollable hysterics.

Dad sneaks me into his new office job after hours to photocopy 100 issues. Since the fanzine has cost us nothing to produce, bar the expense of Letraset and staples, Emma and I sell it for a pittance with the cover tagline: 'It may be crap but it's only 5p.' Our efforts are surprisingly well received and over the course of two years, we produce five issues of *Alphabet Soup*, sneaking the copies into gigs by hiding them under our clothing and flogging them for beer money (the cover price eventually goes up to 10p).

I strike up a correspondence with Chris Donald from *Viz*, who sends us strips to include in the mag, and we become friendly with various fanzine writers, whose network covers the whole country. This proves particularly useful for finding a place to crash at out-of-town gigs and I spend an enjoyable weekend at the parental home of future *Loaded* founder James Brown – at this stage, writing a fanzine called *Attack on B'zag!* – when the Sisters of Mercy play Leeds.

By the time we put out Issue E, we've tamped down some of the more extreme potty-mouth offensiveness. James has landed a job at *Sounds* magazine and offers us a regular column, while *Viz* goes national and Chris suggests we do a parody pop feature for each issue. But we are by then losing interest, painfully aware of how crap the fanzine really is and the pressure of a regular writing gig feels like something we'd doubtless fuck up. Our talents, we feel, lie elsewhere.

———

In 1983, I go to ninety gigs; in 1984, 150 – big gigs, small gigs, student gigs, political rallies, free London festivals, the lot. In later years, when Lush was up and running, the music papers claimed we would 'attend the opening of an envelope', based on our frequent appearances at shows. But we'd been at it for years. Ironically, I went to fewer gigs once I was in Lush than I had done before. Emma and I were muckers together, selling the fanzine, dancing down the front, getting into scrapes and having each other's backs.

Though we've mostly graduated to exploring obscure bands in London's pubs and clubs, we retain our pop fandom and get put on the guest list for the Thompson Twins at the Hammersmith Odeon, where we spend the aftershow crouched and giggling under a backstage table, eating a block of cheddar from the rider. We join a fan-club coach trip to the band's lavish album launch party at Stocks Country Club in Hertfordshire where we run around gawping at the celebrities and generally acting like naughty children at a grown-ups' party. The highlights of the night are a brief conversation with Robin and Liz from Cocteau Twins and being told to fuck off by the singer from Blancmange, who sees through my idiotic attempt at striking up a conversation by asking him the time.

An out-of-town gig, seeing the Sisters of Mercy at Oxford FE College, ends in us missing our train home. While attempting to sleep on the station's benches until the morning service resumes, the police pick us up as suspected runaways and we spend the night in the cop-shop waiting room being harassed by drunks. Still, it's all part of the adventure and our immersion in the gig scene, where everyone we meet seems to be playing in a band. We witness a great many incompetent but enthusiastically received support acts, which inspires us to have a go ourselves. Emma is donated a guitar by a cousin and I buy a Telecaster off a friend and we practise halting renditions of Blondie tunes, plugged into her bedroom stereo.

Despite her parents' objections to our friendship, Emma is allowed to join me for a holiday visit to LA. I'm excited to have her along and we spend hours checking out the record shops and vintage clothing stores on Melrose Avenue, walkable from Mum's new home, though we're disappointed to discover that many of the smaller gigs we find in the *LA Weekly* have a 21+ age limit. We come away agreeing that London – where you can get by on little cash, don't need a car to get around and can go to gigs without an ID – offers an infinitely preferable experience for the teenage music obsessive. Even the initial excitement at uninterrupted 'alternative' record play on KROQ and 24-hour music videos on MTV starts to grate with its ceaseless repetition of the same songs and Emma confesses after weeks of being bombarded with images of flawless models (even the counter-culture outlets on Melrose sell a nude calendar of hot-looking punky girls) that she has never felt so ugly in her life. For fuck's sake, you can't even get any decent cider here.

22

HEAD OVER HEELS

Looking back, I can see how having my own flat, living with a boyfriend and witnessing the lavish life in LA might have made Emma feel envious. But, at the time, her complaints that she is only seen as my sidekick, that people only approach her to ask about me, that 'they all fancy you and I'm just your fat friend', seem ridiculous. I tell her that's bollocks, I get the exact same question all the time – 'Where's Emma?' It's natural, we're associated with one another as the girls behind *Alphabet Soup*. But, whereas I love us being considered partners in crime, Emma feels overshadowed.

Weight is a tricky subject between teenage girls. And, while Emma is clearly not fat, she's just not as skinny as me. I may seem effortlessly thin, even after finally abandoning the habit of chucking up my meals, but my chain-smoking and fidgety, nervous energy no doubt play their part. However, the distinction between a healthy weight and obesity is lost on teenage girls and it's not the only area where Emma feels unfairly disadvantaged. I am 'lucky' to have a flat, never mind the shit I've gone through to end up there, and, though she's now on her second boyfriend, she compares her relationships unfavourably to my own. But, whereas Emma is quickly critical of peripheral details (her current beau is ridiculed for never having eaten an avocado and for being baffled at how to 'open' a boiled egg), I am prone to falling head over heels, convinced that every next lover is The One, which gives a false impression of uncomplicated bliss.

I'm currently seeing Billy Childish, the singer and guitarist in the Milkshakes. He's seven years older than me, plays in a band, paints and writes poetry and I am in awe of him. After a gig at the Hope & Anchor, he'd walked me to the station and literally swept me off my feet by lifting me from the ground in an embracing kiss. He calls my flat for late-night conversations and we meet when he is up in London. I fuck him in the stairwell of Clanricarde Gardens, waiting until my flatmates have gone to bed before sneaking him into my bedroom overnight.

There is, however, one obstacle to my dreams of full-on romance – his girlfriend, Tracey Emin. I understand Billy's reluctance to leave her – she is a fierce, statuesque presence, immaculately turned out, cool as ice and with a figure to die for. But his relentless bad-mouthing of her gives me hope that their relationship is on the wane and it is just a matter of time before we are a couple. He writes me letters, quoting their rows, saying he is 'very visous [sic] to Traci' but things are 'complecated [sic]' so let's just see how things go.

It doesn't take long for Tracey to discover our liaison and her reaction is surprisingly restrained. She unleashes the occasional microaggression – referring to me as That Japanese Slag and pointedly calling me Michaela, insisting that Miki is a nickname I've invented for myself to seem more cool (I wish!) – and corners me in the toilets at a gig, only to bond with me over our shared affection for Billy. It seems she is used to putting up with his infidelities and, so long as I am genuinely smitten and he is more to me than 'just a notch on the bedpost', she will tolerate my presence and refrain from 'scratching my eyes out'.

I'm a bit out of my depth here. Billy's cold treatment of Tracey baffles me, as does her acceptance of it. When I go along to one of his poetry readings, Tracey is compere, smiling proudly and encouraging applause as she introduces each poem, many of which mock in blunt detail her private behaviour and entreaties for affection. It's unsettling to see the object of my slavish desire being so gleefully cruel. Still, Billy is an artist, uncompromising in his determination to write the truth. His truth, at least, which I suppose is what's expected of an artist.

I eventually receive similar treatment. He sends me a book with a scrawled dedication: 'Couple in here for you, girl.' There are two poems: 'Someone Else's Little Jap' and 'Hungarian Japanese'. I'm intrigued that Billy seems so focused on my ethnicity since it is something I try to downplay, but now I think of it he's often pestered me to cook him Oriental delicacies and give him a massage by walking on his back. I'd always laughed this off as a joke, but now I worry that I've disappointed him by failing to live up to the geisha ideal. And while I get a frisson of flattery at being immortalised in verse, I'm indignant about having bits of me selected for use, especially graphic details of my body and our couplings. I don't have the stomach to be a muse.

To be fair, Billy doesn't have a whole lot of material to work with in writing about our time together. I am so cowed by him and flattered that he pays me any attention at all, that I mute any aspects of my personality or conversation that draw anything less than a favourable response. When, after several months, I finally muster the courage to ask where – if anywhere – this relationship is going and whether I will ever be more than his bit on the side, Billy is derisive: 'Look, love, I don't even know how many sugars you take in your tea.'* It's not the answer I was after, but it does at least make my position clear.

In the end, Billy finally splits with Tracey, but I'm not the catalyst. Kira is a year younger than me and, though it's somewhat crushing to be replaced by a younger woman at the tender age of seventeen, I accept that it was ludicrous of me to believe that I would be anything more than a stop-gap morsel to the mighty Billy Childish and snap myself out of binge-drinking self-pity by throwing myself into the next love affair – another bloke in a band, who I've developed a crush on and who I fall instantly in love with after he surreptitiously holds my hand as we sit side by side during a cab ride to an after-gig party in east London.

It's hardly a union of equals. Jake (not his real name) is more than a decade older than me and, though he insists it doesn't bother him in the least, I am painfully self-conscious of saying anything vapidly immature, especially around his smart and witty friends, though they are never anything but friendly and welcoming. Still, it's a proper relationship, unlike Billy, and we head back to his flat after pub nights and gigs, to chat and listen to music, enjoying lazy Sundays in bed, cocooned in intimacy. But as the affair settles into a routine, it gnaws on me that my primary value seems to lie in compliance: maintaining a distance

---

* This, too, is captured in a poem titled 'You Bastard, She Said', my questions compared to 'hungry little pigs' disrupting 'the natural flow' of our 'unspoken understanding' and an observation that it is as unwise to believe in silence as it is in words. I agree with the last bit, at least.

to leave him free to mingle at gigs, meeting him at the pub for last orders when his evenings are otherwise full, turfed out early morning to make way for his busy day. There is no question of him taking time out to visit me in my environment, with my friends, on my terms. When I challenge him, he retorts 'What do you want – marriage?!' Jake is happy as things are, he doesn't want the relationship to change, to grow more 'serious'. I feel like a sideshow to a more important life.

I've learned from Billy that affairs can be a recreational escape from any problems in your main relationship, so I distract myself by embarking on a string of casual flings. Fucking other people seems less problematic than having difficult conversations with Jake and at least juggling a hectic love life keeps me occupied. Who knows? One of them might even amount to something. But they either turn out to be dickheads or are clearly not into commitment and I'm still stuck with the fact that what I really want is for Jake to love me as much as I love him.

A lot of blokes who date teenage girls are under the impression that we are less demanding than older women, too young to want to settle down and clip their wings. What they fail to consider is that a seventeen-year-old can be a mess of hormones and immature, insecure needs. Being unreasonable and demanding is our nature. Ask any parent. All that bullshit about girls maturing faster than boys. Outwardly, maybe, but most of us are still children under the surface. Still, it should be noted that while Billy and Jake were older than me, they were themselves only in their twenties. Sex was the only time when I could act without self-censoring and I can hardly blame them for thinking that it came with few strings attached, since I participated so readily.

I would be immeasurably better off spending time alone trying to work out who the fuck I am rather than trying to fit in with what Jake seems to expect of me, because underneath all the blasé promiscuity is a gaping lack of self-worth. After yet another gig where he is busy all night in the company of everyone else, I decide I've had enough and head off on the long Tube journey home. As I stare glumly into the darkness, blinking back tears of self-pity, a bloke sits down next to me and starts chatting. I know what he wants and I let him have it. We end up fucking in St James's Park and, as soon as the deed is done, he runs from me, clearly desperate not to spend another second in my company.

I feel blank despair at having sunk so low and end up confessing to Jake, in the hope that he'll either dump me in disgust, thereby putting me out of my misery, or be forced to acknowledge how fucked up I am and take better care of me. But, while he seems genuinely concerned at my recklessness, I get the impression that he is fine with me filling my spare time in whatever way I choose, so long as I don't make any extra demands on him.

23

LIFELINES

The Staverton Road house is now so catastrophically fucked that Dad can't find any lodgers. He offers me and my friends rent-free accommodation (we just have to cover the bills) and since our Clanricarde lease is about to end, we agree to move in while he transports Nora – now completely insane and in rapid physical decline – to Hungary, in an effort to find her adequate care. We clean and redecorate as much as possible: layers of dust-caked grease are scraped from the kitchen surfaces, the walls get a lick of emulsion and the garden's 8-foot-high weeds are flattened and burned in a celebratory bonfire. But Dad has been predictably disingenuous about the deal and we discover with horror as one final demand after another arrives that we have become embroiled in a debt amounting to thousands. We pack the house with extra friends to contribute funds, but despite our best efforts, the gas gets cut off over Christmas. When Ivan returns, his solution is to fill the house with fan heaters, merely upping the astronomical electricity bill. Moreover, he has failed to find Nora a suitable new home and she is often discovered sitting naked on the toilet in the dark, muttering curses in Hungarian.

For all the chaos, it's a lively and sociable household, but it is impossible to escape the company of others and the lack of any privacy is taking its toll. And, aside from Nora, I'm the only woman here. Men tend to have a much lower bar over what is deemed an acceptable domestic environment and no woman in her right mind would choose to live in this nuthouse. Dad walks in on one of my self-harming sessions and, visibly shaken, calls an ambulance. I am reluctantly ferried to hospital, where a nurse angrily scrubs and dresses my wounds, loudly declaiming that I should have done the job properly and not waste her time clogging up the emergency services with failed suicide attempts. I sullenly point out that it wasn't me that called the ambulance and I wasn't actually trying to kill myself, but this falls on deaf ears and I am packed off with a letter to my GP recommending psychiatric treatment, which I read and then destroy. I have long suspected that my worst behaviour is evidence of a madness inherited from Nora and the last thing I need is confirmation that I should be locked up in an institution.

At my lowest ebb, I meet Johnny. He plays guitar in the Vibes and the Purple Things and I spend the night with him after a drunken snog at a gig. The following morning, I hastily gather my belongings, ready to clear out before having to be asked. I'm disarmed when he seems crestfallen, inviting me to at least come for a pint at the pub. One day rolls into the next and the next, as we go for walks with his dog, wander aimlessly around the West End and go drinking in pubs. He is hilarious and lively company and feeling so at ease in a burgeoning romance is a novel experience after my recent failed relationships. I worry he is merely too polite to turf me out, so I offer at regular intervals to head off and leave him in peace. But he wants me to stay and comes to stay at mine, too. He meets my friends and my Dad. Can this really be so *easy*?

Johnny confesses that his flatmate had warned him to be careful, as I'm known to sleep around. It turns out half of my reputation is based on lies, but I don't deny my promiscuity and Johnny doesn't seem to mind. He's got form himself – there are long and persistent phonecalls from an ex-girlfriend, who has suddenly decided she wants him back; and when an on-tour affair turns up on his doorstep hoping to rekindle their romance, Johnny spends an awkward hour in the kitchen having to update her on his change of circumstance. But seeing him treat his ex-lovers as friends, with kindness and respect and no hint of upper-hand bragging, makes me love him. He is affectionate and warm, openly talks about his feelings, is friendly with everyone and wonderful fun to be around. He deserves a much better girlfriend than me.

———

Somehow, in the midst of all this chaos, I manage to scrape a couple of A levels. It's not enough to barter my entry into the university choices insisted on by the Queen's College Careers Department, so I apply for a clutch of local polytechnics and secure a place on an English degree course for the following academic year at North London Poly. Emma, too, is taking a year out and, with time to spare, we embark on a springtime trip around Europe.

The Interrail pass allows under-26s to enjoy unlimited train travel around Europe for a bargain price and we set off in April 1986, clueless but enthusiastic, dragging heavy suitcases rather than practical backpacks. In Amsterdam, we feast on hot chocolate and paper cones of chips topped with a swirl of mayonnaise. Emma buys some space cake and we spend the night laughing hysterically at neon lights. Back at our ultra-cheap dorm-style accommodation, a rowdy group of males in the next-door room bang on the wall incessantly and bellow their intent to suck our tits (and worse), but we are tripping and the threat seems distant.

We base a stop-off in Hamburg on an ill-thought-through pilgrimage to the Beatles' old haunts and spend a dismal afternoon wandering up and down the Reeperbahn, unsettled by the clash between seediness and respectability, personified by the well-dressed ladies waiting patiently on the pavement while their stout middle-aged husbands frequent the sex shops and strip shows. Our spirits are revived by the rides at the nearby Hamburger Dom fairground, but we blow far too much cash on waffles and toffee apples and spend a money-saving night in the station waiting room being sexually harassed by drunk tramps.

Berlin is the star destination of our holiday but the Kreutzberg address I've been given as a friendly, free place to doss is no longer inhabited. Thankfully, a trio of squatters in the same apartment block allow us to stay in their vast and well-furnished accommodation. At a Cramps gig, I bump into two girls I've met in London, who show us around the clubs and bars of the city. We're somewhat taken aback that the standard meet-up time here is 11 p.m. and the preferred mode of transport is hitching rides, but in this thriving nocturnal scene it seems mingling on familiar terms with complete strangers is the norm.

I am wildly excited by Berlin's underbelly lifestyle, but Emma often grows tired and heads back to the squat to sleep. It's a fore-shadowing of how we'd eventually respond to touring: me grasping at any opportunity for new friends and adventure; Emma needing her home comforts and wearied by the effort required to engage with strangers. After a further week in Pégomas (near Cannes) and then the glorious treat of Paris in the sunshine, we discover on our return home that the last half of our European adventure has taken place under the radiation cloud emitted by the Chernobyl disaster.

That summer, I dyed my hair red. I'd been colouring it black since I was fifteen, then broke it up with some blond bits at the front and now went the whole hog – bleached the fuck out of the lot and slapped on a pot of Poppy Red Crazy Colour. That crap got everywhere – towels, pillows, my neck and clothes. But it was brash and loud and I liked it. Box ticked at nineteen, never have to revisit that, and it stayed the same for over twenty years. And, after the Vidal Sassoon experience, I couldn't be bothered to go through the fuss of a hairdresser either, so I'd cut it myself, chopping bits off if they looked out of place. It didn't much matter if the back was a mess, it's not like I could see it myself (I still do this).

My sartorial efforts exhibited a similar slipshod attitude. If I found a great dress at a market stall or charity shop, that was me covered for the next year, until it was worn to shreds. I'd buy kitten-heeled stilettos at Kenny Market because they looked cool and a bit sexy, but, by the time I even thought of replacing them, there were holes in the soles where the rain came in. I did like mucking about with make-up, but I used far too much and wore it like a mask. It was more an art project than a beauty enhancement. Mascara was a nightmare because bits would flake off and fuck with my contact lenses and I never mastered blusher – it looked like either bruises or clown paint. But I went to town on the rest.

It may seem odd that such a self-conscious and awkward teenager would have chosen to present themselves in such an overtly eye-catching way. But even before I'd become part of my punky school gang, when I'd tried to fit in with the Queen's College look, I was too sloppy to carry out the necessary checks and maintenance required for smart clothes – everyone could spot a mile away that I was an awkward geek and trying to keep up with how normal people dressed just emphasised my ineptness. Better to abandon conventional attire altogether. It was more fun making up my own rules anyway and, if I was stared at or mocked, I could tell myself they were reacting to the clothes, the hair, the make-up. The stuff I'd put on deliberately, not the girl I couldn't help being inside the disguise.

Of course, I *wanted* to be pretty. My parents were undeniably good-looking, but I felt I had the worst of both. I'd obsess in front of the mirror, pinching my spuddy nose into a slim, tip-tilted button and pulling up the fat under my brows so my Japanese eyes looked wider. For a couple of weeks, I tried to maintain the effect by keeping my eyebrows permanently raised, but men on the street took it as some kind of invitation so I gave that up. But I wasn't alone and the common ground of girls bemoaning their perceived imperfections served as an unhealthy bonding ritual – sharing the things we hated about ourselves brought closeness, but there was a competitive mine's-worse-than-yours edge that ended up confirming the flaws rather than diminishing them. 'Well, my fat thighs are way worse than your nose and anyway my nose is the only thing I can bear to like about myself.' Ah, so my nose *is* big.

Bunny was the first in our gang to tire of this game, exploding in exasperation: 'For God's sake! SHUT UP, you look *great.*' This attitude, if you can embrace it, is the lifeline that drags you out of solipsistic self-loathing. Compliments helped, too. When Billy wrote about the 'dark discs' of my Japanese eyes, I was flattered that they seemed to have a unique and compelling attraction. When I moaned to Jake about my wonky teeth and mouth, he hotly disagreed, insisting I must never change a thing. Johnny even found my massive ears cute. I realise that this plays into a separate trap of only valuing yourself on a man's say-so, but having the very things I felt were ugly being reframed as beautiful was key. Eye of the beholder and all that. But really it was finding my tribe and opening up my horizons that gave me the self-confidence I needed. Life became busy and I found more interesting things to obsess about.

24

G'NIGHT, DAD

Nora died in 1988 and Dad aged a decade overnight. I felt nothing when I heard the news – certainly no sadness, though I'd hoped for some joy at the old bitch finally kicking the bucket. But it was a blank – too late, she'd done her damage. Two years later, Dad moved back to Hungary and for the next ten years he employed a revolving household of eastern European women who he trained in journalistic tasks while facilitating their trips to the west. Their duties included cooking and keeping house, but the reciprocal arrangement seemed pleasing for all concerned and my annual visits provided cheerful holidays of hearty home-cooked meals stretching into late-night chatter and card games. Ivan was happier than I'd ever seen him, full of entertaining conversation and belly-laugh anecdotes, the centre of a sociable and lively household, referred to by the locals in warm if sometimes disapproving tones as 'The Sultan of the Balaton'.

Unfortunately, years of undisciplined eating and having his every need ministered to led to enormous weight gain and related health problems. As time passed, the work dried up and the EU expanded, robbing Ivan of gatekeeper status. The girls drifted off and he was left in diminished circumstances, his household shrunk to a single, once-lively Ukrainian woman called Stella who, stuck alone with my increasingly immobile and demanding father, seemed robbed of all joy and wandered the neighbourhood like a despairing ghost. She'd spend hours sitting on the patio writing long journal entries focused on God and conspiracy theories, resenting the incursion of visitors while apparently trapped in a lonely depression.

In 2007, Dad was admitted to hospital following a stroke. I was there the next day and found him in a dreadful condition, his huge bulk shivering under a thin blanket, unable to recognise me as his daughter. It took me a while to navigate the various bribes you are meant to distribute to get the scantest care in a regional hospital in Hungary and, in desperation, I looked into moving him back to England, but he'd have had to lose about 5 stone in weight before he could even be wheeled on to a plane.

I found a local Balaton nursing home where Ivan could recover until stable enough to return to the villa. I may as well have killed him myself. Dad was used to snapping his fingers and getting his own way by any means available – charm, bullying, emotional blackmail – and living by the rules of an institution was intolerable to him. Thankfully, miraculously, rescue came in the form of his friend Brigi. She'd had long experience of the best of Ivan, who could be that rare kind of friend who engages with your problems, champions your ambitions and does everything in their power to make anything seem possible. Moved by his desperation, she agreed to manage his care – the costs to be compensated via a will ensuring her eventual inheritance of the Balaton property. Dad gloated in anticipation of me receiving news of the arrangement, believing I'd been happy to let him die in the nursing home. But I was, in fact, gushingly grateful to Brigi for alleviating my guilt and taking on a task I couldn't possibly manage myself. It was no sacrifice for me to surrender an inheritance I never for a second thought would come my way.

Brigi was nothing short of a godsend, coaxing Dad to exercise and eat well, keeping him company and hiring a turnstile of physios and home helps, vetted in accordance with his exacting demands. She encouraged friends and neighbours to visit and entertain him with diverting conversation, while keeping a supervising eye on any vultures fishing for handouts from his bedside stash of pension money. But she'd tell me that no medicine or care rallied him as my visits did, so I'd fly in as often as I could – work, family and finances permitting – and we'd spend long, enjoyable hours bantering and laughing, gossiping and reminiscing. He basked in my undivided attention and I was grateful, too, for these last flashes of the old Ivan.

He would speak with regret about Yasuko, claiming he'd dreamed of a huge family and would have ceased womanising, maybe after the fourth or fifth child. I laughed at the very idea: in other words, he would have stopped through loss of appetite, rather than effort. I suggested that he'd have been better off pursuing this domestic fantasy with a homely *Hausfrau* to cook and clean and raise his kids, rather than my ambitious and beautiful mother: a solid workhorse rather than a skittish mare. He'd chuckle in agreement but insist: 'Your mother was the only woman I ever really loved.'

My last visit to Dad is a mercy dash in early September of 2010. Brigi feels he may die at any moment – there is so little spark left in him that she wonders what he is hanging on for and it transpires that there is indeed a burden weighing on Ivan's conscience. One evening, as we watch the sun set over Balaton, he is finally ready to share the truth. The story begins with his mother's marriage, which was a scandal from the start, since her husband, Paul, was Jewish. I'm stunned by this revelation, given Nora's ferocious anti-Semitism, but Ivan assumes that the Berényis' considerable wealth helped smooth over the social embarrassment Nora's family felt at the union.

Little Ivan, who had last seen his father as a toddler, was kept in the dark about his heritage, but, as Hungary and his own family became enmeshed with the Nazis, his paternal parentage became a dangerous secret. As events grew increasingly dire and Hungary began deporting its Jewish population to Auschwitz, Ivan – by then aged eleven – recalls eavesdropping at the drawing-room door during a heated family crisis meeting and overhearing the truth: 'The boy could ruin us. No one must ever find out.' As the war took hold and the family fell on hard times, Nora would take out her frustrations on her son, blaming him for her misfortunes and calling him 'a stinking Jew', cursing the filth that ran in his veins.

I am overwhelmed by sadness for my father as a boy. He was the tainted seed in his Aryan family, made to feel that his very existence could bring disgrace and danger to the people he loved. That his own mother could use this to attack him is unforgivable and I ask him if he ever retaliated. But Dad is quick to make excuses for Nora – she was a single mother, life had been so tough on her. While Ivan at least had school and neighbourhood gangs – wartime held plenty of adventures for a young boy to balance the deprivations – Nora was alone, with no husband and no friends, only her son. She'd been bred for a life of privilege and had no resources for surviving such hardships. 'If you could have seen her when she was young and happy. She could be so lively and charming. The war broke her. Really broke her. Mentally, as well as physically.'

I am undeterred and unforgiving. She was a monster and did unspeakable things to me, too. For once, he doesn't roll his eyes or deflect my accusations with a shake of his head, but looks at me sheepishly, sadly, and says: 'I know, she did it to me, too.'

———————

It wasn't until Dad escaped Hungary and his wayward pal Gabi bundled him around Europe on madcap adventures, chivvying him into heedless womanising, that he regained his confidence and got back his mojo. The relentless promiscuity makes sense, now. More than lust and excitement, it was his cure and proof that he'd got over the past. But love – that was poisoned, because however much he could fuck, he could never trust. An only child, abandoned by his father and abused by his mother, he had no template for a healthy relationship. Just the knowledge that love could turn ugly at any moment, so better to be in control rather than the victim. The leaver, rather than the left.

The night I first told Dad about Nora's abuse, his childhood friend 'Chicago Steve' was also present.* As Dad hauled himself off to bed, Steve lingered, confiding in me that Nora was indeed a 'supremely fucked-up woman'. He said that mother and son were

———

* 'Chicago Steve': son of the renowned Hungarian poet István Fekete.

very close. Too close. When Ivan was thirteen, they still shared a bed together and, sure, there wasn't much room in their place, but there was enough space for an extra bed. I asked him, 'You don't think . . .?', but he backed down. 'Oh, I don't know about that. But it was . . . strange.' I mulled over that conversation long after, but decided in the end that, if something really had happened, Dad would have said. After all, why would he *not* admit it when I'd given him the best possible opportunity to do so?

So my first response to Ivan's revelation is not only shock, but anger. The years I've spent wondering whether it was my fault that Nora abused me, that I possibly encouraged her in ways I wasn't aware of. Dad could have saved me at least a decade of doubt by sharing his experience, rather than shutting me out. And why on earth, after suffering her sexual invasions himself, having finally escaped her clutches by relocating to London, did he bring her into the heart of our home and allow her to share a bed with me? His answer: 'I didn't think she would do it to you. Because you were a girl.'

We have our last conversation the following morning, before I head off for my flight. He looks waxen and frail, too exhausted to rouse himself, so I sit by his bedside, making optimistic plans for my next visit. Brigi has tasked me with broaching the sensitive subject of funeral arrangements. Does he want to be buried or cremated? He's never volunteered his wishes. Dad rallies for a moment and is convulsed by a wheezy giggle: 'You can stick me in a bucket and flush me down the toilet, what the fuck will I care?' No last-minute religious conversions for Ivan, then. It was only ever life – not its aftermath – that engaged him.

I'm at work when Brigi calls the following Tuesday, telling me Dad died that morning. I am not a religious person, but I instinctively look upward and throw a thought to the heavens: *Good for you, Dad. Time to check out.*

It's likely that, if Dad were alive now, we might well have fallen out over some new test he'd cooked up to try my affections. Throughout his hectic life, he'd strained every relationship to its limits, often to destruction, relying on his vitality and charm to attract an infinite number of replacements. But old age and infirmity had robbed him of his powers and left him belligerent and paranoid.

There were times when I wished I'd known Ivan as a friend rather than a daughter, so I could've dodged his bad influence while enjoying the positives – his hilarious turn of phrase, his quick, perceptive mind, his infectious humour and lively charm. He'd never deny you anything if it brought you closer to him and he was a force of life that's not common to encounter. Once met, never forgotten.

I suffered, like all those who loved him, because he took us all for granted – perhaps because he was forever trying to fill a hole where his parents' love should have been. Yet Ivan returned my love, in his way – more than many other people I have known in my life. He never abandoned me, he never stopped caring about me. So even this imperfect love – this infuriating, selfish, pernicious, problematic love – I'll take it and treasure it because it's infinitely better than no love at all. And my world is certainly emptier without his presence.

PART TWO

25

THE BOY IN THE SOUTHERN
DEATH CULT T-SHIRT

It's 1986 and I am nineteen years old, sharing a shabbily executed conversion on the Caledonian Road with Geoff Stoddart, an entertainingly cynical chap with an encyclopaedic knowledge of sci-fi books and cult films, who I've met through gigs. On the upside, our flat is promisingly situated over a wine warehouse and is a mere half-hour walk from PNL, where I am newly enrolled on an English literature degree course.* On the downside, my bedroom has no windows at all, just a tarred-over leaky skylight, where the annoying students upstairs sit out blasting Phil Collins records on repeat. Geoff and I share a cramped kitchen and bathroom with a shifty Zappa fan called Gary who plays inept guitar solos late into the night and almost burns down the entire building by leaving pans to boil dry on the electric hob, but his permanently stoned fug at least means he rarely complains about the noise of our frequent guests and dramas.

---

* PNL: the Polytechnic of North London, now London Metropolitan University.

Geoff is supplementing his dole money by driving for bands and our flat plays host to stray musicians needing a bed for the night. His owning a vehicle means I have the luxury of being ferried to and from nights out, though I abuse this by abandoning any last vestiges of self-control and drinking to lunatic excess. Poor Geoff is often tasked with peeling me off the floor from gigs and, on one pass-out occasion, carries me from the car in a fireman's lift – a gallantry I reward by vomiting down his back.

College is a steep learning curve. I'm used to spending a whole year studying a single Shakespeare play – here, we're expected to get through one a week. But many of the other students feel similarly overwhelmed and the immediate proximity of the Nelson Mandela Bar, situated in the basement of our Kentish Town campus, offers a sociable watering hole to congregate and share our grievances. We're a lucky bunch, though. This is an era before student loans and annual fees. You get a grant you never have to repay and can claim housing benefit and sign on in the holidays. And it's easy to get by on very little money: my clothes are home-sewn or from charity shops, I live on a diet of chicken wings (10p a pound at Brixton Market) and boiled veg, transport is cheap and the student bar is subsidised.

It's liberating to be entering a new environment at the same time as everyone else, rather than as a mid-term interloper trying to break into established cliques and many of the students are living away from home for the first time, far from family and old friends, which makes them eager for new connections. Chris Acland and I bond early on, our common interests signalled on first meeting by my bright-red spiked-up hair and his home-made Southern Death Cult T-shirt. Keen to escape the confines of the halls of residence, he becomes a regular visitor to our flat and gets on famously with Geoff, Johnny and all my friends. In fact, Chris gets on famously with everyone.

There's a certain breed of chippy northern male, prevalent at the poly, who are intent on playing up their working-class credentials to establish an upper hand over the 'southern wankers'. They're as determined to sniff out and condemn any signs of affluence as the snobby girls at Queen's were to jump on any shortfall of wealth. But Chris is blissfully free of such status jostling and when his Lake District roots provoke assumptions of entitlement, he straight-facedly informs everyone that he was a pupil at the Burneside School for Privileged Little Boys. When asked why he became a vegetarian, he ignores any mocking challenge and dig at effeminacy, explaining: 'I just did it 'cos it was trendy.' It's a disarming tactic that makes him instantly popular. That and his good looks, humour and charm – none of which he seems remotely aware of or plays to any advantage.

The Freshers events and themed bar nights laid on by the well-funded Ents Society encourage social mingling and within weeks I am friends with a varied bunch – Dave, Meriel, Tanya, Mike, Simon and Steve. The pitch of conversation is relentlessly piss-taking and any hint of taking yourself too seriously is pounced on with scoffing one-liners. Everyone takes these ribbings with the intended good humour, but Chris is unique in that he genuinely never seems to harbour any secret pride that the teasing may have rumbled. When I mention that he seems to have sparked some romantic interest from a fellow student, he puts on an exaggerated serious face, nodding earnestly: 'Mm-hmm, ohhhh yeah, go on, that's very interesting.' Poke fun at some profound observation he made in a seminar and he'll mime puffing on a pipe, grimace his face into an elderly professorial mien and, in a mincing David Starkey voice, say: 'Well, I'm very taken by the works of Melville and have some unique observations about his magnum opus.' Any heated disagreements about musical tastes will have him doing impersonations of Elvis's kung-fu period – stiff hands raised, one-shoulder shrug, lip curl and 'Uh-huh-huh'; or throwing 'Start Me Up'-era Mick Jagger shapes – elbows out, hands on wiggling bum, cockerel strut and 'whoo-yeah!' yelps.* The one and only thing that Chris has no sense of humour about is Tottenham Hotspur.

Chris's explanation for supporting a team 200 miles from where he grew up is that his older brothers had first dibs on local sides and, as a child, he had a thing for knights (Spurs being named after Sir Henry 'Harry Hotspur' Percy). But, however random the initial affiliation, he is unswervingly, obsessively devoted. A bad result will throw him into a depression and no amount of coaxing will snap him out of the black mood. It's difficult to accept that this always affable, jokey lad will walk scowling from a social gathering after a Spurs loss, apologising for the desertion but determined to take his misery to a private space and wallow in anguish alone. But as I grow to know him better over the subsequent decade, I learn that this is the flipside of his sunny personality: an inability to share his troubles, whether trivial or crippling, for fear that he is 'bothering people with his problems'.

---

* This will, in later years, morph into a Bobby Gillespie impersonation that includes hand-claps and star jumps. I should add that Chris loved Elvis, the Stones and Primal Scream – recognising their more ridiculous affectations and playing them for laughs in no way diminished his affection.

Emma, too, has made new friends. She's started a humanities degree at Ealing College of Further Education and is dating Kevin Shields, the guitarist in My Bloody Valentine. The first I hear of this romance is on a visit to her new flat, when during the walk from the station she shyly informs me that he will be present. It's touching to see Emma so enamoured and Kevin is engagingly sweet and chatty. The three of us spend a pleasant afternoon drinking tea in her draughty bedroom and I discover, during the course of our conversation, that Emma has also joined a band – playing bass in the Rover Girls. I'd attributed recent failures to return my calls to some possible misstep on my part, so it's actually a relief that she's merely been busy enjoying herself. But I'm more than a little jealous that she is playing gigs.

Half the people I meet these days seem to be in a band and joining one feels tantalisingly within reach. I've been plugging away at the guitar, aided by Johnny's patient instruction, but Emma's enthusiasm for our collaboration seems to have cooled. While I continue to invite her along to my every social engagement, the arrangement is not reciprocal and I worry that she has moved on. I dutifully attend her Rover Girls gigs, dancing down the front in enthusiastic support and trying not to overstep any boundaries that might piss her off and cause her to shut me out further.

My eggshell-treading pays off and Emma thaws, offering me the chance to join the ranks of the Rover Girls' backing singers – three girls dressed in OTT party frocks who contribute shouty vocals, punctuating shrieks and wacky dance moves to the band's surf covers. I tag along to a rehearsal and give it my best shot, gamely squealing along to the chorus to 'I Fell in Love with a Kebab Man', but faking the required bouncy personality is exhausting and I'm further alienated on the lift to the station in the back of the van where the girls communicate in ickle-baby voices and spend the journey taking turns to wave the arm of a tiny stuffed panda out of the back window cooing 'hewwo' at motorists. A day later, I am sporting a vast bruise where I had been thrashing a tambourine against my leg and regretfully concede that this really isn't my bag.

But it seems that the Rover Girls isn't really Emma's bag either. While playing with a full band is fun, her role is limited and the music isn't to her taste. As for her romance, she complains that Kevin does nothing but talk about the Valentines, which irritates her and ignites her competitive streak. We make renewed efforts to work on our own band, meeting up to practise covers of Abba and Delta 5 songs. We even have a name – the Baby Machines, nicked from Siouxsie and the Banshees' 'Arabian Knights'. And I've written a few songs: 'Truth or Fiction', a reworking of a lyric that an ex once proposed as the basis for a band that never happened; a three-chord anthem about *EastEnders* (which is exactly as awful as it sounds); and another about ligging at gigs.

It's all a bit *Alphabet Soup* and our halting efforts are nowhere near the stage of being ready to play live. I worry that Emma is merely biding her time to sever ties completely, since she continues to keep me at arm's length socially. Whatever her complaints, she is primarily occupied by her new friends, new boyfriend and new band. I am stung by the rejection and fret that I'm being left behind.

26

INTO THE FRAY

Opportunity finally knocks in the summer of '87 when I get chatting with Richard Smith, the lead guitarist in the Bugs. Their double-bass player is about to move permanently to San Francisco and the band is on the look-out for a replacement. 'I'll do it!' I chirp, having never picked up a bass in my life. Johnny assists me through a crash course in learning their album of '60s trash-punk wig-outs and I pass the audition with flying colours, probably because I am the only candidate.

Johnny, Geoff, Chris and I are now sharing a house in Tottenham. Rent is cheap, since we are a mere five minutes' walk from the Broadwater Farm Estate, which continues to invite bad press since the 1985 riots; and Chris is ecstatic to be living a stone's throw from White Hart Lane. Our landlord is indulgently patient with frequent late payments, uncomplaining when we accumulate a menagerie of stray pets and, though he refers to me as Marie throughout our two-year residence, touchingly concerned about my wellbeing during the dramas of my on–off relationship with Johnny. This happy community is swelled by a bunch of PNL friends moving into the neighbouring street, whose household of seven provides soap-opera levels of entertaining gossip and intrigue and plenty of company for a regular pint at the local watering holes.

I'm having a blast and it's thrilling to finally be in a 'real' band, though I am learning on the job and often feel out of my depth. But Richard and his brother Martin (on lead vocals) and drummer Geoff C., cheerfully insist I'm doing a great job. I find Dave's (second guitar) incessant mansplaining a bit of a struggle, but it soon transpires that his macho bone-headedness is thinly tolerated by the others only because he owns the band's sole means of transport − a dilapidated Bedford van amateurishly daubed with the Bugs' logo and christened 'The Beautiful Mad'. I knuckle down to the challenge of official band membership, putting in the hours of practice, schlepping up to Colchester for rehearsals and buying myself a 1960s Burns bass.* Johnny's enthusiasm for vintage guitars has rubbed off on me, but my choice is primarily aesthetic, based mainly on the intriguing 'Mad Dog' setting on the Burns's dial, alongside the more traditional 'treble', 'bass' and 'jazz'. Within weeks I have played my first-ever gig at the Golden Lady in Stoke Newington, where initiation jitters are subsumed by the cacophonous on-stage energy as Martin throws himself around the stage and rolls on the floor in frenzied abandon. In November, we record a four-track demo (with me nervously chiming in on backing vocals) and lark about in a graveyard for a band photo session. By the month's end, I have a full five shows under my belt and am heading off on tour to Germany and Austria.

---

* When I eventually leave the Bugs, I allow them to use the bass for an upcoming tour and I never see it again, despite repeated pleading. I do hope it found a good home.

It's a riot from the off, the overnight ferry crossing spent swigging duty-free vodka, though I don't have the required sea legs for the choppy waters and spend the latter hours hugging a toilet, summoned from pass-out sleep by a tannoy announcing our imminent docking. The Bugs' three-week expedition covers a zig-zagging route of small clubs and youth centres (*Jugendzentren*) around southern Germany, but none of us has come adequately dressed for a Bavarian winter and scant funds mean we subsist on a diet of Smirnoff and Flips (peanut-flavoured Wotsits/Cheetos), so I am most often starving, hungover and cold. At an outing to a kebab stall, I knock back an aniseed-flavoured shot and for ten terrifying seconds I feel like I'm going to simultaneously vomit and shit myself, before a cocooning warmth spreads over my entire body and I feel like I've imbibed a magic elixir. It's the first time I've been warm in days. Since opening the vehicle's windows to the icy winds is not an option, we travel imprisoned in a noxious fug of cigarette and dope smoke. Every journey in the van requires a push-start and frequent stops to allow the overheating engine to cool, which makes us late to every show. But our local hosts and audiences are remarkably forgiving and we often play our set twice over to rapturous reception. Being an integral part of these raucous nights feels incredible and, though it's an exhausting life and we're mostly sleeping on people's floors, I am used to living in disruption and at only twenty years old, young and resilient. The excitement of the gigs, the camaraderie of the gang and the adventure of being abroad are well worth any hardships.

As the tour rolls on, Dave's increasingly antisocial behaviour gets on everyone's nerves. During gigs, he sneakily fiddles with everyone's amp settings while boosting his own, edging his backing-vocal mic to stage centre and bellowing over Martin's lead vocals. Worst crime of all – he doesn't share his cigarettes or on-the-road snacks and he never, ever buys a round. But Dave's unpopularity cements bonds within the rest of the touring party, who retaliate with pranks – stuffing rollie butts into Dave's harmonica and devising in-jokes and catchphrases ridiculing his sour-faced carping. It's my first taste of how on-tour banter can be a coping strategy, but also how falling out of favour will make you an immediate pariah – trust me, though, Dave deserves it. It's also my first on-the-road fling, though it's arguable that Geoff C. and I are driven as much by a need to pool the warmth from our undernourished bodies as any carnal attraction.

By the time we play our final show in Vienna, the van is on its last legs and so are we. Geoff celebrates his birthday by imbibing the bar's entire stock of mini-mescal bottles, along with the maggots steeped inside and ends up running around the venue half naked, laughing and sobbing in alternating delirium. When money goes missing from the tour profits, Dave is the only suspect and the brothers Smith hatch a serious plot to garrotte him and dump his body before our homeward-bound border crossing. As we load up our gear at the end of a hectic night, I get punched in the stomach by a Christian Death fan who tries to drag me off for an orgy with his goth girlfriend. I am rescued by Dim (our roadie/soundman/driver), armed with a chair leg, who wrestles me back into the van as we beat a hasty retreat. The Bugs make it back to the UK in one piece, in time to see in 1988 with a New Year's Eve bash at the George Robey, supporting Ug and the Cavemen and the Surfadelics.

Though Emma and I are no longer the close unit we once were, she occasionally responds to my persistent invitations and we often cross paths at gigs. Touring with the Bugs has proved my worth and means I am no longer chasing her coat-tails and, with her interest in the Rover Girls waning and her relationship with Kevin on the rocks, she channels her energies into writing a Shop Assistants-style ditty pointedly titled 'He's a Bastard', keen to make immediate headway with our band. I suggest Chris and Meriel to join on drums and vocals and, though Emma is wary of being swamped by my friends, a first rehearsal proves both members' worth: Chris is a seasoned drummer who has been in punk bands since the age of thirteen and Meriel possesses a coolly melodious singing voice, also plays guitar and is a songwriter herself. 'The Baby Machines' is ditched as a band name and after a brief flirtation with 'Devotchkas' (a term used for girls by the leering protagonist in *A Clockwork Orange*), we settle on 'Lush' – suggested to Emma by a friend who has no band to attach it to.

When Emma decides to switch from bass to guitar, I enlist Steve Rippon, another PNL pal. Steve doesn't actually play bass, but I am aware he has some musical ability after being treated to a listening party of his solo home demos – painstakingly recorded via a layering process from one tape to the next, with the percussion backing tapped out on a cassette case. He's a little less part of our gang – five years older than the rest of us and living with his long-term partner Irene, who has a sensible grown-up job as a teacher. But he is also witty and dry and a fount of knowledge on sport and '70s music and Chris could do with having another bloke in the band.

Some early patterns are established. Only Chris is a competent enough musician to jam, so songs are written individually, submitted to the rest of the band via barely decipherable home-recorded cassettes and then tweaked in rehearsals. Steve already has his hands full learning to play the bass while standing up and shows little interest in writing basslines for our songs, so we write them for him; and after Emma tasks me with writing the vocal melody and lyrics for a tune referred to as 'D-slidey', which I develop into a sing-song diatribe against Page 3 pin-ups titled 'Female Hybrid (Grotesque)', she subsequently – and wisely – decides that she is best off keeping control of her own songs, which is fine since Meriel has already set a precedent by being fiercely protective of her own compositions and resists all collaboration.[*]

Emma pours some angst into a number called 'Three Months', which refers to the length of time it's taken for her to get over her split with Kevin; I take one of my old rejected songs, a sledge-hammer feminist anthem titled 'Cinderella', and rework it into a more poetic, metaphor-stretching take on drowning in the patriarchy, newly titled 'Sea Salt' (clearly, the Critical Method: Feminism unit at PNL is having an influence). Any sagging incompetence in the performance is masked by the judicious use of an overdrive pedal and Chris's tendency to play everything at oi-punk speed, in the hopes that mistakes will either be drowned out or go by so fast that no one will spot them.

With everyone on board and a setlist of songs taking shape, Emma is impatient to crack on. She's become friends with Jeff Barratt – who handles the press at Creation and Factory and runs the Phil Kaufman Club at the Falcon in Camden – and gets

---

[*] In future songs credited to both me and Emma, I provide lyrics to her music. But otherwise our songs are written entirely separately from one another.

casual employment as his assistant.* This gives her some insight into the business side of running a band and after playing her final gig with the Rover Girls in February, she wastes no time booking our first Lush show.

---

* Jeff goes on to set up Heavenly Records, whose early releases include Saint Etienne, Andy Weatherall and the Manic Street Preachers.

27

SHIT OR GET OFF THE POT

Lush play our first gig, third on the bill to the Rosehips, on Sunday 6 March 1988 at the Falcon in Camden. I manage to break a string on the first song and am so overwhelmed by nerves that our twenty-minute set goes by in a blur. But our attending friends rally with morale-boosting compliments and we are immediately offered a follow-up show. This second gig, according to my diary, is 'a total disaster that I'd rather not dwell on'. We all acknowledge that we sound like shit and need to get better and resolve to put in the necessary practice, but I'm running on empty and overstretched as it is. I was up late the night before, celebrating my twenty-first birthday and my frazzled condition is not improved by a Bugs gig the night after, supporting the Purple Things, where evidence of my on-tour dalliance with Geoff C. causes explosive scenes with Johnny. I'm not able to handle the fall-out from my actions and shamelessly gaslight Johnny with 'it was nothing' dismissals. The truth is, I'm not used to facing the music. Any obnoxious, reckless or self-destructive behaviour I exhibited as a teen was hidden from Mum and either condoned or ignored by Dad, so I'm hostile to call-outs, however inexcusable my behaviour.

It's a relief to be heading off to LA for an Easter visit to see Mum and I put the break to good use, making an effort to sort my head out, catching up on a backlog of essays and knuckling down to some songwriting using a beautiful 1965 vintage Fender Jaguar that Mum has generously bought me as a birthday present. Earlier in the month, Lush recorded a four-track demo and it was apparent that Meriel's song 'Skin' and Emma's latest, 'Sunbathing', were head and shoulders above my own efforts, so I need to get my act together – not least because in my absence, Lush will be playing a show with Johnny standing in for me and there's a distinct possibility that I may soon find myself surplus to requirements and kicked out of the band.*

Taking a cue from Emma's fuck-you paeans to failed relationships, I write 'Pint of Bitter(ness)', purging myself of love-life angst with a self-consciously petulant lyric that consigns any remaining vestiges of affection I might harbour for Geoff C. to the bottom of a beer glass. Well, that's what I tell everyone. In truth, it's as much driven by my current feelings towards Emma and Meriel, who have both distanced themselves from the cyclone of my self-inflicted dramas. In rational moments, I'm able to recognise that my needy demands are an insufferable test of their loyalty, but, at my worst, I feel unjustly abandoned and rejected. While the song, whose title is eventually trimmed to the less clunky 'Bitter',

---

* 'Sunbathing' is the first hint at the direction Lush's sound will eventually take, though this version is recorded at around four times the speed that it eventually ends up when Tim Friese-Greene produces the track as a B-side to 'Sweetness and Light', two years later.

is of little significance in the final body of Lush's work, it does mark a move towards more subjective and introverted lyrics where my songwriting, much like my diary, becomes an outlet for grappling with a well-stocked cupboard of personal demons.

I fly home, rested and reinvigorated, armed with a list of resolutions to become a better friend, girlfriend and band member, but my positive mood is derailed by a customs officer at Heathrow who eyes me with hostile suspicion and, having methodically destroyed half the contents of my luggage, decides that my guitar is doubtless packed with illegal substances. I argue that it's unlikely that a drug smuggler would choose to draw attention to themselves by having bright-red hair, but apparently, 'girls like you tend to carry for their boyfriends'. I point out that his appraisal seems a bit sexist and he instructs his sidekick: 'Take it apart. 100 per cent it'll have heroin inside.'

The sidekick knows a lovely vintage guitar when he sees one and is gazing at my Jaguar with protective sadness, aware that taking it to pieces would be an act of irreversible vandalism. He offers to put it through the X-ray machine instead if I submit to a strip search. Two females accompany me to a sterile room, barking orders at me to hand over each item of clothing for their nose-wrinkling inspection and making sniggering comments about 'fishy smells' and 'discharge problems' as I'm made to bend over and pull my fleshy bits apart for torch-beam scrutiny.

An hour later, under further barracking, I'm told that the scars on my arms are proof I'm a junkie. Seriously? I'd have to be the world's worst addict to have made that kind of mess with a needle. Fine, they can keep me here until I've shat out everything in my system but they're wasting their time. This show of defiance prompts some whispered discussion among the officers, but I am released, with the unhelpful observation that I was only pulled aside because I 'looked guilty'. I have, on my many tours and travels, encountered decent customs officials, firm but polite, who are simply doing their job. But I've also met my fair share of power-abusing cunts and for them I reserve a front row of panoramic-view seats on the kamikaze flight into the mountainside of my vengeful imagination.

———

Lush play a spate of pub gigs, with me newly coopted into singing backing vocals. At one show, where we are second on the bill, the opening act's mullet-haired singer takes our set as a personal insult and gives me a lecture on how shit we are. I don't disagree – it's only our fifth gig – but I'm baffled as to why he's so annoyed. Over the ensuing months, I get used to the occasional snide comment, but having witnessed some of the back-slapping camaraderie between any number of patently abysmal male-led bands, I'm beginning to suspect that the real outrage is being uppity girls who think they can cut it with the boys. It's fine to be female if you're under the aegis of an overseeing bloke; not so fine if you're driving the vehicle yourself.

Emma, who has taken a year out of her college course to continue working with Jeff Barratt and commit to Lush, is now the de facto manager of the band, sending out demos and negotiating gigs. We play with the Pastels and My Bloody Valentine and she books us a show at her own college where we experience a brush with fame, supporting a jazz band featuring Fred Harris, a presenter on *Play School*, on saxophone (I'm being sarcastic, but he was genuinely friendly and we really were rather thrilled). But, when Johnny has to take over my guitar duties for yet another gig because the Bugs have a clashing home-crowd show at Colchester Arts Centre, I get an awkward talking-to from Emma and Meriel, who make it clear that my half-arsed commitment to Lush has become a drag.

It's actually a relief to be forced into a decision. I've been trying to have it all for fear of missing out, unwilling to disappoint any-one and in denial that I'm doing exactly that. But the Bugs has become so burdened with complications that any excuse to bail is a blessing. With Geoff C. out of the picture, I've now started an affair with Richard. Flings were one thing when I'd been with Billy and Jake, but Johnny has done nothing at all to warrant my betrayals. In my diaries, I scrawl endless pages claiming to still love him, but interpret the fading of all-consuming passion as somehow his fault. I seem to have turned into my dad, who wouldn't recognise a happy, stable relationship if he was in the middle of one – which I am. Was. Johnny and I finally split and are now faced with the challenge of living under the same roof while we run around shagging other people without restriction.

Not to excuse my own shabby behaviour, but cheating and promiscuity are relatively rife around me. I just happen to be more reckless and brazen about it. Chris has had a few dalliances himself and we often share our highs and lows during beery con-fessionals – I rely on his good humour to make my trespasses less histrionic and provide reciprocal reassurance for his pursuit of a commitment-free good time. When he witnesses fresh cuts on my arm one night, I am shocked to see he has tears in his eyes.

The usual responses to my self-harm range through accusations of attention-seeking, embarrassed dismissal or a practical effort to mop up the mess, so I am moved by his empathy.

Inevitably, this closeness leads to occasional sex, but since we know each other's faults well, both of us are wary of taking things further. However, active denial can be as much of a draw as desperate pining and within months we are struggling to keep our increasingly frequent assignations a secret. It all comes out at a Lush gig, causing an acrimonious end to an otherwise triumphant night, where we received our first ever demand for an encore. Emma is livid, partly because she has become best buddies with Chris's most recently ditched girlfriend, but mostly because she fully expects me to fuck things up, potentially leaving the band without a drummer. Meriel is similarly snippy, long ago exasperated by my lack of any discernible moral compass. Steve is the only band member who doesn't immediately assume that this situation is wholly under my control and instigation and merely shrugs with affable lack of concern. Even Johnny seems relieved that of all my conquests, Chris is the one who has settled into seriousness.

Chris and I vanish off for some holiday time, allowing the fuss to die down. I survive a week of wild camping during a trek down the north Cornwall coast, which is by turns stunning and taxing. My previous experience of the British countryside has been restricted to school trips, car-window views between major cities and a heavily populated Glastonbury weekend, so I am unaccustomed to hiking precarious paths in changeable weather and am grateful to be in the company of a seasoned country boy.

Tell a lie, I *have* been in the countryside. Johnny and I went up to the Lake District the summer before for a weekend to visit Chris's home, where I was chased by cows, went rowing on Grasmere and somehow managed to climb a craggy hill in a pair of kitten-heeled faux-Victorian boots while beset by a combination of vertigo and agoraphobia. I was captivated by the idyllic environment, not only the breathtaking local scenery but also Chris's warmly welcoming family and home. His parents – father: posh, eccentric and loudly jolly; mother: posh, cosy and quietly jolly. And Granny Biddy, visited daily in a rose-trellised cottage up the road. There was a cavernous barn where Chris and his two brothers and the local punk bands they'd dabbled in, had rehearsed and the framed family photos displayed an Enid Blyton childhood of countryside rambles, local football matches and barge holidays. I marvelled at the surroundings of his upbringing and concluded that he must be the most well-adjusted person I'd ever met.

Once a band is up and running, it develops its own momentum, but during this embryonic period, each member is only as valuable as their latest contribution. Talent, of course, is paramount (however underdeveloped, in our case), but hands-on effort is also key: there's no label, manager, agent or roadie, so everybody needs to muck in with admin and grunt-work tasks wherever possible. And, if you can't make a practical contribution, at least be positive – good-humoured camaraderie and enthusiastic support go a long way, because at this stage, the five of us in that rehearsal room are the only people in the world who give the slightest shit about Lush.

Meriel, however, has become less amenable to the demands of the band. Having moved in with her boyfriend, she seems to be morphing into him, parroting his opinions, shunning our crowd to socialise with his and even dressing like him. While the boys and I greet news of every gig booking arranged by Emma with excited anticipation, Meriel is tetchy when Lush's schedule interferes with her coupley plans and, though she's come up with a new song (a choppy monotone stomp called 'It Has to Go'), Emma hates it even more than she dislikes my latest effort, an unmemorable dirge with yet another tortuous water-themed lyric titled 'Other Fish', which I at least have the good grace to admit is shit and bin without complaint. Meanwhile, Meriel's resolutely static on-stage performance is drawing murmured criticism from the Creation staffers and press contacts on whom Emma increasingly relies for feedback and advice about the band.

To be fair to Meriel, she's been given some fucking terrible songs to sing and has never felt comfortable stuck on stage without a guitar. We figured that understandable nerves and her own admitted reluctance to make a fool of herself could develop into an enigmatic coolness, but she comes across as bored. In fact, she seems to have tired of every aspect of Lush. Her foot-dragging casts a deflating pall and an early exit from a rehearsal to attend yet another can't-miss domestic arrangement with Ethan sparks an exasperated discussion of her shortcomings.

I grew quickly and warmly attached to Meriel when we first met and we made a good team – her level-headed maturity a balancing foil to my reckless hedonism. When Dad failed to fill out the required forms for my student grant, Meriel generously subbed me a huge sum until I could chase up the funds and repay her. For my part, I yanked her out of reclusiveness, dragging her along to gigs and parties and engineering an ice breaker at a PNL social with a philosophy student she'd been pining after for weeks. But she cooled on me once she hooked up with Ethan and I was bruised by the rejection, so my loyalty has worn thin.

When the last straw breaks and Emma throws down an ultimatum, no one feels inclined to disagree. I volunteer to do the dirty work ('She's *your* friend') and spend a terrible afternoon in Meriel and Ethan's flat breaking the news. I fooled myself into thinking that she would be relieved, convinced that she was merely finding the right moment to sever ties herself, but she is in fact shocked and upset. Though we part amicably and continue to be friends, I feel like a thorough Judas.*

---

* I manage to claw back some karma when, in 1990, we tour with Pale Saints, who are on the lookout for a second guitarist. My tireless and hyperbolic promotion of Meriel's talent and personality lead to an audition and she ends up becoming a permanent member.

28

A NEW SINGER

Emma places an ad in the *Melody Maker*, listing Blondie and Hüsker Dü as influences, and we audition a selection of potential lead vocalists. Our first candidate informs us that she is a songwriter and wants all her material included in our set. She is also agoraphobic and will need the band to cover the cost of taxis, since she can't travel on the Tube. Another launches into an operatic rendition of 'Truth or Fiction', all OTT enunciation and theatrical arm gestures; the next is worryingly racist. One girl with a sweet, pure voice seems the perfect fit, but she is only in the UK temporarily, working as an au pair and is due to return to the Netherlands in six months. Most ask how much they will get paid (errr . . . nothing) and some request that we transpose the songs to fit their vocal range, which is completely beyond any of our abilities.

I feel a little hypocritical standing in judgement over the singing talents of others when we are such ropey musicians ourselves. We want someone good, but not *too* good: committed enough to turn up for rehearsals and gigs, enthusiastic enough to get excited at a bottom-of-the-bill pub night, confident enough to perform without being embarrassingly showy – someone who mucks in and whose personality fits with our sense of humour and who doesn't have excessive demands – such as actually making any money. So not a tall order in the least. The full repercussions of kicking Meriel out of the band sink in during a depressing debrief in the pub and it's decided that – for the next couple of gigs, already booked – I will have to step in. I'm the obvious choice, since I am already singing backing vocals and my horrified reluctance is brushed off with the promise that our hunt for a permanent replacement will continue.

I play my first gig as lead singer supporting the Sun Carriage at the Falcon. Johnny is standing in on guitar, so I can fully concentrate on the task at hand, but we're almost cancelled when the headlining act's drummer refuses to share his kit. Just to be clear, Chris does have his own, but it's at home in Tottenham. No third-on-the-bill support at a half-sold pub gig would insist on cluttering the stage with their own drumkit and normal etiquette would only stretch to providing your own snare and a bass-drum pedal. Luckily, Colm from My Bloody Valentine lives just five minutes up the road and loans us his equipment to save the day. Everyone is encouragingly supportive of my shaky debut and Simon Williams, reviewing the show for the *New Musical Express*, tactfully avoids being too specific about our performance by chucking in a thesaurus of flowery metaphors.

But as October turns to November, we still haven't found a singer. Emma flatly refuses to go through the torture of yet another pointless round of auditions and lays out the facts: we either split up or carry on as we are. It seems I have no choice.

And, with gigs booked through to the end of the year and beyond, I have no time, either.

Being a half-competent guitarist with the odd backing vocal to chime in on is a far cry from the multi-tasking involved in singing and playing throughout a whole set. Whereas, before, I was positioned at the side and could hover around my amp to hear myself over the on-stage din, I am now tethered front and centre to the mic, with Chris's deafening punk-rock hammering inches behind me. It takes so much concentration to tune my vocals to any stray musical note discernible in the cacophony of drums – like a mobile phone running down its battery to scan for a signal – that I stumble on lyrics and guitar parts, forgetting which verse I'm on.

Moreover, permanently facing the audience inevitably involves off-putting eye contact and while the band fiddle with their tuning and equipment between numbers, I feel the weight of responsibility to fill awkward silences – acceptably fleeting when you are in the audience but agonisingly long when you are on stage. The standard announcement of song titles and 'This one's about. . .' introductions feels crushingly embarrassing and my every halting effort to break the dead silence sounds like an apology. In short, my performance becomes a prolonged panic attack and I yearn for the days when I could actually enjoy playing. Any hopes that I might be cut a little slack are crushed when, at yet another pub-gig support, I decide to calm my nerves with some Dutch courage. It seems I am alone in thinking that a few relaxing ciders rather improved my performance and Emma ragingly confronts me after our set, stabbing a finger in my face and snarling: 'Don't you EVER get pissed again before a gig!'

Our first show of 1989, fourth on the bill at the Cricketers pub in Kennington, nets us a huge *Melody Maker* review with a massive photo of me and claims 'Lush will be bigger than the Middle East within months'. *Sounds* predicts 'Travelcards are a necessity; Lush are going places', which Chris adopts as a piss-take catchphrase every time we get the Tube. We are racking up write-ups on a weekly basis and score a full-page *MM* interview (on my twenty-second birthday) barely a year after our first rehearsals with Steve. While the plaudits are flattering, they are worryingly premature and punters expecting to witness the Next Big Thing are disappointed to find that Lush are a stumbling band fronted by a painfully shy and barely audible vocalist. A couple of years back, during the *C86* 'shambling bands' period, we might have passed muster – but times have changed. We are not raw and chaotic enough to get away with a messy performance and the more complex, melodic elements of the new songs are lost in the uncoordinated din.

The press buzz bumps us up from bottom of the bill at My Bloody Valentine's sold-out show at the University of London Union, our biggest gig to date. Following the soundcheck, our excitement is doused when we overhear the Sperm Wails, now demoted to first on, ranting in their dressing room that going on before Lush is 'a fucking insult'. When we walk out on stage to a palpably frosty reception, Emma greets the crowd with 'Hello, we're Lush' and a voice at the front moans 'Oh God', which prompts a dispiriting ripple of laughter.

Lush are barely out of the gates and the backlash has already started. And the accusations of hype aren't entirely unwarranted. Half our first reviews are penned by friends from our fanzine days and Emma is on familiar terms with several music journalists via her association with Jeff Barratt, who continues to offer us slots at the Falcon, so it's not entirely wrong to assume that our frequent bookings and press reviews have a whiff of nepotism about them. But it's also unfair to claim that we are entirely devoid of any merit and a lot of the sour grapes are directed primarily at Emma and me being girls, with claims that we only get attention because the press want some eye-candy to fill their pages. The fact that we alone are responsible for writing the songs is rarely credited (and frequently doubted) by the growing number of Lush's detractors, who relish dismissing us as talentless lightweights. And yet the songs really are improving.

Emma's 'Thoughtforms' has a lilting, unusual 9/4, 6/4 time signature. I write lyrics for her dreamy, melodic number 'Etheriel' – a portmanteau of 'Ethan' and 'Meriel' – mourning the loss of my once-close friendship with our former lead singer; and for the icily soaring 'Scarlet' – my words a sly dig at blokes shagging much younger girls – which Kevin Shields tells Emma he can 'imagine being played in a stadium' (though she's not sure this is meant as a compliment). My own compositions are designed to ease my burden while playing live. Hence, 'Second Sight' forces Emma to carry most of the song with a backing vocal and features a mid-song change of pace led by the drums, while 'Baby Talk' allows me to abandon my guitar almost entirely to the rhythm section and Emma's punctuating slide guitar, until a final noisy wig-out where I can lose myself and let off steam in some thrashing away from the dreaded vocal mic. While less refined than Emma's songs, they provide some welly for the set and shift some of the spotlight to Chris, who is still our best asset live and Steve, who I feel is often a little out of the action.

We record a new demo, which Emma distributes to various record labels. A slew of majors take the bait and are put on the guest list for one of our shows, where every last one of them beats a hasty exit before we finish our set. But Geoff Travis at Rough Trade has expressed an interest (despite informing us that we are 'the most hated band in London'), as has Ivo Watts-Russell from 4AD. This is genuinely mind-blowing. The two labels' output makes up a good chunk of my album collection and I've often bought records purely on the basis that they are released under their aegis. 4AD in particular occupies a special place in my heart and it's staggering to think that we might end up with our music positioned alongside the Birthday Party, Bauhaus, Cocteau Twins, X-Mal Deutschland, Throwing Muses and Pixies – so many of my favourite bands.

Pale Saints are booked into the support slot of our April Falcon gig, so Ivo can watch two potential signings strut their stuff on the same night and they outright blow us off stage.* They cleverly avoid any awkward gaps by playing seamlessly through from start to finish, each song segueing into the next with meticulously executed interludes until the final crowd-pleasing head-nodder, 'Sight of You'. Our set, by contrast, feels like it's held together with sticky tape. We pack up and go home, convinced that we'll never hear from Ivo again.

———

I sit my final exams (by some miracle, I end up getting a 2:1) and blow the last of my grant money on a van for the band – a rusting ex-British Telecom Dodge/Commer that we pick up via

---

* Our man with a van at this stage is Jamie from anarcho-punk band Blyth Power, who I have only just realised is future Kills guitarist and Mr Kate Moss, Jamie Hince.

an ad in *Loot* from Tooting Bec – and an amp for Steve, who is still playing Emma's bass from Rover Girls days and shows no intention of making any financial investment in the band. Chris is the only member of Lush who can drive, but only barely and reluctantly, so every journey is a white-knuckle ordeal. Still, it's handy for Spurs away games, so he doesn't complain too much. But, with college finished and no future prospects, I'm pondering whether to join a clutch of fellow graduates who are heading off to a TEFL course in Broadstairs.

All plans are shelved when we get if not a green, then an amber light from Ivo. It appears that a major obstacle to us signing to 4AD is the label's plugger, Howard Gough, who is vehemently against the idea and describes us as the worst band he's ever seen. This, I feel, is a little harsh and thankfully Ivo seems to agree. Seeing promise in the songs, he sets us up to record some demos with John Fryer, the label's long-standing in-house producer, at Blackwing Studios in Southwark – to help prove our worth.

Fryer is unfazed by our nerves and makes quick and easy work of recording and mixing three tracks in three days. Though the tempo sounds rushed to me now and there is no evidence of the guitar effects that will eventually become part of our trademark sound (just 'clean' or 'distorted'), when Fryer solos the harmonising vocals, I'm amazed by what double-tracking and reverb can achieve, given that I've had to wrap my arms around myself during every take to stop myself from shaking with stress. As we listen to the completed tracks on the 'big speakers', the four of us are quietly impressed at how good we sound.

Ivo, too, is pleased with the results and suggests we record another three tracks, then put out the lot as a mini-album. We're presented with a contract and I'm informed about something called 'publishing'. I've been under the impression that we'll just put 'All songs by Lush', but apparently this is not how it works. Emma argues that it's only fair that her work (and mine) should be credited and is already sick of people making sexist assumptions that 'the boys probably write all the songs'. Since Emma is the only one of us with insider knowledge of the business, we nod along with her decisions, leaving her to be the main channel for negotiations with Ivo. This suits me, since I often end up tongue tied in the face of his quiet and thoughtful reserve, worried that my loud-mouthed jabberings will make him think I'm an idiot. Though he is friendly and conversational with all of us, he clearly sees Emma as the leader of the band and the better songwriter, commenting on 'Second Sight' that yes, he can see what I was aiming for but it doesn't *quite* work, does it? That's fine, I get it. In any case, it's not about individuals, we're a band.

There's an argument that Lush would have benefitted from more time to improve before courting the limelight. But, if we'd had to wait longer, we might all have moved on to 'proper' jobs and Chris might have abandoned London altogether and headed back north. With our first record out on a well-respected label, making a living off music has become a realistic goal. So what if we're still a little rough around the edges? Fuck it, we'll catch up – seize the day and all that.

29

SCAR AND *MAD LOVE*

4AD's chic offices on Alma Road in Wandsworth feel very grown up and more akin to Mum's LA lifestyle than the shabby London haunts I am used to and I'm a little intimidated at meeting the crew behind the label's arty, high-brow image. In fact, everyone is surprisingly down-to-earth and welcoming and flatteringly enthusiastic about our music. Debbie Edgely, Ivo's girlfriend, does the label's press and is chatty and warm; Simon Harper, who heads up the international side, remains one of the funniest people I've met in my life – a true master of the understatement. I'm less nervous around our label boss, too, since Chris started referring to him as 'Uncle Ivo'. We are given free rein to raid the archives for records and I am pinching myself that this is really, actually happening.

Vaughan Oliver and Chris Bigg are the talents behind V23, the design team responsible for the iconic packaging of (most) 4AD records and I'm thrilled that our music will be used as inspiration for their artwork. Vaughan talks us through the various elements of the mini-album's sleeve design, which features blurry mauve and blue stripes scarred with vertical gouges (photography by Jim Friedman).

He has a novel idea to print on the inside, too, and bows out the sample sleeve into an oval aperture, explaining that it will be bright pink and have two facing images – cards from a language-teaching course, one for 'elder sister' and another for 'tongue' – that touch when the record is removed. The entire demonstration is delivered with dead-pan calm, which I receive with respectful, thoughtful engagement, but the vagina-like effect and the hints at cunnilingus have me exploding into shocked laughter. Vaughan meets this with wide-eyed innocence, as though the thought had never occurred to him and it's *me* who has the smutty mind. I come up with the title *Scar*, inspired by the sleeve's vertical scratches.

In an effort to improve our confidence live, Emma and I are sent for singing lessons with vocal coach Tona de Brett, a trillingly posh lady who has worked with an impressive list of clients, from Elizabeth Fraser to John Lydon. I dutifully follow her instructions on technique – relaxed posture, mindful of breathing, expression elastic to enunciate scales of 'proper-copper-coffee-pot' and 'rubber-baby-buggy-bumpers' – then instantly forget everything the second I am anywhere near a microphone. Still, the lessons give me focus and the tools to improve and Tona's effusive 'Marvellous!' 'Wonderful!' exclamations of encouragement help boost my confidence.

Scar is released in October and we play as many gigs in these last three months of the year as we have to date. With our PNL pal Mike on driving duties, we head off on a support tour with indie power-poppers the Darling Buds. They are accommodating and friendly and we are buoyant about playing our first gigs in new cities, but the drives are long and exhausting, not least because the fully weighted Commer slows to a crawl on every uphill incline. On an overnight drive from Newcastle to the next day's London show, we get pulled over by the police on a deserted roundabout at 3 a.m. by an officer claiming we were doing 90 miles an hour. Mike, exhausted and down to his last thimble of patience, points out that the van wouldn't do 90 if you dropped it off a cliff.

In December, we tour with psych-trance rockers Loop. 4AD provide some money for crew: Steve Smith (former bass player in the Vapors) is doing our sound and we now have a proper van (with seats in the back!) driven by Adrian, a cheerful if rather scatty Ozric Tentacles fan, who is also tour-managing. Howard, our former nemesis at 4AD, is accompanying us throughout for 'moral support'. He's a little brusque and a bit of a loudmouth, but he seems to be warming to us, both as a band and as people, and we believe him when he says that a gig was good. Particularly as he was so dead against us at the beginning. Emma's new beau Russell Yates and his pal Kevin McKillop, known as Moose (which, confusingly, is also the name of Russell and Kevin's band), ride along for half the gigs, adding to the party atmosphere. Both are avid Spurs supporters and Chris and I have been regularly attending matches together, so there's an added gang camaraderie between us.*

---

* In eighteen months' time, me, Chris, Russell and Moose join Simon Raymonde of Cocteau Twins to record a one-track flexi together as the Lillies – for the Tottenham fanzine, *The Spur* – titled 'And David Seaman Will Be Very Disappointed About That', celebrating a 3–1 win over Arsenal in the FA Cup semi-final. Much was made about my enthusiasm for football in the music press, like it was such an exceptional thing for a girl to comprehend the rules of the off-side trap. But the very notion of female commentators, pundits and journalists was inconceivable back then and the sport was entirely run and discussed by men. I'd grown up regularly watching matches on TV with Dad, who also took me to see his beloved Ferencváros in Hungary and I enjoyed going to Spurs games with the gang, but to be honest, the relentless post-mortem analysis and obsession with stats bored me – I was more into getting carried away with the action and joining in with the chants.

At the Glasgow show, the PA goes AWOL and Loop put on a spirited instrumental set by playing through their amps, which on this miserable cold night, the crowd is demonstratively appreciative of. The review for *Sounds* rejoices that 'we are spared the mewling, stumbling and bumbling Lush. Come an independent Scotland and they won't be allowed across the border, with any luck.'* It's quite an achievement to receive a scathing review for a gig we didn't even play, but the brickbats are bothering us less, especially in the wake of the overwhelmingly positive reception to *Scar*. Our star is on the rise and we're beginning to believe in ourselves.

———————

With just one day to recover from the tour, we are in the studio recording *Mad Love*, a four-track EP with Robin Guthrie – two days for drums at The Church in Crouch End, two days at Cocteau Twins' studio, September Sound, in Twickenham. Emma has been in touch with Robin for a while – she sent him our earlier demo and he responded with interest, but he was either too busy or overruled by Ivo (depending on whose story you believe) to produce *Scar*. He's now keen to have a crack at 'Thoughtforms' himself and Ivo has given 'De-Luxe' the thumbs-up as the lead track after recognising its potential from our live show.

I'm fully star-struck by the prospect of working with Robin, having been a fan of his music for years, and, though it's daunting

———————

* I can only assume that the writer was eaten up with bitterness that we'd progressed from supporting his band at a pub gig in Brixton eighteen months before.

to record vocals with someone used to the astonishing talent of Elizabeth Fraser, it transpires that she too is frequently overwhelmed by nerves and Robin is well versed in calming insecurity to coax a performance. He's incredibly patient, having to drop in and out for each line to mute my gulps of air, which are louder than my singing. Emma, too, feels in good hands: Robin is at his happiest experimenting with guitar sounds – the walls of his studio are lined with banks of effects units – and the tracks swoop and chime, poppier than *Scar*, but still retaining an energetic, raw edge.

I see in the new decade with a Christmas trip to LA and buy my first twelve-string guitar. The Jaguar, though beautiful, was too delicate to survive the thrashings of our noisier numbers live: the strings would slip off the bridge and retuning between numbers was a chore, so I swapped it for a more solid Les Paul. Too solid, though and built with men in mind – it weighed a ton. So I trade it in for a 1967 Gibson 335, hollow-bodied and light, with an elegant slim neck that better fits my female hands and skinny fingers. LA was all heavy rock and hair metal at the time, so the jangly twelve-string was a bargain and I am captivated by its chiming tones, which perfectly complement the layered, effects-driven guitar parts that Emma and Robin have developed.

I get to debut my new instrument at a show in Nantes, celebrating an exhibition of Vaughan's work. It's our first gig abroad and an opportunity to bond with the 4AD family. Some of the bands baulked at being grouped together under the label's umbrella, feeling their individual identity was being subsumed by Ivo's Svengali image, and we've had one French interviewer assume that Ivo writes all the songs, dishing out tracks among the artists like some Stock, Aitken and Waterman hit machine. But the rapturous reception we receive, slotted in between the

Wolfgang Press and Pale Saints, demonstrates the overwhelmingly positive power of 4AD's draw abroad. And *Snub TV* and *Rapido* cover the event, which means we'll be on the telly!

Our first video, for 'De-Luxe', takes place on a winter shoot in the Kent countryside. It's not exactly glamorous, huddled in the motorhome for warmth and the discomfort is compounded by a genuine fear of breaking our necks, as we balance precariously with our instruments, high up in the branches of a tree. Steve, who can always be relied on to go along with any band decisions so long as it doesn't require too much effort on his part, is so traumatised by vertigo and frozen with cold that he throws a totally out-of-character fit and refuses point-blank to go back up the tree after a break. I find it all rather exciting, though you wouldn't know it from my rabbit-in-the-headlights performance. Much of the video consists of the four of us wandering about or standing woodenly, looking a bit glum. But it gets played on *The Chart Show*, which means it's a success.

When we record a Peel Session, Robin comes along as moral support to ensure we aren't ridden over roughshod by the in-house team, who have a reputation for treating bands as nobody upstarts. Emma's slide guitar draws a withering put-down from the prickly tape operator, who sneers, 'Oh God, bring on Ry Cooder,' but producer Dale Griffin is so taken with my vintage twelve-string that he is uncharacteristically tolerant of Robin's backseat instructions during the mix. Though I'd hoped, like every band in the UK, that we might be embraced by John Peel, whose late-night radio show has influenced the tastes of generations of music lovers, his interest is only momentarily engaged by our cover of Abba's 'Hey Hey Helen', which appeals at least to his sense of humour. But we are never invited back.

We get an *MM* cover, along with a slew of positive reviews and our first major *NME* spread. Photographer Kevin Cummins has come up with an idea to have us all naked and body-painted, a concept that he claims Emma proposed during a drunken bar chat, but which Emma hotly insists she has no memory of. Feeling snookered into embarrassing 'sexy' photos, I propose a damage-limitation compromise that the photos are waist up and each band member is daubed with one letter of LUSH, ensuring at least that all four of us will be featured and not just the girls paraded as cheesecake pin-ups.*

Debbie tactfully liaises between Kevin's eye-rolling impatience at our fussing and mine and Emma's panicked efforts to keep our tits safe from his camera. Emma's wearing a white bra, which can be painted over, but mine is black so I end up with a pair of Emma's white tights secured around my chest. I like Kevin, but he can fuck right off with his 'Oh, for God's sake, I've seen it all before' bullshit. I didn't join a band to be treated like meat. Which just shows how much I have yet to learn.

---

* When we play at the end of the year in Japan, we are given a stack of promotional posters to sign, showing just me and Emma from the session. We scrap the lot.

30

A GOOD (SOUND) MAN(AGER)
IS HARD TO FIND

It had always been an uphill struggle projecting Lush's fragile vocals and tricky harmonies over the loud drums and guitars, through the minimal and often ropey PAs in the smaller venues we played. And trying to get the monitors loud enough so we could hear ourselves and each other was almost impossible. Back then, you had to be Madonna playing Wembley to have in-ear monitors; they weren't something you used for a Tuesday-night gig down the Dog & Trumpet. In-house equipment was brutal and crude and often broken. And, if Emma and I couldn't hear ourselves on stage, we'd sing out of tune and the songs would sound awful. We'd discovered mouldable waxy earplugs you could buy from the chemist and I used one to mimic the effect of sticking a finger in your ear, to amplify my voice in my own head. But it didn't solve the problem of feedback all over the stage – ear-splitting squeals from the vocal mics that made my fillings jump, wompy swells from the bass that hit me in the gut and drowned out all notes – so I had nothing to tune my vocals to.

Occasionally, a sympathetic and friendly in-house sound engineer would try his best to make it work, but more often they were grumpy at having to make the extra effort. Bands with loud blokes bellowing into the mic could be noisy as they liked, but girls either needed to turn down the instruments or have a powerful voice. I definitely didn't have a powerful voice, so soundmen (and they were *all* men) would shake their heads and mutter, whacking down the fader in response to any feedback so I couldn't hear myself at all. I can't help thinking that, if there had been more women doing these jobs back then, they might have empathised with our struggles. Or at least I might not have felt so pathetically *female*.

So the arrival of Pete Bartlett (recommended by Steve Smith, who was fully booked after the Loop gigs), for our first headline UK tour, was a godsend. He had a ton of live experience and had been in several bands, including an '80s female-fronted pop group called Siam, so he was used to working with women. He was also an excellent bass player and lived by the creed: never trust a front-of-house sound engineer who isn't a musician themselves. You need someone who knows what it's like to be on the other side of that mixing desk.

Pete knew just what we were up against and was all over it – tweaking the levels front-of-house, rushing up to the monitor desk to deal with feedback, repositioning mics and amplifiers, fully engaged and constantly reacting. He was worth his weight in gold. Previously, we'd been easily cowed by blokey crew who insisted our vocals were the problem, not the house equipment and certainly not their skills. But Pete had no patience with amateurs who talked the talk but didn't deliver or lazy twats who couldn't be bothered to do their job. And he was fast. No hours-long soundchecks spent pointlessly finessing every moment in every song. Pete knew that when the punters came in, the sound would change completely, so you got everything balanced and then there'd be a lot to do in the first few songs. During the gigs, he'd rush up to the balcony, to the back by the bar, in the alcoves at the side, checking to make sure that the sound was good in every corner of the venue.

It took a lot of trial and error to build a crew who did what they were paid to do and didn't piss us off. Who realised that we weren't interested in them bragging about groupies and porn and didn't take kindly to having all our guitar settings changed because 'it sounds better now' (it didn't). Or bore on about the 'proper lads' band' they'd just come off tour with. Or lick their finger and stick it in Emma's ear. Or go 'phwoarr' when she was getting on the tour bus in front of them. Or who were nice but shit at their job – or not nice and still shit at their job. Pete was there throughout, until the very last gig: on our side, rooting for us, involved, gossipy, funny, opinionated and a great friend and confidant. Which is *exactly* what you need on tour.

––––––––––

Assured that we sound good out front, I am able to relax on stage. Our new songs are more complex, so my eyes are generally focused on the frets, checking I'm playing the correct chords, which gets over the problem of any sudden, distracting eye contact. I rest my top lip on the mic to avoid drifting out of range – my voice is quiet anyway, so the closer I am, the better. Though I get occasionally banged in the face if the moshpit gets a bit lively and end each gig with smeared lipstick, forgetting about the audience allows me to lose myself in the music and sway to the rhythm without feeling self-conscious.

When the song ends, I'm back in the room, but now that I am enjoying myself, the gaps don't feel like an ordeal. I've become more aware, too, that everything you do on stage is magnified and the audience picks up on it. Showing nerves or upset either brings out the bullies or makes those rooting for you uncomfortable in sympathy. So I laugh and chat between numbers, slapping down any 'Get your tits out!' heckling, faking breezy assurance. In Newcastle, when Chris suffers a mental block with 'De-Luxe' and we have to restart the song three times, I mask our rattled confidence with jovial banter and the crowd responds with appreciative cheers and moshpit mayhem. On the final night of the tour in Bristol, I am serenaded by the audience, celebrating my twenty-third birthday.

———————

Chris and I moved into a one-bed flat in Camberwell the previous summer, which likely spelled the beginning of the end for us as a couple. We love each other, but with the band fully taking over our lives, it's all got a bit intense. Chris's time-worn method for dealing with problems is to isolate himself into private brooding and, if that doesn't work, flee to the Lakes to recharge his batteries with bracing perspective-restoring walks and the comforting bolt-hole of his family home. But there is no privacy in our tiny flat and the band's relentless schedule allows no time for escape. With college finished, I have no end-of-term breaks for recuperating visits to LA and Japan and cut off from the companionship of my old housemates and confidants in Tottenham, all my neediness is dumped on Chris.

In public, Chris maintains his cheerful, affable exterior and never lets his good humour slip; in private, he resists opening up, because talking about his problems is 'boring'. I grow weary of everyone else enjoying 'fun Chris', while I am lumbered with his increasing uncommunicative moodiness. Ever intolerant when my demands aren't met, I've started to stray, which Chris – like every boyfriend before and after – discovers by reading my diary.

We split up and Chris moves out and, though it's sad and a little messy, we manage to reset to being close mates and muckers, with the added affection of having once been in love. Now free and single, we throw ourselves into party mode, mingling with the bands and players on the lively London scene. Much of this ligging is facilitated by Howard, who prides himself on being able to chisel free entry into every gig and aftershow party in the capital. 'Leave it with me,' he says and we do.

With a background at major labels, hustling to promote the bands in his charge for radio play and TV appearances, Howard has a network of contacts all over the music business. His mantra is 'Think big, act big, be big' and he has no patience with any indie proclivities to wilful obscurity, which makes him both an asset and an anomaly at 4AD. This can-do positivity is expressed through an Essex-boy cocaine-boosted machismo that I'd normally run a mile from, were it not tempered by his enthusiasm for being in our company – embracing us as mates rather than a band he's been tasked to work with.

Steve can't stand him and neither can most of my friends. They see an entitled and thuggish ex-public schoolboy and wonder how on earth I and particularly Chris – with his down-to-earth northern punk ethic – can tolerate his presence. I don't disagree; Howard can be overbearing and he is rudely dismissive towards people he has no use for. His barely coherent political opinions – regardless of his worship of the Clash and fond reminiscences of Rock Against Racism gigs – ally with the views of right-wing tabloids and I recall in a later meeting where our accountant explained the concept of self-employment and tax, Howard taunted that we'd be 'voting Tory within the year'.

But despite his boorish traits, we're swept along by Howard's self-confidence. He is breezily dismissive of any self-doubt and, when Emma gets morose, dwelling on negatives, he clutches her in a matey hug and laughs, 'Oh, shut up, you moany old cow!', which literally no one else could get away with. He also excuses my wayward behaviour with a laugh – 'You're fucking mental, you are!' – and treats Chris with protective fondness, like an older brother. Steve remains unconvinced, though he appreciates the effort when Howard sources him a rare Japanese release of an obscure Neil Young LP.

But, most importantly, Howard champions Lush – bigging up our music and performances, to us and to everyone else. He really believes in us. So much so, that he's offered to leave 4AD and manage us full time. Steve observes that Howard may be experienced in the biz but he has literally no track record at management. But he doesn't labour the point. After all, we're a year into being a 4AD band and no one else has volunteered. Howard may be a bit of a wanker, but he's *our* wanker.

31

SWEETNESS AND LIGHT

In August, we record another EP – *Sweetness and Light* – with producer Tim Friese-Greene. Ivo is a long-time fan of his output with Talk Talk and, given his increasingly strained relationship with Cocteau Twins, is keen to steer us away from Robin Guthrie. Tim is drily amusing in conversation and uncompromisingly intense at work. We play through the title track hundreds of times in the rehearsal room, perfecting the arrangement and tweaking the drums. Tim sits in a corner, looking at the floor and shaking his head – an action we interpret as disapproval until Emma blurts out, 'What's wrong? Is it really bad?!', which prompts him to look up, baffled, explaining he's just getting into the music.

Where Robin is a fiend for digital electronics, Tim is all about experimenting with live sound. Guitar parts are recorded to perfection and then again with the mic positioned 3 inches further from the amp. A percussionist comes in to play an egg shaker and make noises with a wet cloth. Emma is put in a darkened room with an amp, a guitar and a candle for illumination, then told to make random noises. We spend an evening trying out various two-syllable words for me to mutter at the end of the song's breakdown section, completely inaudible on the recording but a key punctuation in Tim's ears.* In the end, there are forty-eight tracks to mix down on 'S&L' – drums, guitars, bass, vocals, percussion, other experimental shenanigans – and it's taken six weeks to record and mix three songs.

Chris is so traumatised by having his playing pulled apart and analysed in meticulous detail that he flees to the Lakes the second the drums are finished. Believing his ability was being questioned and undermined has made him jittery; I thought he'd be flattered that the drums were the backbone of the song and there was so much attention spent getting them absolutely right. Steve was barely there – off as soon as possible to spend the school summer holidays with Irene. And, although Emma was in her element (she wrote all three of the EP's tracks, though I did write the lyrics to 'Breeze'), the epic length of time it took to record and mix was too much attention, even for her. Still, the hard work paid off. 'S&L' remains one of Lush's best-loved tracks and I am close friends with Tim to this day. However, my mind is on other things since I've missed my period and fear the worst.

I'd have to wait some weeks to get an abortion on the NHS so I'm encouraged to go private. All my friends (not that they know from experience) advise me it's best to get it over with as quickly

---

* The timing of this breakdown section is tricky (eight and a half bars, if you're interested) and it becomes my role, for every single Lush gig ever after, to provide a count-in nod for everyone to resolve to the beat.

as possible. Though I've always defiantly claimed that I'll never have kids, now that I'm pregnant, I'm not so sure. But it's out of the question. Not because of the lack of a stable relationship – I don't realistically expect to ever have one of those. But I'd have to leave the band and find a whole new life. None of my close friends have children (in fact, when my daughter is born a decade later, I am the first of our friendship group to have a baby) and I know I'd end up cut off and isolated. My worst nightmare. And I'm barely able to look after myself, let alone a child.

But you dream, don't you? Maybe having a baby will ground me, make me more responsible. I know nothing about raising kids – no siblings or close extended family, I've never even babysat – and my parents aren't the best example. But maybe my own shitty childhood experiences will be of benefit, because I understand what it's like to be small and vulnerable and to need protection from a cruel world. On the other hand, maybe I'll be just like my parents. Worse still, maybe I'll be like Nora.

I arrive at the clinic to be met with a pro-life protest. It's not called that yet – we're a few years from the screaming crowds and murders of doctors and, in any case, this is Britain, not the US. A middle-aged woman with a pained, pitying expression hands me a leaflet about Jesus and I shuffle inside. I am sharing a room with a woman in her forties. She is garrulous and upbeat, housewifey and Irish. In fact, almost all the other patients seem to be Irish, too.* My roommate tells me she has five grown children already and is 'not bloody going through all that again. Knowing my luck it will probably be twins!'

---

* Abortion only becomes legal in the Republic after another twenty-seven years and is still only available in Northern Ireland if your health is at extreme risk.

I opt for a general anaesthetic, rather than a local one. I don't want to be conscious when it happens. I am given Valium, which plasters me to the ceiling. When I'm wheeled into surgery, the anaesthetist pats my arm and says, 'Who's been a naughty girl then?', and I slip into unconsciousness. Post-op, I am sobbing and bereft and submit gratefully to the comforting hugs of my roommate. I'm aware of the argument that 'it's just a cluster of cells' and that may be true in purely physical terms. But it's also hope and dreams and love and a life not lived, both mine and the baby that never will be.

The women gather together and I listen to them recount their stories and the lies they've had to tell in order to 'cross the water' for the procedure. Some are convivial and chatty, others defiantly refuse to feel bad about what they've done (and why should they?). Some, like me, are morose and quiet and the chatter is good for us, brings us out of our lonely contemplation. One woman confides in me that she's here because her boyfriend didn't think it was the right time for her to have children. She's had liposuction on her legs and hips to keep him happy. I look sadly at the moon-shaped indents all over her thighs. The scars are terrible, but she's prompting me to say that her legs look great, so I do.

The next morning, as I pack up to leave, my roommate is telling me she's off to Spain for a holiday with her husband and I wish her well. When the doctor gives her the forms to sign, he unnecessarily informs her that she was, indeed, pregnant with twins. 'Told you!' she bellows, winking at me and brushing aside his expectations of remorse. Good for her.

In September, we head off to LA to secure a US licensing deal. We're accompanied by Howard (probably the reason Steve has passed on the beano), who's in his element, ferrying us about to be courted by the money men. A stretch limo whisks us from the airport to the Mondrian Hotel, which has a poolside cocktail bar and huge double beds and not one but TWO phones in every room. It's a far cry from the shabby hotels and guest houses we're accustomed to in the UK. The staff are all wannabe models and actors – men in designer suits and women in figure-hugging lycra – and the MTV Awards are on, so the place is crawling with celebs. We share a lift ride with Michael Hutchence, Kylie Minogue and Queen Latifah. It's all impressively lavish and glamorous. Howard secures an open-top Mercedes and we visit Hollywood haunts and tourist spots. I have, of course, seen it all before, but it's so much more fun enjoying LA with my mates.

Tim Carr, A&R at Warner Brothers, came to see us play in the summer and the label is footing the bill for this trip, but there's no harm in checking out the competition. We are swept along to brunches and meet-and-greets and bombarded with 'We love you guys' schmoozing. At a meeting with Columbia, we perch awkwardly on a sofa surrounded by bods with clipboards. Emma nudges me when she spots one note taker's scribblings – 'We already have Ultra Vivid Scene' – implying another 4AD band is surplus to requirements. The room is plastered with images of glam-metal band Warrant, whose 'Cherry Pie' single is on 'heavy rotation' on MTV. The video is all big hair and wacky gurning, featuring a hot blonde on rollerskates in case any fourteen-year-old boys have missed the sledgehammer single entendre. Chris straight-facedly comments how he hopes Columbia will achieve a similar success for Lush, which the collected staff take completely seriously, either gushing about Warrant's amazing energy and talent or casting nervous side-eyes at each other, signalling: 'Do these idiots think they'll be as big as Warrant?'

In this ocean of fakes and phonies, Tim is a breath of fresh air. He plays up to the irony-free American stereotype, repeatedly checking, 'That's a joke, right?', though he is in fact whip-smart and mischievously sarcastic and we trust him to keep us from drowning in the vast roster of a major US label. After a thirteen-date UK tour for *Sweetness and Light*, we are back again across the Atlantic to promote *Gala* – a compilation of the tracks from *Scar*, *Mad Love* and *S&L* – repackaged as an album for North America and Japan.*

It's a short, whistle-stop tour that begins in Toronto and then sticks to the East and West Coasts, providing a chance for some press, radio and meeting the Warners muscle. We end with two LA gigs, the first at the Wiltern Theatre supporting Cocteau Twins, where Mum and I are in the audience together watching their set, moved to tears by the performance, sharing the moment. Two nights later, at our own gig at the Lingerie Club, Mum is charming and chatty with my friends and the crew and the Warners folk find her delightful. I know she's doing her social-butterfly bit, but I don't resent it for a second. This is my world and my crowd and I'm touched that she's making the effort.

---

* *Gala* was named after Salvador Dalí's wife. Emma had come up with this earlier as a potential title for *Scar* so for once we didn't have to agonise over a name. Ivo, who always valued art above commercialism, loathed the entire concept of *Gala* as he saw the component mini-album and EPs as distinct artefacts, inseparable from the original V23 artwork. I don't disagree.

Dad saw us play at the Town & Country Club just a month ago and I was similarly beaming at his praise. He scrubbed up for the occasion, which I appreciated, though bizarrely he had a Peperami sausage sticking out of his top suit pocket ('In case I get hungry'). I know I've given my parents a hard time in these pages, but they were 100 per cent behind me with Lush. They never once questioned what I was doing or pestered me to get a 'proper job'. I'm not sure Dad had a clue what to make of the music, but he relished seeing me out there and enjoying myself. He'd always advised against getting bogged down before I reached thirty: 'Make the most of being young. There's plenty of time for all the other boring shit once you're older.'

32

PUBLIC IMAGES

It's all very well saying that you don't much care about appearances, but, when your image appears in publications and music videos, it's stripped of whatever gregarious personality and sparkling conversation you may hope adds balance and you're evaluated on looks alone. Like the gauche teens you now see trout-pouting on Instagram, my awkward inner shyness screamed out from every frame. The clothes I was comfortable in looked shabby through the unforgiving glare of a camera lens and what seemed passable make-up for a night out brought out under the blinding lights of a photo shoot a sickly pallor and showed up every flaw. To achieve the same impact as 'real life', the make-up had to be thicker, darker and heavier. This is hard to judge if you don't know what you're doing and, in any case, I had none of the cosmetics or skill required. Which is why we needed a make-up artist.

It felt glamorous sitting before the brightly illumined mirror, ready to be transformed from humble caterpillar to splendid butterfly. But I was disappointed to discover that it wasn't enough to simply sit back passively and expect miracles and I'd have to provide my own input and opinions: 'Would you like me to do natural or a bit bolder? How do you want your eyes? What about eyelashes? Lip liner? A bright shade or more subtle?' And I'm thinking: *How the fuck should I know? You're the professional. Work your magic.*

What exactly *is* 'natural' anyway? Does it mean I'll look like I have no make-up on at all? I don't want that. And, if 'natural' is designed to bring out the flush and glow of your skin and subtly accentuate your features, then the colours are invariably all wrong, designed for white northern European skin and the usual shading tricks don't work because my face has all the wrong shapes. So no, not natural then. In the make-up room for a Sky TV interview, a flustered woman had plastered me up like a geisha – all orange and yellow around the eyes, squared-off black brows and geometric, angular lips. I should have stopped her as the disaster was unfolding, but I thought all the terrible details might miraculously cohere and at the end, I'd come out looking fabulous. I scrubbed it all off in the toilets and quickly applied my usual face.

The cavalry arrived in the form of Sarita Allison, who did make-up jobs for several other 4AD bands. She gauged my cluelessness and guided me gently through the process, assuring me she'd tweak elements until I looked – and felt – right. Emma, too, had little confidence with cosmetics beyond the basics and required the same patience. I've seen films where girls bond over styling each other's hair and make-up in some flossy boudoir, but it's not something Emma and I ever did ourselves. We were too busy talking or laughing or making up stupid names for bands or putting together the fanzine or playing music or making plans. We never had a pillow-fight in our underwear, either.

Sarita would affectionately berate me over my unbrushed, wonky home haircut and complete unfamiliarity with moisturiser. Her proven results made me trust her entirely and I followed her beauty tips and cosmetic application with studious attention, stocking up at home with her recommended products and making at least some effort with a grooming regime. Appraising my scruffy outfits with a critical eye, she encouraged me to abandon the familiar tacky charms of Kenny Market and cross the road to the young designers' pop-up stalls at Hyper Hyper, where I'd find better quality gear.

As luck would have it, the sporty look was in and cotton lycra was popular – affordable, functional, un-creasable. I bought stretchy black tops and leggings with white go-faster stripes down the sides, which unlike the cheapest high-street versions wouldn't bag and sag but held their shape and colour, flattering my figure. Shorts were *de rigueur* and I stocked up on several pairs: velvet with a sequinned stripe down each side and a couple in denim (short and snug, but not buttock-exposing), along with a short onesie in a batik print and a flared mini-culotte dress. My favourite purchase, which I practically lived in, was a long-sleeved, scoop-neck black-and-forest green panelled mini-dress (again, in cotton lycra) that hugged at the top and flared out at the bottom.

The genius of these outfits was that they doubled as stage wear, so I could get away with one set of clothes for everything – daytime, socials, photos and gigs. I'd have cycling-style shorts under the dresses, to avoid any upskirt embarrassment, along with thick unladderable lycra tights. The fabrics of my snazzy new wardrobe were so durable they defied destruction, so I could continue with my slobby habits, deeming clothes clean enough to wear so long as they passed the sniff test and ignoring 'dry-clean only' labels by swilling them about in the sink if I thought they'd get destroyed in a washing machine. They always came out fine.

Being outwardly presentable gave me more confidence on the inside. When I turned up to one session after a particularly wasted night and very little sleep, Sarita made me drink a litre of water and applied a cold compress and eye-drops to help calm my bloodshot eyes, sighing: 'Oh, Miki, what are we going to do with you?' But I'd been paying attention and had learned that half the job is faking it: if you're knackered or tense or unhappy, it shows – so don't show it. Breathe, unclench your teeth, relax your shoulders and look at the lens like it's a friend. Try to feel natural even though you're posed with one leg forward and a hand on your hip in a way that you would never normally stand. It's all about trust, really. If the photographer is telling you it looks great through the camera, you have to believe them. And I enjoyed being told I looked great.

The others warmed to it less. Chris felt like a ponce and Steve's expression (and indeed, clothes) never changed whether he was on stage, in a pub or waiting for a bus, so he wasn't about to start posturing now. Though Emma got a buzz from seeing herself looking gorgeous on screen and in print, she'd refuse to comply with a photographer's instructions if they made her feel silly or uncomfortable and her pleasure was further diminished by my encroaching presence. She'd huff with irritation if I was positioned at the front of group photos and grimace at the final cut of videos, where my lip-syncing presence dwarfed everyone else's screen time.

During our adolescence, when Emma had felt overshadowed by her loud and attention-seeking friend, she solved the problem by carving out a separate work and social life where she had space to grow her identity. With Lush, her songs dominated our records, both in number and in quality, and my obvious difficulty with becoming the lead singer gave her a novel opportunity to be the confident one. She was the person with the network of contacts in the industry; I was the sidekick who would whisper excitedly 'What did they say?!' after some journalist or label bod had engaged her in conversation at a gig. But now she was stuck once again with me hogging the limelight.

There's an inevitable focus on the lead singer in bands, even more so when that singer is a woman and has bright red hair. But Lush had been born out of a defiantly indie scene – anti-star, anti-contrivance – and I had no desire myself to be singled out as frontwoman, carrying the full weight of the band's public image. It smacked of the whole 'Blondie is a band' struggle and I was no Debbie Harry. But I'd noticed that it didn't bother Emma at all if the boys got ignored. When Chris and Steve were cropped out of our *Melody Maker* cover, her response was: 'Well, we *are* the songwriters.' So it's really not about the band, it's about Emma.

I try to redress the balance. In sessions, I position myself at the side of the group. When we peruse the contact sheets to select our promo shots, I allow Emma first pick on the ones she likes best. This doesn't always work as she often bookmarks images where she might look great but the rest of us are caught in an awkward expression or have our eyes closed. When I point this out, she'll throw her arms up and flounce: 'Fuck it, I don't care anyway.' When we score the cover of *Time Out*, I lead the charge in insisting that the rest of the band be featured and they compromise with an insert of the band alongside the solo shot of me. And when the *NME* put me forward as Laura Palmer for their Christmas edition photo feature of bands dressed up as TV icons, I decline (I love *Twin Peaks* but am not keen on being featured as a naked corpse anyway) and we do *The Liver Birds* instead, where Emma is smiley and cute cast as Sandra and I am happy to be full-on ridiculous as Carol in a ginger wig and garish '70s pant-suit (again, no sign of the boys).

None of this makes enough difference. Every live review that features a solo shot of me, every interview dominated by my photo, prompts a resigned sigh, however much I voice my agreement that it's lazy and reductive for promo to focus so much on the lead singer. It's Emma's talent and Emma's drive that has made Lush a success and she resents anyone thinking otherwise. And, though none of this is my fault, it's me she takes it out on.

33

MONEY (WHY A LOT IS NOT ENOUGH)

If there's one sure-fire way to set a cat among the pigeons, it's money. Until now, we haven't had any and, though we moan about being skint, we don't expect any different. Chris, Steve and I have spent the last year on a government initiative called the Enterprise Allowance Scheme. In theory, it's meant to encourage entrepreneurship by launching the unemployed into a business start-up; in reality, it's a cynical ploy to keep the jobless figures down. We were required to attend some pointless training days (jumping over laminated pictures of sharks to illustrate the risks you have to take in business) and endured a quarterly accounts check where a bored clerk gave my double-entry notebook a cursory glance. In return, we got £40 a week and were freed from the fortnightly ritual of having to sign on at the local dole office, which allowed us to go on tour without having our benefits cut. But you can only be on it for a year and our time is almost up.

Howard has left 4AD and set up a management company with Ray Conroy, who himself has a long history with the label. Lush is Howard's baby and Ray brings with him Frazier Chorus and

Colourbox, while also becoming the main caretaker for Moose (not least because Moose himself wants nothing to do with Howard) and the two share duties with Chapterhouse. They plunder their major-label contacts and land Lush a deal of £80,000 (in today's money, about twice that figure) with Island Music Publishing. It's a staggering sum and beyond my comprehension. But I'm about to get a harsh education in how music-business finance works.

I won't go into the complications of how publishing companies shell out an advance and then get repaid in a percentage deal that means you are reimbursing more than you borrowed. If you have a mortgage, you'll understand. But it's basically, as Howard puts it, a big fuck-off loan, with your songs held as collateral. When we'd first stumbled into 4AD after recording *Scar*, we'd been booked into a meeting with an in-house publisher at Beggars Banquet, which was presented as yet another routine hoop-jump in releasing the record. Ivo seemed a bit embarrassed about it and with good reason. A guy behind a desk offered us £500 a song and rattled off some guff about how they had the muscle to get our music used in films and ads, but even I could see £3,000 for the rights to *Scar* was an insult.

Way back when Emma had insisted that we get songwriting credits for our records, I didn't think it meant much beyond a name on a label. Now, it transpires, there is real money to be made. Emma insists that this is our money – mine and hers – because we write the songs. And it's true – there's no collaboration, apart from my lyrics to some of her compositions. We don't build songs in rehearsals or in soundchecks; they come to the band fully formed, with basslines, drum parts, vocal parts, the lot – all written by either me or Emma. So while the boys can kick back between tours, Emma and I are tethered to our portastudios, coming up with material for the next record. But is that because they're not willing to put in the work or because they're not given the opportunity?

Steve once ventured to submit an idea he'd been working on and we tried a variety of approaches in rehearsal until Emma impatiently snapped, 'Look, it's just not working,' and all further effort was abandoned. She was right, it didn't fit with Lush, but she didn't need to be quite so rude about it. And a fleeting shock crosses Chris's face when I explain how this publishing deal works, before he recovers his usual bluff composure: 'Yeah, no, that's great.' I'm worried about how the financial imbalance will affect the band and put it to Emma that £80,000 is a huge sum and we can afford to be generous.

We barter the percentages: my concern is having more parity between band members, but Emma is comparing her slice to Howard's 20 per cent management fee and (rightly) insists on a demonstrable gap between his take and hers. We settle in the end for 25 per cent between Chris and Steve, with Emma and me splitting the remaining 55 per cent. Oh and we only get half now and half after we deliver an album. So not such a staggering sum after all. Dad, who is done with London and planning to move back to Hungary, 'borrows' half my first cheque to carry out repairs to the Balaton house (it takes a decade of persistent hassling from me to be repaid), so at this stage I'm no better off than the boys. But I'm outraged that Howard, who is raking in a commission from all the other bands he manages, is earning more from Lush than either Chris or Steve, who have no other means for an income. I put this argument to the band lawyer, but am told that yes, it seems unfair, but that's just how it is.

Buoyed by the publishing deal, Howard suggests we abandon 4AD for a major label, which admittedly would go some way to ameliorating our money issues. But on this, the whole band are in agreement: no. We love being on 4AD and are keenly aware of the gravitas the label adds to Lush. You can't put a price on that. Howard negotiates a generous five-album deal, which allows us to pay ourselves a wage of £100 a week – more than any of us has ever had to live on. Ivo tells me to my face, only half joking, that we're greedy, to which I snippily counter that the licensing deal we signed with Warners, of which we don't get a penny, more than covers what the label is paying. He was also happy enough to talk us into giving an extra percentage point on *Scar* for John Fryer, failing to explain that this would come out of our already measly share of the profits. In any case, after our wages, legal fees, accountancy, Howard's 20 per cent cut, rehearsals, individual band expenses and the myriad other dribs and drabs it costs to run a band, we're hardly living like millionaires.

———

The money from 4AD allows us to splurge on new equipment. With Pete's collaboration and advice, Chris gets a new Yamaha kit, Steve a Fender bass amp, I have a new Mesa Boogie Mark IV amp and some nice new Boss pedals and Emma is kitted out with two amps for a stereo sound and a Roland GP-16 rack effects unit that breaks down so often we need a second in reserve. She and I get four-track Fostex portastudios and a Roland drum machine each, which gives my songwriting a new lease of life. I've tried playing the drums but I don't have the coordination and the R-5 lets me translate what I can hear in my head but can't physically perform, calculating mathematically where the accents and changes should be. And, with a fully realised drum track to work from and a bass riff recorded on top, I can experiment more with guitars and vocals, moving away from my usual open chords and trying different blends of harmonies, building the song and hearing whether the dynamics I've imagined in my head will work.

Emma's demos frankly sound no different from when she was having to use a standard tape recorder and was warbling the melody over an acoustic guitar. Except now with an added click track or a pre-set beat. But she's always had a remarkable talent for holding a complete song in her head and going through the chore of recording it all properly and allowing the rest of the band in on the secret isn't something she can be bothered with. She never masters the complicated and temperamental tech that she's now set up with for live shows and rehearsals, either. If the problem doesn't fix itself by turning the power off and on again, she'll fume, then shout strangled obscenities and finally switch it off: 'Fuck it, Pete can sort it out.' Any offer of help from me is waved away with concerns that I'll do irreparable damage.

The portastudios allow us to dish out cassettes of complete songs, along with recordings for individual parts. Because Emma's ropey recordings pay no detailed attention to the drums, there's some trial and error required to translate her ideas as she explains to Chris what she's envisaged. My experiments with the R-5 mean I have a better grasp of precisely where you can place a snare hit or a hi-hat accent to achieve the results she's after, which I'm keen to contribute to bring out the best in Emma's songs. But the effort I've spent finessing my own demos belies that they aren't set in stone and I'd benefit from some input and ideas – rethinking the tempo or the arrangement or making changes to the overall sound. I have a song, 'Untogether', which I just can't quite make work. I know there's a good tune in there but it sounds messy and rushed and I get no help from Emma, who looks bored and impatient with my failure to sort out the problem myself.

I'm getting a tetchy, competitive vibe from Emma these days. Increasingly, my songs are abandoned after a couple of run-throughs with a tired and exasperated 'I've got a bad back' excuse for her to sit down and disengage – a complaint that miraculously disappears when it's time to move on to her own songs. And Emma's material is becoming more demanding, paying no heed to our individual ability or personal style. I know I wrote the lyrics for 'Tiny Smiles', but the jazzy scales and tricky intervals are a struggle for my limited singing talent. Emma winces at the flat notes and when we overhear a band next door rehearsing, she wistfully comments on the female vocals, sighing: 'It must be great to have a proper singer.'

I put a lot of this sniping down to the disparity in public attention – from the press, on stage, just being recognised while I'm out and about. I've been told by others that it's hard for Emma to stomach and I've seen other bands struggle with this issue myself. I try not to feel aggrieved and figure I'll get the chance to make my songs work once we're in the studio. Not that I've got a concrete plan, of course, just keeping my fingers crossed, as ever.

34

OUR FIRST PROPER ALBUM

The promotion for *Gala* amounted to almost fifty gigs in total – the earlier US/Japan dates, then a return to America on a co-headline tour with Ride and some stadium shows with the Sisters of Mercy and Jane's Addiction. But it's now, finally, time to knuckle down and begin work on our first 'proper' album. Though we've been happy with all our records to date, the John Fryer sessions were so early and raw that it feels like a backward step to consider him for producer. And it took six weeks for the three tracks with Tim Friese-Greene – at that rate, we might still be recording our album at Christmas. Robin Guthrie is the obvious choice: *Mad Love* was well received and he's become a champion of the band. He's seen us live numerous times and also recorded our cover of 'Chirpy Chirpy Cheep Cheep' for the anti-poll tax album *Alvin Lives in Leeds*, directing us to 'speed it up for fuck's sake and enjoy it!'. So we're used to working with him and confident he'll bring out the best in our songs.

It's suggested we do everything at September Sound, as the studio is purpose-built for Robin's requirements and will make every process quick and easy. Robin suggests using a Simmonds kit, played into a sequencer to trigger sampled drum sounds, which Chris, never one to rock the boat, nods along with. But, if Tim Friese-Greene's drum bootcamp was tough for Chris, playing on the unresponsive pads, which don't have the feel and resonance of a proper kit, is torture. As soon as the ordeal is over, Chris vanishes from the studio, with assurances from Robin that any discrepancies can be fixed via digital wizardry. This is going to be very much a 'studio album' and, though we've demoed several of the songs, there is no 'routining' – working on the arrangements in a rehearsal room, as we did with Tim – so many of the songs are unfamiliar and Emma and I are still writing more tracks while in the studio. We still aren't competent enough as musicians to simply rattle off an accomplished performance for a part we aren't familiar with.

Like Chris, Steve also can't get out of there fast enough. I sympathise with Emma that his bass-playing hasn't much improved since the early days – the two of us have had singing lessons and our songwriting has demanded we develop as guitar players, while Chris enrolled himself on a drumming course to brush up his skills, making jokes about paradiddles and show-off twirling his sticks. And, though Steve did make the effort in the early days with some bass lessons, in rehearsals he's taken to listening to the cricket commentary via an earpiece plugged into a portable transistor radio, *while playing the songs*! Ah well, Steve is Steve. I'm happy with the basslines he's recorded for my songs, so long as they're in tune and in time. But Emma is a hard taskmaster and gets frustrated if her compositions aren't played exactly as she wants them. She oversees every element of her songs and is uncompromisingly critical if every note isn't perfectly executed. If it's hard for Steve, it's a fucking nightmare for me.

Some songs are fine. I'm never confident enough to belt it out and there's a lot of comping, trying to get one usable vocal by patching together several tracks. But I get good at double-tracking, matching a previous take exactly. Robin is patient and encouraging, coaxing my performance, though his 'come and have a listen' prompt, calling me from the vocal room, makes me nervous as it offers no indication of quality. I listen to the playback and look at him for clues – 'Sounds alright to me,' I venture. 'Alright? It sounds fucking brilliant,' and I beam and breathe a sigh of relief.

If Emma agrees, it's encouraging to see her delight as her songs take shape. But at other times I find her staring glumly at the mixing desk, refusing to make eye contact and I know something's up. I listen out for any glaring fuck-ups, offering, 'Is that second line still a bit flat?', to which Robin might respond: 'Mmmm, mebbe a bit. S'okay, we can fix that.' At which Emma suddenly explodes, 'It's the same note as the other verse! Can't you just SING IT IN TUNE?!', and I gulp and nod, 'Sure, let me give it a go,' while she exhales in 'look at what I have to deal with' frustration. It's like she thinks I'm trying to sabotage her songs on purpose.

Robin does his best to mediate, occasionally pointing out that a little wobble is acceptable if the delivery has charm and character. But Emma's not having any of it. She wants it to be perfect, so I try different headphone mixes, singing to the track slowed down a little, trying alternate lines, sometimes individual words – whatever it takes to get it right. I rely on superstitious rituals to help calm my nerves – making sure I've eaten, making sure I've *not* eaten, sipping herbal teas or just hot water and honey, standing in different ways, hands on hips or arms relaxed, employing all the Tona de Brett tips from her lessons. But the simple truth is that I'm just not a good enough singer and any confidence I've gained over the past year is seeping out of me.

There are songs where I become so cowed and quiet, deliberately tuning flat or sharp to compensate for whatever it is that's wrong with what I've sung before, that I'm barely enunciating. All personality has been sucked out of my performance and we might as well sample me singing a single note and play the entire fucking vocal on a keyboard.* And it's not like this works in reverse. If I attempt to correct Emma's guitar solo or wrongly worded backing vocal on my songs, I'm met with impatient complaints that 'it's really difficult to play/sing' or 'I don't think it actually works'. So my songs are all wrong as well.

I'd been particularly proud of 'For Love'. There was a cynical sadness in the lyrics that contrasted with the bright, chiming music, capturing my mixed emotions. The song had a catchy bassline and some inventive transitions, along with a particularly satisfying key change that resolved to the chorus, which Robin paid the utmost compliment to by saying 'That's really good. I'm gonna nick that.' But as we record my guitar, he points out that there's a chord that doesn't work. I can see Emma smirking, enjoying my crestfallen state. I worked so hard on that song and it's wrong. I'm flooded with disappointment at myself. Even my best song is shit and I flee the room lest I burst into tears. Robin fixes it – it's just a matter of changing minor to major (or vice versa, I can't remember), but this atmosphere is crushing

---

* When, later in the year, we record B-sides with Mark Freeguard, Emma decides to sing the lead for 'Astronaut' herself. I'm privately delighted when she realises it's not as easy as she bloody thinks and the vocals end up barely audible in the track, awash with effects.

me. I'm all about needing an environment of togetherness and mutual support, not having my every contribution scanned for possible imperfections, then held up for scornful criticism, which makes me feel hopeless and defensive.

Emma, however, seems to thrive in this competitive atmosphere. When Howard enthuses about 'For Love', earmarking it as a possible single, I am quietly thrilled. Within a week, Emma turns up at the studio brandishing a demo of 'Nothing Natural' and confidently announces: 'I've got a new song and it's *definitely* a single!' We spend less time on my songs, more on hers, not least because she demands perfection whereas I don't like to ruffle feathers. But honestly, I give up. If it's that important to her, let her be Queen Bee. I immerse myself instead in cooking meals for the studio, strolling around Richmond and shopping for ingredients, then secluding myself in the kitchen to serve up home-made soups, pasta sauces and stuffed mushrooms. Cooking has always been good therapy for me and my culinary efforts win unadulterated warm appreciation, even from Emma, allowing me to feel I can at least do something right.

It's not all bad, of course. Recording at September Sound means Robin is in his own environment, so it's quick and easy work to record guitars as he has all the effects at his fingertips. He is fun to be around, engagingly chatty and mischievously gossipy. And he has great ideas, bringing out the bright, pop edge of our songs. He strips back and rethinks 'Untogether', releasing its potential and prompting me to write new parts that complement the new, spacier feel. It's exactly the collaborative nudge I need.

And Emma blossoms working with him, the two of them ensconced in the studio, experimenting with guitar sounds. Robin loves his gadgets and will brandish some pedal he's been sent from Japan or plug in an instrument simply to share the pleasure of some newly discovered setting in one of the multitude of racks mounted and stacked around the mixing desk. Emma has ideas for sounds – which she describes through adjectives or by vocalising an approximating noise – but she's not interested in the technicalities of how to create them herself. This isn't a criticism. Not everyone wants to pore over YouTube videos to find the perfect effects pedal or spend hours fussing with settings to get the exact right swell or delay. For Emma, it's all about the song and Robin is great at interpreting her ideas and making them happen.

Emma, Robin and I spend a night recording a cover of Dennis Wilson's 'Fallin' in Love'. Freed from the 'my song/ Emma's song' competitive pressure, we are effortlessly productive, excitedly chiming in with ideas. My vocal goes seamlessly and Robin and I are loudly cheering when Emma executes the tricky keyboard solo. She is giggly and playful and fun to be with. At the end, Robin kicks back in his studio chair, smiling and happy: 'That was fucking great, no?' And I'm thinking, *God, why can't it be like this all the time?*

———

Ivo had been reluctant for us to record an album with Robin, but he'd never been entirely clear why. As the weeks of recording rolled by, some of the possible reasons became apparent. Cocteau Twins had been on 4AD for almost a decade, but the relationship had soured and was on the verge of collapse and Robin's calm and matter-of-fact exterior had begun to slip. He rarely missed an opportunity to launch into a 'let me tell you' takedown against

Ivo. I politely nodded along but found it uncomfortable – it's like having one of your parents slag off the other.

I'm aware now and was shortly after these recordings, that Robin had a notorious cocaine habit. We weren't much exposed to it, because we didn't much indulge ourselves. Drugs were for parties, not work; casual, not compulsive. So when his various acquaintances started turning up at the studio – people that both Emma and I found irritatingly boorish, not least because they were occupying Robin's attention and interrupting our work – we failed to spot the enormous quantities of drugs being delivered. We just assumed these people were dropping by to hang out.

Robin starts to go AWOL. I wait at the studio all day and when Emma turns up for her evening guitar session, she's livid that no work has been done. On one occasion, he vanishes on a four-day bender and we progress instead with Robin's studio engineers Mitsuo Tate and Lincoln Fong (also bass player in Moose – such a small world!). It's not ideal and Emma and I wonder together what the fuck is going on. But we don't want to shit-stir by running with complaints to Ivo, which, given the situation between 4AD and Cocteaus, seems disloyal to Robin. Howard is no help either. An enthusiastic snorter himself, he's reluctant to criticise anyone else's habit. Robin's interest trails off and we more or less finish the recordings without him. During the mix, he is often preoccupied and grumpy. Whether it's the drugs or the stress from the imminent split from 4AD, I don't know. But it feels like we're holding him against his will.

One happy side effect of Robin becoming a problem is it gives Emma and me a common cause for complaint. This was often the way – when Emma's dissatisfaction was focused elsewhere, my input and support were valued. Compliments worked well, too. When I apologised for stumbling with the vocals for 'Monochrome' and 'Nothing Natural', explaining I was getting a bit choked up because I found the lyrics so moving and emotional, Emma blushed at the flattery.* And, when I informed her that my lyrics for 'Covert' were inspired by Anaïs Nin's *A Spy in the House of Love*, which she had bought me as a birthday present, she yelped in delight: 'Really?!' She was a sucker for praise, I should have learned that and used it to disarm her.

But there's no such thing as money in the bank with Emma – the next threat and any previous goodwill is forgotten – so competitiveness is restored the second we have to compile the album. Emma makes zero mention of my songs, so I have to fight for them myself. Neither of us can see beyond getting our fair share and, though Ivo, Howard, Robin and the boys put in their ha'p'orth, none of them wants to get in the firing line of our bickering power games, so the album ends up being too long, too sprawling.

Emma comes up with the title, which I instantly, unfairly, shoot down and scoff at. I've grown just as hostile to Emma's ideas as I perceive she is to mine. But happily, I'm outvoted. *Spooky* is released in January 1992 and goes to number seven in the UK national album charts – truly a triumph and a cause for celebration.

---

* 'Monochrome' – my personal favourite on the album. I sided with Robin that it should be the single, but Emma had set her heart on 'Nothing Natural' and I didn't want to lose my one chance with 'For Love', so that was that.

35

LOVE AND REVENGE

I've decided that I'm simply not built for relationships. I find good people, we fall in love and then I ruin everything with my fucked-upness, which I don't seem able or willing to control. My stab at abstinence lasts all of three weeks – I have a radar for available men and it's impossible to switch it off. I need to find someone who doesn't want a serious relationship; someone who's only after a bit of fun. That way no one gets hurt.

When I first meet Travis (not his real name), he is completely off his tits on ecstasy, rallying the Milk Bar crowd with bug-eyed, whooping dancing. I've never much liked clubs, finding them hostile and elitist. They like to maximise their kudos by keeping a queue of punters waiting outside for an unnecessarily long time, which I find irritating and rude. The thrill, I suppose, is having your worth validated by some idiot tastemaker on the door deeming you cool enough to gain entry. Even better if you're a recognised 'face' and can barge to the front with no apology. But hanging out with Travis demystifies some of the stuck-up unfriendliness and it's a new scene to explore. He's part of the Primal Scream organisation and, like all of the band's carefully selected entourage, helps burnish their druggy, bad-boy reputation.

When word gets around that we're seeing one another, I get warnings from acquaintances concerned for my welfare. I imagine they think I'm being coerced into demoralising sexual acts, but I'll be honest with you: Travis is all talk and the tankload of drugs he's on means there's not much going on in that department. And, anyway, I'm just after some shallow fun, hanging out with the in-crowd. Travis and I enjoy a Christmas trip to Rome, carousing in the clubs and tourist attractions. We fail to smuggle a bottle of Champagne into the Vatican City and neck it on the spot, like legends in our own private movie, racking up the anecdotes for future self-aggrandisement.

The worst elements of Travis's crew model themselves on rock 'n' roll tropes, which means the females around them are expected to conform to clichés, too. They toy with women for entertainment, the boys lined up like a row of hyenas, pointing and cackling at some girl who can't tell whether she's being admired or ridiculed. That's the point, though – it doesn't matter what she does, they're in on the joke and she isn't. Another, judged as fancying herself too much, is mocked among the boys for her 'revolting camel-toe'. But, while I'm relieved to be spared any cruelty, acceptance is no less troubling. I'm told that I'm sexy, that when I dance I look like I'm having sex, that my tits look amazing in that dress, that I have an amazing body. Travis refers to me as 'my bird' and gets conspiratorial winks from the lads. Bobby Gillespie, high as a kite at some do, silences my chatter by cupping my genitals and fixing me with a stare as he licks his lips, while Travis grins collaboratively: 'I know, she's goooorgeous, isn't she?' I go with the flow, accepting that these are the

rules if you want to be part of the entourage, weighing my discomfort against the perks of free clubs and drugs.

On New Year's Eve, Travis fails on his promise to get my
friend Melissa (another Queen's College friend) into some happening event and kvetches and sulks when I refuse to dump
her at the door. I understand that his slavish worship of 'The
Scream' means everyone else comes second, but I'm not about
to leave her alone on the street, half an hour before midnight,
having dragged her along myself. I'm here for the ride, not to
burn all my bridges. And keeping up with Travis's voracious
consumption of ecstasy is taking its toll. I often end the night sat
in a corner, startle-eyed and chewing my mouth, too far gone to
move. I'm realising that I don't have what it takes to be a carefree 24-hour party person.

And neither, actually, does Travis. There's a troubled sadness
he reveals during quieter moments: the violent stepfather, the
terrible insecurity, the self-hatred of having to act like a clown in
order to be liked. Away from the pack, he can be thoughtful and
caring, but Travis has no intention of toning down the lifestyle,
however much it damages him and I'm not the type who is content to offer soft, feminine condolence so he can simply offload
his shit on me and return to the party unburdened.

One of his friends, *NME* journo Jack Barron, who is older and
wiser, can see where this is headed: 'Don't fuck him about, Miki,
because, if he falls, he'll fall hard.' But I wave away the warning –
Travis is a party animal, I'll be replaced as soon as it's over. And,
in any case, I've already slept with at least three other people during this period and fully expect Travis has, too.

———

Debbie has taken a six-month break from 4AD and John Best, who runs a PR company called Best in Press (this becomes Savage & Best shortly after when he joins forces with Jane Savidge), is babysitting the label's press. The frequent promo for Lush means we are often in each other's company and one thing leads to another. I'd thought that his marriage was a guarantee that our casual affair could never turn serious, but it has. When I look deep into his eyes, there's a force like a rush that makes us both laugh in wonder: 'What was *that*?!'

We break up, numerous times. I have no desire to become a homewrecker and the guilt and responsibility of splitting up a marriage is too much for me to handle. Meanwhile, John's friends try to talk him out of a reckless mistake and he seeks out a therapist for help. It's a fucking awful time for everyone involved, especially John's wife, but our love is fierce and selfish and everything pales in comparison. After months of on–off, back-and-forth drama, John and I end up together.

Unlike me, John isn't used to thinking of himself as a bad person and often spirals into self-flagellating sadness. So we talk – sharing our anxieties, exploring our pasts, eager to learn everything about each other, however sad or dark or fucked-up. Within the year, we've bought a flat together. John is thirty to my twenty-three and guides me through all the grown-up stuff – sorting the mortgage, decorating, helping set up the front bedroom for me to write and practise my music. He even has a car! I've never been so well looked after in all my life and feel like a proper adult.

With several of my exes, even the modest attention that Lush received would prick their competitive pride. They'd rarely engage with what I did for a living and any mention of the band might trigger a take-down, thinly veiled as a joke. One used to walk past the framed posters of Vaughan's Lush artwork in my flat, football-chanting 'Ego! Ego!' *every fucking time*, though I was happy for him to talk about his band until the cows came home and regularly cheered his gigs. John shares my joy in any praise or success the band achieves and it's a relief not to have to tiptoe around a man's ego. In any case, neither of us is the type to think ourselves special. We both love what we do, but know it's not the be-all and end-all, however glamorous it may look to others.

John finds my slobby ways endearing, jokily calling me a 'slattern' and laughing with incredulity that I 'wash my face like a navvy'. He books me in for a proper haircut and I sit in the chair while the professional dye-job is being carried out, observing that I look like a glacé cherry.* He buys me a Pam Hogg dress (on the cover of this book), which I wear on stage and for photos and recommends clothes shops to check out when I'm touring in the US: Anna Sui and Betsey Johnson become favourites. John is interested in clothes and style and I benefit from his critical eye. It sounds a bit *Pygmalion*, but it's flattering to have someone care about how I look and I trust his guidance.

I cook us Japanese meals and bring him to Balaton to meet Dad. Mum and John get on great guns in LA, both chatty about photography and fashion, and he fits in with my friends and enjoys their company – always a non-negotiable must for my boyfriends. He's on the look-out for a junior at Savage & Best, so I recommend Melissa, who's been looking for a change of career, and he trains her up as part of their team. When Lush headline

---

* It's not something I take to. The bleaching and dyeing take hours and I revert to colouring my hair at home, where I can crack on with more constructive things than leafing through magazines and having tedious conversations about holidays.

two gigs for *Les Inrockuptibles* magazine in France, with Blur and Pulp supporting, I'm wowed by Pulp's show and charmed by their down-to-earth and friendly company and insist John comes to see them.* John is reluctant: Pulp? *Pulp?!* They're also-rans, dead-end indie. No one cares about Pulp.

But I drag him to their gigs, in London and out of town, and he agrees that they've turned a corner, taking them on the roster at Savage & Best. It's amusing to recall that no one was interested: one editor witheringly responded to a request to review their album: 'What – more songs about Spangles?' But John champions them, which in turn helps get them proper management (they ask Howard, but he turns them down) and then a deal with Island. I'm overjoyed to have played a small part in both Pulp and John receiving well-deserved kudos, delighted to be involved in his career.

But for all the joy and compatibility, in the first two and a half years of being together, I'm at home for barely ten months – and two of those are spent recording *Spooky*. Our lives are at the mercy of Lush and peripheral to its demands and there is little time left over to nurture and grow our relationship.

———————

Travis is less than pleased to learn that I'm shacked up with John. Apparently, blokes in bands are treated like heroes for fucking and

---

* Blur are already Emma's territory, so I spend little time with them, not wanting to step on her toes, but they aren't my cup of tea anyway. I first encountered them at a party some time ago, two of them nudging each other and sniggering, 'Our mate really fancies you,' while another hovered in the background posing expectantly. The puerile first impression is confirmed at the gig in Lille, when Damon and Graham smash up the dressing room – not the riotous rock 'n' roll act of hedonism that implies; more like two spoilt brats having a tantrum about the gig not going well, while the French promoter shrugs at their behaviour and the rest of the room watches nonplussed.

dumping any number of women, but the reverse isn't true and I need to be punished. I receive hoax phonecalls from his friends: startling bellows, gleeful braying insults or elaborate set-ups where I am drawn into conversation before the hilarious gotcha reveal is embellished by Travis's shrieking laughter in the background. When I'm on tour in the US, John is woken at 3 a.m. by a call claiming that there's been a terrible accident at the venue. He contacts the club in a panic and the baffled staff member assures him nothing untoward has happened – Lush are safely on stage. For the rest of the night, John is left jeering messages on our Ansafone: 'Hey, *Georgie* Best! What's it like spongeing off your Lush girl?' 'How's the wife, Georgie Boy?' On and on, until the tape runs out.

I try to follow my bandmates' advice: 'Ignore it. He'll get bored once his broken heart has healed.' But I'm beginning to question this framing of Travis as the bereft ex-lover nursing his wounds. We were together for all of three months, half of which I was on tour for, and he already has a new girlfriend. He's not pining for me, it's his pride that's bruised.

The pestering continues. There are more phonecalls and messages, I receive religious publications in the post that he's subscribed me to and, on the day of a Primal Scream release, the police barge into our flat prompted by a fake 999 call (from a phonebox near Travis's office, I later discover). Debbie Edgely calls me in a panic about a tabloid getting a tip that I was so heartbroken over splitting with Travis that I'd tried to end it all by slashing my wrists. I say, let them print it, I'll rinse them in court. I have legions of witnesses who can testify that that's bullshit. They don't run the story, but it's clear to me who was behind the 'tip'. When we play Melbourne, Primal Scream are in town and when I am heckled throughout our show, the promoter informs me that Travis and his cronies were responsible.

I try to reason with him – I'm even friendly when our paths cross – but he claims outraged innocence, twisting my accusations in an attempt to prove that it's *me* who's obsessed. Friends suggest elaborate revenge plots, but the last thing I want is to spend even more time and energy on him. And I worry if I retaliate, it'll make things worse. As John says, it's just so fucking *tedious*. We change our home phone number.

At Reading '94, several years after this shit first started, I finally snap. Travis has been following me around all night in the hotel bar party, positioning himself within my earshot and eyeline, heckling me with jeering insults in a falsetto yodel: 'Wooo, look at me, I'm Miki from Lush! I'm in a SHIT indie band! Hahahahaha!!!' It would be nice to have someone leap to my defence, but he's always so exaggeratedly off his nut that people find his antics funny and allowing it to bother me makes me look like I have no sense of humour.

One of his former cronies from the Primal Scream entourage engages me in quiet commiseration, telling me his current girlfriend, another of Travis's exes, suffered similar nastiness. And it wasn't even her who left him – she was just punished for moving on. It's a revelation to discover I am not the only one who has been a victim of Travis's malice, that it's him, not me, who's at fault. It's all the encouragement I need and I march over, pin Travis to the wall by his neck and threaten to slice his bollocks off if I ever hear so much as a fucking peep out of him again. 'That's right,' he wails, 'make a scene. In front of all the press and the photographers!' I tell him he's pathetic and walk away. It was as easy as that. He never bothered me again.

36

BASS GODS

Howard has been cosying up to the Americans and I've got to hand it to him, everyone at Warners seems to love him. He's been schmoozing US agent Marc Geiger, fishing to get Lush on the next Lollapalooza festival and hangs out with Perry Farrell, singer in Jane's Addiction and curator of the on-the-road festival, for extra leverage. With his sights set on conquering the US with a storm of press and 'heavy rotation' on MTV, Howard seizes on the promo and insists we use a proper 'classy' fashion photographer for the band photos (Jurgen Ostarhild, whose shot from the session is on the cover of this book). He sits in on the video meeting for 'Nothing Natural', boiling down the priority to a single mantra: 'Look good, look good, look good.'

On the day of filming, Emma and I are presented with a rack of Barbarella-sexy space outfits. Emma sidesteps this indignity by announcing that nothing fits her, while I select the least-worst option of a sparkly T-shirt and silver shorts with body-wrapping straps. Sarita is instructed to pile on the make-up and I can barely open my eyes from the caterpillar-heavy false lashes. Thank fuck

Howard managed to talk the director out of the diaphanous designer shirts decked with campy Pre-Raphaelite cherubs that he'd originally intended for the boys.

On the plus side, Emma is alongside me in every shot, so any screen-hogging fears are allayed and even Dad calls me to comment that she looks amazing. I also rather like my visible discomfort at the hefty eyewear, blinding lights and hair-blowing industrial fans, which seems to subvert the OTT glamour. Warners are happy that the video gets played on MTV – a bit – and it's picked out for praise by Kurt Cobain, which is kudos. But as Howard fills us in on the relentless and packed schedule of tours and promo for the year to come, Steve calls a meeting to tell us that he's decided to leave the band.

———

There's no animosity. Steve has fulfilled his youthful dreams of playing in a band and feels he's ticked all the desired boxes: having his photo in the papers, recording an album and touring the world. Anything further would be more of the same and he and Irene have their own bucket-list plans for a year-long globe-trotting holiday before a permanent move to Ireland. I suspect there are other reasons, less easy to discuss. For two years, our recording schedule has clashed with Irene's holidays and the *Spooky* sessions were a trial. Moreover, Steve never took to Howard, who is now firmly in position as our manager, and, though the deals we signed have been generous, it's clear we won't be driving around in sportscars anytime soon. Emma has recently bought a top-floor flat off Portobello Road, facilitated by her chunk of publishing money and John and I are settled in Kensal

Rise, though Mum helped me with our deposit – and neither address is the chi-chi paradise they would later become. But the disparity in our incomes means home ownership is beyond the pocket of the boys. On tour, too, Emma and I have our own hotel rooms, while Chris and Steve cohabit. I offered to keep costs down by sharing with Emma but I knew she'd object – I'm often an incidental beneficiary of her demands. But it all adds to the impression that the boys' needs are secondary.

Emma isn't particularly bothered about Steve's departure. She likes him as a friend, but found his lackadaisical input increasingly hard to tolerate. I found it rather hilarious that he wore his standard comfy jeans/trainers/jumper for the 'Nothing Natural' video, while Emma and I were glammed up to the nines, and live he'd have one of Emma's basslines taped to the stage on sheets of paper because he hadn't learned it. But I agree that his failure to show up for our last photo shoot – and several soundchecks – was a pain, as was his barely-there input during rehearsals and recordings. It had started to look less like charming eccentricity and more like he couldn't be bothered to make the effort.

But it's a blow for Chris. He and Steve share an irreverent sense of humour and blokey sports talk, which offered relief when the business of the band got stressful. And Steve gave no shits at all about the fickle music scene that was increasingly consuming our lives, the details of which he would chuckle about dismissively. Chris trusted him as a close mate and opened up to him, one time confessing how inconsolably sad he was that his much-loved whippet, Solomon, had died. It became a private joke between them, mock-crying 'Solomon!' if either of them was having a sad moment. But it's Howard who insists on trying to prevent Steve from leaving, pointing out that losing an original member could have a huge impact on the band. He arranges a separate meeting, offering to solve any undisclosed problems, but Steve's mind is made up: no hard feelings but the looming treadmill holds no appeal and he wants to get out while he's still able to enjoy it.

We find a replacement through Polly Birkbeck, who works at Food Records (Blur's label). She and Emma have become friends and now flatmates and she puts forward Phil King. He's been in a number of bands (the Servants, Felt, Biff Bang Pow and his own solo project, Apple Boutique), knows the Creation crowd well and has several press friends in common with us, since he was occasionally employed as a picture researcher at the *NME*. After a get-to-know-you pub drink, we welcome him into the band, without so much as an audition. Frankly, we're just relieved to find someone whose personality fits and Phil is engagingly self-effacing, has an entertaining stock of band anecdotes and is playfully eager to enjoy a bit of gossip. We take the piss that at thirty-one, he is even older than Steve, which Phil accepts with good-humoured eye-rolls.

Steve plays his last UK tour (for the *Black Spring* EP), which culminates in a 'surprise guests' support slot at Ride's fan-club-only Christmas bash at ULU. His last words on stage and as a member of Lush are: 'Follow that, Phil!' And, with a gleeful wave and a big cheer from the crowd, he's gone.

37

SHOEGAZE

The UK reviews for *Spooky* are mostly negative. Even the good ones are lukewarm. They blame 'The Great God' Guthrie's production, claiming he's swamped our sound in Cocteau Twins mush, drowning out the lyrics, which 4AD's arty packaging fails to feature, leaving listeners clueless. It's implied that this has all been imposed against our will. Emma and I are framed as victims, too cowed and controlled by men in power – Robin, Ivo, Vaughan,* Howard – to show what Lush are *really* capable of. Come on, girls, stop letting the blokes trample all over you!

But it's not just the album, it's the length of time it's taken to release it. That first big *Melody Maker* review was almost two years ago and there are no concessions made for the album's-worth of material we've released in the interim: *Gala* isn't a 'proper'

---

* Vaughan did in fact offer to include the lyrics but we declined. On this point, I concede that we were being pointlessly obscure and, on future albums, the lyrics were included in the sleeve design.

album, so it doesn't count. And neither do the months of touring it had taken to promote each release. So we are deemed lazy as well as over-rated. This is exacerbated by our every night out being documented and exaggerated, in the weekly *NME* and *MM* gossip columns. The impression is that Lush have been ligging about on the London scene, parading ourselves for column inches, while we should have been working on our album. Our self-deprecating and jokey demeanour in interviews is proof that we don't take ourselves seriously and half our reviews and features focus on discussions about backlash. It's all a bit meta.

And, oh God, then there's the whole 'shoegaze' thing.

The term is coined at a Moose gig by Andy Ross, head of Food Records.* Russell has his lyrics taped all over the floor of the stage and Andy makes the comment to a journalist, bemoaning the crop of wishy-washy student bands who hide behind their fringes staring at their pedals – rather than pogoing about and performing high kicks like Damon, presumably. The term catches on: Madchester is framed as cool, exciting and working class and now Lush, Moose, Ride, Chapterhouse and Slowdive (My Bloody Valentine are, by now, exempt, with Kevin hailed as a genius) are lumped together and sneered at for being middle-class and dull. David Quantick assumes the pseudonym 'Lord Tarquin' and pens a weekly *NME* column called 'Memoirs of a Shoegazing Gentleman', casting the bands as boarding-school poshos – all 'Toodle-Pip Rah Rah', Latin prep and euphemisms for wanking. Moose – whose mum had worked in a factory and dad is employed as a labourer – bristles at being ridiculed for

---

* Moose says it was supporting Lush; I think it was Chapterhouse, but I can't be sure.

his supposed privilege and Chris feels like an idiot when he's featured, along with 'Tim from the Charlatans' and 'Stephen from Chapterhouse', in another piss-take regular, 'The Shoe-gazer's Beard-Growing Competition', which makes laughs from the notion that they are so fey they can't grow a single facial hair between them.

But you take it on the chin. Plenty of bands get shafted in the press and for the weeklies, there's a build-'em-up, knock-'em-down aspect that is in-built. The *NME* and *MM* are in direct competition with one another, both published by IPC and they have pressure to keep the readership interested. That means ramping up the hype – buy our paper every week or you'll miss out on The Next Big Thing! And once everyone is thoroughly sick of hearing about a band, they can be mercilessly pilloried for entertainment. It's the nature of the beast and everyone accepts it. In any case, the jokey shoegaze stuff isn't far off the sort of thing Emma and I did in *Alphabet Soup*, writing comic caricatures of goths, psychobillies and casuals, so we find it amusing. And, even when Steven Wells writes a hit piece for the *NME*, tearing into us for everything we say and do and how we say it, we know he's the paper's attack-dog, so we don't take it personally.

I have friends in bands who tell me they NEVER look at the press. Promo is a hoop you have to jump through, why torture yourself by reading what they say? But I am going out with John, who is a PR and half of Emma's and Phil's mates work for the music papers, which means I get to see every barbed comment aimed at us. I can deal with a reviewer not liking the band, but the personal attacks get to me. I'm humiliated when Silverfish do an interview revealing that their song 'Fucking Strange Way to Get Attention' is about self-harming, dropping unambiguous 'flame-haired indie chanteuse' hints that I am the subject.* On hearing that I've been appalled at having my sex life speculated on in a gossip column, one editor retorts that, if I'm going to drop my knickers to every pop star I meet, I've got it coming. Charming.

There were no social-media platforms back then where you could put your side of the story, only the music papers themselves. And woe betide anyone who wrote in and complained – you'd get barbecued in the editor's comments. But Lush got plenty of hyperbolic praise, too, and there were benefits to getting so much press, good or bad. The UK papers had an influence in America where Anglophiles lapped up the information. It meant there were fans who had followed us before we ever played a note in the US, so we had a foothold already, before even the Warners publicity machine and their home-grown magazines started spreading the word. And, though we were initially wary when American interviewers asked about 'shoegaze', they seemed to have no idea it was intended as a slur and chose to take the term as purely descriptive, morphing it into a compliment.

We film a video for 'For Love' (the song charts at thirty-five, making it our first top-forty single) and do a photo session with the new line-up. Phil is a seasoned poser (and I mean that in the nicest possible way) and looks effortlessly cool, so Howard is over the moon, rubbing his hands in excitement: 'We look GREAT!' We've got a new album, a new set and a new rock-solid bass player (no offence, Steve). Time to head off on tour.

---

* Back then, self-harm was little understood and attention-seeking was a common accusation. I blamed the paper more for the indiscretion, aware that bands can often shoot their mouths off in interviews and later be appalled at what's printed. I never got an apology, but we remained friends.

38

COMMOTION IN MOTION

I love touring. It's pretty much everything I wanted as a kid and never got enough of: company, attention, a chance to shine and endless opportunities for distraction. I'm both nervous and excited in anticipation of the gigs and loading up my baggage and heading up the motorway feels like the start of an adventure. The crew have gossip and anecdotes from other tours they've been on and there's a support band – a whole *other* group of people to make friends and hang out with. For the UK leg, we've got Spitfire and Emma is dating their drummer, Justin Welch, so she's upbeat and sparky throughout.* Chris gets on famously with him, too, and at a triumphant headliner at the Town & Country Club, the band's twin go-go dancers join us on stage to strut their stuff during a rapturous 'Sweetness and Light' finale.

I have just enough time to have my wisdom teeth out and recover, then it's off to the US for a solid month and a half.

---

* Justin Welch – later in Elastica, then long after that playing drums for our Lush reunion and now with me in Piroshka.

Howard tried to convince us to save money on visas by hiring a US crew, but no fucking way – he's not the one who has to be in their company night and day, packed into a tour bus. We've found our people and we're keeping them. In fact, since I've mentioned the bus, allow me a moment to eulogise. Our first experience was on the Ride tour a year earlier. Not only was it our first full-length US tour, it was also our driver's – a former pilot who was switching careers. Ron had motored from Florida to pick us up in Boston and, on his maiden voyage, misjudged the height of his vehicle while driving under a bridge. We spent the first week with the front half of the roof missing, the gap covered in plastic sheeting flapping furiously in the highway winds. But no matter, after years of neck-aches from sleeping upright in vans, the self-contained home on wheels was bliss.

There's a kitchen, which we stock with snacks and drinks and a bathroom replete with signs saying 'Don't Shit on the Bus' (so number ones only). The snug bunks have a curtain for privacy, with a reading light and pockets for my books, diary and contact-lens paraphernalia. After a show, we pack into the front lounge, excitedly going over the night's events; then as the mood mellows, some drift off to bed, conversations splinter off, others head to the back lounge for a movie or music. If I wake in the night, I'll sit up front with the driver, hypnotised by the endless road while pontificating on the meaning of life. And, in the morning, everyone emerges dishevelled, brewing the coffee, chatty and expectant of the next day's events.

Though I've been visiting LA for over a decade, those trips centred around seeing Mum. Her world was an oasis for the well-off that bore no connection to my life in London or the wider context of America. So driving across the vastness of the States and watching the landscape change from rural to urban is a new experience. Occasionally, one of us will shout 'Scenic wonder!' to alert everyone to the majestic landscape at the window: golden cornfields stretching to the horizon, great salt lakes reflecting the sky, distant blue mountains following us for miles. We park up at truck stops, bewildered by the surfeit – steak and eggs, toast, hash browns and a stack of blueberry pancakes. That's *one* breakfast?! When we drive through Detroit, I am told it's a slum, yet the houses are detached and have porches and gardens. They are dilapidated compared to the Hollywood properties around Mum's neighbourhood, but I'm used to the packed terraced housing and high-rise estates of London and this much space seems like a luxury.

These are naïve observations, but we are naïve. There's no internet or social media to familiarise us with the daily lived experiences of people on another continent, so the surface differences are a point of fascination. Chris notes that 'football (soccer) is the fifty-third most popular sport in America; the fifty-second is tractor pulling' and, when we are taken to a Phillies game, I'm confused that the sport on the field is not intended to be watched with unwavering attention and instead people wander off to get a beer or a hot dog or take a leak and sit chatting on the stands, only occasionally responding to the action. A bit like cricket, I suppose. It just seemed cooler in the Peanuts cartoons I'd grown up with.

The gigs are different, too. There's a kind of casual, feelgood atmosphere. People are out to have a good time, so they give you a chance to settle in, primed for entertainment. It's not as *brittle* as it is at home, that frosty pressure of 'Come on then, I've paid my fucking money, impress me'. Here, they've come to whoop and cheer anyway, so they're on your side already. I'm not criticising one or the other – it's as rewarding to win over a tough crowd. But like I say, it's just different.

The first half of our tour is with Babes in Toyland, the second is with Flaming Lips. I know nothing much about either band's music, but the Babes are another of Tim's signings and Jo Lenardi, vice president of alternative marketing at Warners – a bigwig title that belies her warm and open friendliness – had championed the Flips (as Chris and I call them). It may seem surprising, now, to have such contrasting bands playing together, but back then, before 'alternative' became capital-letter Alternative – i.e. mainstream – US audiences were more open to diverse music and didn't demand that all the bands on a bill sound similar.

The hours between doors opening and going on stage are when my anticipation turns to anxiety. The backstage rider is filled with temptations of snacks and booze, but, if I graze too much, I'll be lethargic and leaden on stage and I can't risk drinking before a show, so I head out front to watch the support. If I don't connect much with a band's music at the beginning of the tour, I'll find something to love by the end. Being just another punter in the crowd lets me forget that I'm about to play a gig myself. It's infinitely preferable to nervously pacing the insular and sterile environment of the backstage area.

Babes in Toyland are wild, cathartic and compelling on stage, earthy and friendly off. Lori, their drummer, is herself an experienced tour manager, which makes every show fuss-free work for the crew. When the Babes come off stage, they are sweaty and buzzing from performing and joyfully drink everyone under the table. I'm in awe of their effortless, tough confidence. I may look like I'm relaxed on stage, but it's a fragile shell. If the gig goes well, the nerves start to abate, but, if not, it's an effort to maintain the façade. And the same applies off stage – when bad vibes start to spread, I hide any troubled emotions under manic good cheer, but the Babes are refreshingly open about their feelings. Michelle might say to Kat, 'Why are you being such a bitch?', and Kat will just shrug, 'Ignore me, I'm in a shitty mood,' and everything is fine. Wow, I wish we could do that.

Flaming Lips arrive uniformly sporting specially made badges bearing the legend 'Bogus Opening Slot', implying they are here against their will. Chris and I ignore the passive-aggressive signals and launch into a charm offensive, plying them with beers and good cheer from day one. When their soundman blows a PA speaker during their set by maxing the volume, Pete goes nuts and the situation escalates into a near fight when our tour manager nixes their elaborate stage set – just some fairy lights strung around their equipment, but yes, it's more hassle for the crew to facilitate the changeover. I say: 'Let them have their lights, but come on, lads, give us a break with the sound levels.' We want everyone on the night to put on their best show, so the crowd gets the best entertainment possible.

It takes a couple of nights for the Flips to thaw, but once they drop the pointless hostility, the mood relaxes and everyone bonds. They ditch the badges and laughingly admit to being 'assholes'. Chris and I watch them every night and shower them with well-deserved praise. They are travelling in a van, so we offer lifts in the bus. Michael is laid-back and laconic, Ron is childlike and sweet. Wayne is a bit aloof, but friendly enough and Steven is self-deprecatingly humorous and prone to boyish bursts of enthusiasm. A bit like Chris. He is also a remarkable musician and entertains us one evening with a rendition of 'For Love' on the piano in the fancy LA hotel bar, making the song sound more delicate and beautiful than I'd ever imagined.

———————

We are playing seven, eight then nine gigs on the trot and days off are taken up with travel and a relentless schedule of promo. Where touring in Britain might involve a couple of interviews with regional papers or eager fanzine writers, in the US, every city has its own radio station, video show, local press and the college equivalents, along with in-store signings and meet-and-greets (more cynically referred to as 'shake-and-fakes') with independent record stores and regional Warners reps. Howard wants the US label to be fully engaged with Lush, so I understand the logic of showing willing enthusiasm, but it can be exhausting having these events scheduled before soundcheck, after soundcheck – sometimes even after the show. Chris and I spent a day recording about 200 radio idents ('Hi, this is Lush and you're listening to W-A-N-K in Buttfuck, Ohio') before the tour even started.

Emma, in particular, finds this a slog. She's fine doing the necessary stuff – things that she sees will make a difference, like MTV and national press – but she resents having to jump through hoops to 'keep Warners happy'. Me, Chris and Phil are generally uncomplaining, but Emma spits barbed comments about how she's not willing to grovel with fake smiles and vapid small talk and seems to resent our compliance. I've made it clear we're absolutely fine with her opting out if she's not in the mood, but perhaps she thinks it makes her look 'difficult' by comparison.

And I actually *like* some of it. I get to meet interesting and friendly people who are queuing up to speak to me. And I enjoy signing the posters and albums and bits of paper for fans waiting by the bus after a gig. I know I'm basking in the attention, but so what? I well remember the pleasure I got from musicians – like Tom Bailey – being friendly to their fans. It breaks the monotony of repetitive conversations within our entourage, which tend to revolve around Emma's complaints about Howard, 4AD, Warners, the press, the gruelling schedule, the shit sound she had on stage, the unreliability of the GP-16, last night's hotel, her bad back. All the negatives, basically.

When Emma is happy, it's clear to the world. She will be full of quick-fire banter and skipping about in irrepressible glee. There's no artifice in her, she wears her heart on her sleeve. But I wonder if she's aware of how *very* bored or pissed off she sometimes looks and how upsetting it is to be on the receiving end of her temper. When Emma is angry with me, which she makes clear by glowering and flouncing out of the room at my approach, I take it to heart. If I ask the boys or the crew, they'll either shrug or claim they haven't noticed. No one wants to appear to take sides or make a bad situation worse, so I'm never any the wiser. I pour out my angst in my diaries – why, how, when, *what* have I done NOW?!

Of course, you're only hearing my side of the story. I imagine there are plenty of reasons: I can be tiresomely needy and over-sensitive; in-your-face and playing to the gallery in company; and am prone to blaring my undiluted opinions in conversation. You can probably make your own list from what you've read in this book already. And my inability to simply leave her alone and ignore the situation only makes matters worse because she thinks I'm milking it for attention (I also second-guess people too much).

I'm reminded of how angry Emma would get as a teenager, when her mother would invade her space when it suited her and calmly talk over objections, ignoring her obvious resentment. So, excuse the cod psychology, but I have some idea of why the constant company of the tour bus and no control over who walks into your space or conversation, makes her irritable and intolerant; why she believes her passive-aggressive behaviour might be easily overlooked and even her rages require no apology and will simply be forgotten and reset instantly. But I am not impervious and, when hostilities between us escalate to full-blown rows, I brood on the harsh words, which are never discussed or taken back.

The gigs – the whole point of why we are here – provide the best antidote. There's nothing like having a crowd of people rapturously cheer everything you do to lift your mood and make you feel appreciated. Chris, too, is a tonic for dragging me out of negative thoughts. He will give me a bolstering hug if I'm blue and remind me to enjoy how lucky I am – on tour! In America! Come on! On stage, too, he's the one I turn to for a laugh or a nod of recognition. Phil is generally in his own world, looking cool and enjoying the attention of the audience. If I catch his eye, he immediately panics that he's done something wrong, so I try not to distract him. Emma often looks pissed off on stage and it's impossible to tell whether she's merely concentrating or there's genuinely something bothering her. The occasional heckles of 'Cheer up, Emma!' from the crowd certainly don't help.

So, if the on-stage sound is bad or the crowd is unresponsive or Emma's guitar set-up is playing up for the umpteenth time, I mask any problems by ramping up the performance, smiling, moving to the music, addressing the crowd with whatever non-sense comes into my head and making wisecracks that Chris punctuates with a comedy *G'doof-tish* on the drums. If I've gone on stage feeling sad or troubled, I'm determined to ensure that by the last song, I have something to celebrate, lifting my spirits with the energy and adrenalin, playing our music and *feeling* how good it is. I recall, years later and long after Lush, my boss asking how an office job could possibly appeal after being on tour and didn't I miss it? My reply was that, if I could have a door in my house that led straight to the stage so I could play the gig and then be instantly home, that would be fantastic. The rest of the shit I could do without. Then again, it depends on the tour. And we are about to embark on the tour of a lifetime.

39

LOLLAPALOOZA (JOINING THE CIRCUS)

Perry Farrell had lavished unexpected praise on Lush, describing us as 'music to soothe the savage beast' and, in April 1991, we were invited to play four shows supporting Jane's Addiction, who were in the middle of a year-long enormodome tour for the double-platinum album *Ritual de lo Habitual*. To give you some idea of the scale of perspective: three days earlier, Jane's Addiction had headlined before a packed house of 20,000 at Madison Square Garden, while we were coming from the rather more cosy closing show of our month-long co-headliner with Ride at the 1,000-capacity Theatre of the Living Arts in Philadelphia.

Taking the stage in the echoing vastness of a hockey stadium felt like leaping into a chasm. I expected certain death – boos and bottles for being too indie and too female – but we were thrilled by the unexpectedly lively reception. Perry would every night come off stage to hang out in our dressing room – which was a touching gesture from the big star to the minuscule indie support, although in retrospect it may have had something to do with him wanting to spend as little time as possible with his own band (five months later, they'd split up).

So we already had an 'in' for Lollapalooza '92 and Howard's relentless courting of Warners and Marc Geiger and bonding with Perry whenever possible, also helped distinguish us in a sea of contenders jostling for a precious festival slot. There's an argument that Howard put in the effort at least as much for himself as for the good of Lush, insisting from the outset that his managerial talents would be crucial throughout the entire tour – we'd have to pay for all his expenses, along with per-diems – but it felt grudging to deny him his reward. He'd pulled out all his stops to get us on board and seemed to want this more than we did.

In the weeks before the tour started, Emma and I worried about being the only women on a seven-band bill with the Red Hot Chili Peppers, Ministry, Ice Cube, Soundgarden, the Jesus and Mary Chain and Pearl Jam. We were used to being in a male environment, but this was on an entirely different level – one that aggressively radiated muscle and testosterone: Ice Cube's occasionally misogynistic and homophobic lyrics; the possibility that the name Pearl Jam was some sort of euphemism for sperm; and one disconcerting exposure to the Chili Peppers on a late-night TV show hosted by James Whale, where the band, stripped to the waist and on their knees, performed an a cappella rap about 'pretty little pussy lips' and 'pumping that labia till it pouts'. This recital had been rounded off with a lot of raspberry-blowing, followed by co-host Cleo Rocos being upended over the back of a sofa, while Anthony Kiedis shoved his face up her skirt and the remaining members tousled her hair and licked her neck and shoulders. Throughout the ordeal, Rocos was all rictus smiles, kittenish mews of 'help!' and desperate eye-signals as she struggled to prevent her breasts from spilling out of her dress, live on air. It made for uncomfortable viewing and I was, frankly, terrified about what we were letting ourselves in for.

But fuck it, I wasn't about to let a bunch of sweaty lads intimidate me out of the opportunity of a lifetime – the tour would, if nothing else, be character-building. Hopefully, solidarity with fellow Brits the Mary Chain might provide a refuge and I crossed my fingers that our bottom-of-the-bill status might work in our favour, allowing us to slip under the radar of any negative attention and casting us as plucky underdogs.

————

As it turns out, there are hundreds of people involved in the Lollapalooza production, loads of them women and the vibe is laid-back and friendly. Moreover, fears that our opening slot means we'll be playing to empty venues are swept away by Pearl Jam's non-diva insistence of sticking to their second-on billing, negotiated well before they'd gone on to become one of the biggest bands in the world. As a result, huge numbers of their fans arrive early and seats fill up as our set progresses. By the time we launch into our end-of-set number, we're pleasantly surprised to have a sizeable crowd clapping and whooping our efforts.

This arrangement is less agreeable for the Mary Chain, who have the difficult task of playing after a band who are vastly bigger than themselves. Pearl Jam's roof-raising set, often culminating in singer Eddie Vedder throwing himself from the side-stage scaffolding into a frenzied crowd whipped into pandemonium, is a tough act to follow. By the time the Mary Chain have set up their gear and got the smoke machine going, much of the packed house has filtered away to refuel with beer, grab a bathroom break or load up with merch.

This does nothing to sweeten the Reid brothers' guarded demeanour. Indeed, they seem to have turned up at Lollapalooza determined to have a bad time. From the off, they are casting disdainful aspersions about the travelling rock circus and we often overhear the brothers loudly arguing from behind the closed door of their dressing room while their girlfriends sit hunkered down in the corridor outside. At the end of the tour, as William Reid and I drank a beer in the LA sunshine, wondering how we'd got through it all, he said rather sadly that he regretted missing out on so much of the fun. But their shows are fantastic and I watch almost all of their thirty-five gigs, either from prime front-section seats, abandoned in the exodus after Pearl Jam, or in the moshpit, jumping up and down with the hard-core fans.

Soundgarden's lead-heavy rock is more of a challenge. I grew up ignorant of the charms of heavy metal, so Pete provides an educational crash course in the wonders of Deep Purple to facilitate my appreciation. I put in the effort because Chris Cornell is not only a very charming and friendly individual but also one of the most dazzlingly handsome men I've ever clapped eyes on and it's a physical rush just to bask in his gaze. Of all the stars my visiting female friends want an introduction to, he is top of their list.

I have a stab at engaging with Ice Cube's performance, gamely waving my hands in the air on command and shrieking in response to the repeated enticements for competitive audience participation – 'All the guys on the right, say oh-oh; all the ladies on the left, say oh-oh.' But the hulking bodyguards patrolling the stage with plastic super-soakers carried two-handed and cross-body, as you would a loaded submachine gun rather than a brightly coloured toy, saps the songs' menace for me. As Phil observes: 'It's a bit *cabaret*, isn't it?'

The only possible response to Ministry's set is awe-struck submission. The cacophony of industrial pounding, pile-driving guitars and Al Jourgensen scream-growling like Beelzebub over nerve-shredding samples is like being crushed by the Apocalypse. The ranks of punters in the seated section howl their approval, while those in the back fields go full-on tribal, hurling everything they can get their hands on high in the air (not, thankfully, at the stage) – drinks and food containers, clothing, shoes, clods of earth dug from the lawns and the occasional person tossed 20 feet up from a blanket – all silhouetted against the last blush of the sunset and the occasional illegal bonfire. It's like witnessing a frenzied sacrificial ceremony.

I try, I really do, to maintain interest in the Chili Peppers' headline set that follows, but no amount of go-go dancers, flame-spewing fireman's helmets or underpant-clad acrobatics can engage my attention after Ministry's thundering performance. At this point, I am frequently too far gone to concentrate on much other than making sure I'm not left behind as our bus heads off on its next overnight drive.

———

From the kick-off in San Francisco, Lollapalooza's vast travelling circus offers plenty of exciting diversions. Our crew gleefully report that the tour is rife with cocaine and argue that this is at least partly medicinal, since the gruelling schedule of post-show pack-up, overnight drive and early set-up requires something more bracing than a round of coffees. I'm not sure our own bus driver is operating on truck-stop fare alone, given that he's managed a two-day journey in just over nineteen hours, pulling into the hotel car park thirty hours ahead of schedule. However, the Lollapalooza production, whose job it is to manage the entire roadshow, are having none of it. The tour has barely taken off when one self-appointed dealer is caught selling pilfered passes outside the venue and instantly banned from the tour, much to the alarm of various travelling personnel who were relying on his services to get them through the next nine weeks.

Our own initial pursuits are more innocent. Emma commandeers one of the many golf buggies used to navigate the extensive grounds and finds bonding opportunities by either offering breakneck lifts to various members of the touring party or narrowly missing collisions with them. For me, some early photo sessions provide a friendly introduction to a couple of the tour's major stars. Our old friends Fuzz and Lesley from Silverfish show up to the opening gig, so we cheerfully don their gifts of *Hips, Lips, Tits, Power* T-shirts as a good-luck talisman for our first performance. Fuzz himself is so seduced by the carnival that he fearlessly tackles the 200-foot bungee-jump. Chris and I accompany him to the launching cage, but despite some persuasive 'You're up here now, you might as well' cajoling, stick to our original plan to simply enjoy the view.

By the time the tour has progressed through its first week, we've become less overwhelmed by the sheer size of the operation and learned to navigate some of the privileges on offer, enjoying thrilling close-up access to the performances from side of stage and heading into town with our tour passes on display, to get freebies and discounts at local music shops. These laminated

IDs are allocated via a complicated process designed to outfox any would-be counterfeiters and Production impose a staggering fine if you need a replacement. Phil, who frequently vetoes any photograph of himself unless it meets a number of exacting standards, spends several days considering the $200 charge to swap the hastily snapped Polaroid of his Lollapalooza Access All Areas pass for one of the many carefully posed photo-booth images he carries around for just such an emergency.

As daily familiarity with the colossal venues makes them less intimidating, we're able to enjoy playing our music rather than approaching every gig as an ordeal – Chris grinning ear to ear and no longer panicking that he might fall off the drum riser, Phil edging his cool bass-god stance ever closer to the front of the stage and Emma beaming a delighted smile at any ripple of applause, while I even manage some relaxed chit-chat: 'Pay attention, everyone, you're about to hear the only waltz of the day.'

And we're flattered to glimpse the occasional member of other bands' entourages watching our performance from the side of the stage. It may seem from the other side of the barrier that everyone backstage must be all over each other enjoying some vast VIP love-in, but breaching initial inter-band rivalry can sometimes prove tricky. In this respect, the crew are in a better position to break the ice than the performing artists, since their daily routine necessitates communicating across factional boundaries during set-ups and changeovers, where the offer of a helping hand always goes down well.

Indeed, most of my own early social forays are with Ministry's crew, a great number of whom seem to have no discernible role and are along for the ride purely because Al or Paul Barker enjoy their company. Despite their uniformly forbidding biker-gang appearance (aside from one fresh-faced and notably untattooed 'stage manager' named Fritz with whom, thirty years on, I am still good friends), they are to a man gregarious and friendly. I often hunker down side of stage with Turner Van Blarum, a mohawked Texan man-mountain bearing the official title of 'bone tech', whose job it is to furnish Ministry's stage set with a macabre collection of animal skulls and skeletons. He provides me with my greatest souvenir of the tour – a 4-foot-long sheep's spine that I inexplicably manage to get through Heathrow security on my journey home.

An early brush with the Chili Peppers proves more awkward. During an evening meet-and-greet, they exude rock-star aloofness, scanning the room over my shoulder for more impressive company. So I'm pleasantly surprised when Anthony ('the "h" is pronounced') extends an invite to join their imminent departure to 'attend the ballet'. I'm embarrassingly credulous when attempting to appear friendly and my gushing response – 'Oh wow! I love ballet!' – is punctured when it's spelled out that this is in fact code for 'strip club'. For a Limey like me, this conjures up visions of creepy old men in desolate pubs dropping coin tips into a pint pot. But, however glamorous the US counterpart, I find the whole notion of naked women being ogled by entitled men a depressing set-up and retort: 'Why the *fuck* would I want to go to a strip club?!'

Despite being at least as famous as the Chili Peppers, Eddie Vedder's recent and rapid rise to global celebrity seems to have him running for cover. Hitching a ride on our bus one afternoon to escape the persistent attentions of a camera crew, he is self-effacing and humbly appreciative of Pearl Jam's success, but wary of the Eddie-focused limelight. He is still traumatised by the now-notorious theft of his journal earlier in the year and, as a diary writer myself, I proffer my sympathy, although I get the impression that Eddie's loss is a significantly bigger deprivation to world culture – private insights and experiences worked for lyrical inspiration – than my own pages of drunken ramblings and paranoid obsessions.

Eddie is earnestly engaged with the politics of the day and voices eloquent concern over the imminent US election (which Bill Clinton would comfortably win). Despite my frequent LA visits to see Mum, I know little about US politics, though I am staggered to learn that America is poised to make abortion illegal (Eddie himself has launched an impassioned on-stage plea to the crowd to boycott the Domino's Pizza stall in view of its founder's anti-abortion stance). Mere months earlier, the UK yet again voted in the Tories, guaranteeing their unbroken governance for another five demoralising years. Your average lefty musician back home will snarl that their country is a shithole, governed by cunts and populated by morons, so I am intrigued by Eddie's wistful reference to his homeland as 'God's own country'. Despite his criticisms of the political status quo, he states that America is the greatest place on earth and expresses the conviction that anyone, in any other country, would without hesitation give their eye teeth to move there. The statement is made as a matter of fact, almost apologetically, but I ponder that in the UK, I've only ever heard the most nationalistic Billy Britain express this sentiment.

As fellow minnows in the celebrity pool, another early bonding opportunity comes through table-tennis tournaments with members of the Jim Rose Circus Sideshow, whose second-stage act consists of an updated take on the Victorian freakshow carnival. Joe 'Mr Lifto' Hermann, whose act consists of hanging skin-stretching weights from his earlobes, tongue, nipples and penis, becomes an early regular in our dressing-room hangout zone, as does ringmaster Jim – who along with maintaining a street-barker monologue throughout the troupe's twice-daily performance invites audience members to stand on the back of his head while he lies face down in a pile of smashed beer bottles. Slug has a sword-swallowing act that also involves chewing through a buffet of bugs and larvae, foreshadowing the *I'm a Celebrity* challenges by twenty years. He later renames himself Enigma and embarks on a full-body jigsaw-puzzle tattoo that he intends to fill piece by piece, with the eventual aim of becoming blue all over – a concept I find more disturbing than the collective derangement of all the JRCS acts.

This camaraderie leads us to participate in Matt the Tube's segment of the sideshow, which I (enthusiastically) and Chris (less enthusiastically) agree to. Other bands have taken part, so how bad can it be? A perspex canister is ceremoniously filled with beer, chocolate sauce, ketchup and Pepto-Bismol (to guard against any stomach upset – ha ha), all of which is forced via a plunger down a 7-foot clear plastic hose, slid up Matt's nose and down into his stomach, a process he plays up with exaggerated winces and heaves. The plunger plunges and the canister is emptied – cue massive congratulatory applause. But wait! Now the plunger is pulled back and the contents re-emerge and the noxious liquid is decanted into a pitcher from which glasses are filled and we all drink a toast. Chris and I gamely mug along, downing the brew in one long gulp to the wild response of the gathered crowd – groans, gasps, cheers, screams and the occasional flurry of drama as some queasy observer passes out and hits the deck.

Emboldened at surviving the bile-drinking, we accept the invitation to join Ministry on stage in Toronto. Having hit it off during a gig-free day, after a bands-vs-crew game of Capture the Flag, drummer Bill Rieflin and keyboardist Roland Barker patiently walk Emma and me through the chords to 'So What' and find me a suitable guitar for the occasion. The white Flying V that I settle on certainly looks the part, but it has a neck like a plank and is about four times heavier, in every respect, than my slim, hollow-bodied Gibson 335. On the plus side, there are already five guitarists in Ministry's sprawling on-stage entourage, so I figure my cack-handed fumblings will probably go unheard and Emma and I throw ourselves enthusiastically into a full-on head-banging axe-wielding rock-out.

These cross-band guest appearances become increasingly common as the tour progresses. Ministry's crew members gee up our lunchtime crowd with a more meaty intro than my customary Mary Poppins-prim 'hello girls and boys' by bellowing: 'Are you ready, Lollapalooza?! I SAID ARE YOU READY, LOLLAPALOOZA?! Comin' atcha at a hundred miles an hour all the way from the beautiful UK, 4AD recording artistes LUSH!!!!' On later dates, Emma and Chris provide snare-drum fills for Soundgarden and Sharkbait; I join the army of guitarists wigging out for Pearl Jam's rendition of 'Keep on Rockin' in the Free World'; and various members of Pearl Jam, Ministry and Soundgarden bring their talents to Lush with some 'one of the girls' cross-dressing (I've never met a bloke who didn't jump at the chance at a bit of drag).

But much of this is yet to come and a mere month into the tour we manage the coup of simultaneously opening Lollapalooza and headlining it – albeit on a technicality. Coming from the temperate climes of the UK, where you have to go as far back as 1987 to find a weather front worthy of a Wikipedia entry (I myself spent the Great Storm drunkenly dancing in a garden in Tottenham with Chris and Meriel, screaming 'It's really windy, innit?!'), I'm not attuned to the meteorological devastation that regularly clobbers the US. So when weather warnings are issued for the second date in Jones Beach, my only thought is that some sort of hat might be in order, in case the rain gets a bit out of hand.

To be fair, as the noonday sun bleaches the bleachers, everyone else is similarly blasé that the storm will consist of nothing more than a passing shower, even as I jokily introduce the end of our set to darkening skies: 'One more song before the rain starts!' As the last chord rings out and we saunter off stage, a bolt of lightning splits the sky with a deafening thundercrack and a biblical downpour drops from above. The ensuing hour is pandemonium, every hand on deck clearing the flooded stage, evacuating the venue and desperately scrambling to dismantle scaffolding, tents and equipment before the whole bloody lot gets blown into the ocean (much of it does). Al takes it upon himself to cheerlead the troops by joyfully roaring 'Splice the mainsail!' and 'Land ho!' through a loudhailer, but it is genuinely terrifying and more than one person needs to be rescued from the sea. Driving away from the carnage, we creep out of town at a snail's pace through the howling cyclone, amid felled lamp-posts and upended cars.

Back in the hotel bar, the amassed Lollapalooza folk gather, excitedly exchanging survivor stories and dining out on Al's insistence (broadcast across the premises via the ever-present loudhailer) that all tequila-based drinks are on him. Unfortunately, Justin – who along with John has joined the Lush tour for a week of East Coast dates – is two years shy of drinking age in the US and not only banished from the bar but, on the insistence of hotel security, confined to Emma's hotel room. Several members of Ice Cube's entourage suffer a similar restriction – I hadn't realised until spying a printed sheet of personnel details how very young many of them are. I count my blessings I'm twenty-four, with free rein to enjoy myself.

40

LOLLAPALOOZA
(TESTOSTERONE OVERLOAD)

We're a month or so in and Bill Rieflin is well and truly one of the girls. He dons one of Emma's dresses, my fishnets and some of Mr Lifto's make-up stash to play guitar with Lush on 'For Love', so Emma and I decide to match the cross-dressing spirit for a second appearance with Ministry. This is frankly much easier male to female, where a skirt and lipstick are enough to make the point and our efforts at cosplay – suits, slicked-back hair and eyeliner moustaches – look more Laurel & Hardy than bad-ass macho. Still, it leads to one of my only exchanges with Ice Cube, who is seated on the steps outside his trailer. He shoots me an up-and-down glance, stating, 'That's just *wrong*,' and meets my smiling explanation – 'Well, every woman has a bit of man in them and vice versa, right?' – with a shake of his head and a frown. I don't think I convinced him.

William Reid has his own run-in when his leisurely stroll through the backstage lawns is interrupted by one of Ice Cube's soaker-toting bodyguards aiming a jet of water at his girlfriend's chest. This prompts a red-mist response from William, who, uncowed by the 2:1 ratio in height and weight, instantly steams in for a scrap. It's a scuffle made all the more surreal by the fact that they are surrounded by Ministry's elaborately costumed dancers who are practising their voguing. No one gets hurt but most witnesses score William kudos points for fearlessness.

My last stab at social interaction is daubing a lipstick message on his dressing-room mirror when our backstage facilities share an adjoining door: 'Hey Cube! Come say hi to Lush – we're next door!' It's a well-meant invitation to help demolish our rider, but I am later informed that when the posse turns up there's a lot of muttering about 'lack of respect', so I guess it didn't go down well. Ultimately, the only Lush member to make any inroads is Chris, by participating in some basketball play and enjoying a friendly exchange with one of their number who is wearing a Scotland football shirt. Of course . . . SPORTS! The go-to staple of all male bonding. *Kuh*, why didn't I think of that?

In other ways, too, the default machismo of the tour occasionally brings me up short. For every tattooed, testosterone-oozing roadie who confounds my expectations by being an absolute sweetheart, there'll be another to confirm the stereotype. One particularly wizened and monosyllabic member of Soundgarden's crew carries with him a collection of obsessively curated photo albums containing trophy Polaroids of random women he's enticed to go topless in exchange for a backstage pass. Access to this gallery of tits is apparently an exclusively male privilege, though I'm told that 'to be honest, after three pages it's like looking at someone's beermat collection'. I'm assured by witnesses that far from tear-streaked girls being violated against their will, it's an altogether transactional affair: the women hoick their tops

Glastonbury '87: Emma, Meriel, me,
Steve and Chris – months before we'd
even formed Lush!

Above: On tour with the Bugs, existing on a diet of rollies and vodka, freezing in Bavaria.

Below: From terrified singer supporting the Darling Buds in October '89 to the first signs of confidence, armed with a twelve-string guitar, on our March '90 UK headline tour.

First European tour: Amsterdam stroll
(with Ian Masters, Pale Saints).

Emma and I as *The Liver Birds* for the
NME Christmas edition.

Raiding a wig shop in Los Angeles for another *NME* photo shoot.

Life on the road (*clockwise from above*): Pete and Emma in my beach-themed hotel room; make-up time; with John Best; Tim Carr A&R; with Chris and Howard – time to call it a day and go home.

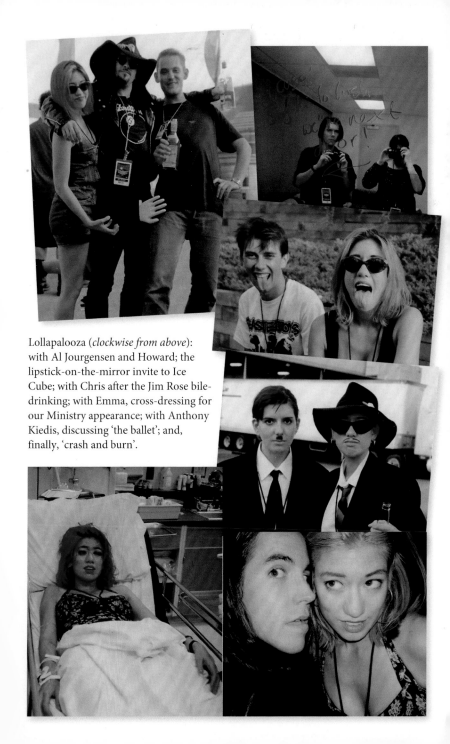

Lollapalooza (*clockwise from above*): with Al Jourgensen and Howard; the lipstick-on-the-mirror invite to Ice Cube; with Chris after the Jim Rose bile-drinking; with Emma, cross-dressing for our Ministry appearance; with Anthony Kiedis, discussing 'the ballet'; and, finally, 'crash and burn'.

Above: Going stir-crazy in Domfront.

Left: 'Enjoying' the equestrian distractions of Rockfield.

Below: Robin Guthrie shows up in Rennes for the *Split* tour.

Above: 'Single Girl' video shoot – Simon Kunz and Polly Kemp as groom and bride (both had appeared in *Four Weddings and a Funeral*).

Left: Chris, Emma and Phil at the 1995 *NME* Brat Awards.

Below: KROQ Weenie Roast, interview with MTV video DJ Kennedy.

Above: Chris's thirtieth birthday, on stage in San Francisco, serenaded by Elvis impersonators.

Right: Home for the wedding – hen night with Bunny, Melissa and Maxine.

Below: Wiped out.

up with a bored eye-roll, snatch their earned pass and are gone before the image has even developed. But my sheltered indie sensibilities are shocked by the bluntness of these flesh-for-perks exchanges and I can still remember, in indelibly vivid detail, the thong-clad woman in the Dallas car park with a Bon Jovi back-stage pass tattooed on her right buttock; the undeniably sweet but vacuous girl I found in our dressing room one afternoon wearing a pair of hotpants that consisted of a denim belt and a single frayed thread hanging down her bum-crack; and the frankly terrifying rock chick screeching 'Who do I have to blow to meet Eddie Vedder?!' at a bouncer stationed at the entrance to the backstage area.

I'm not keen to be cast as part of the meat market and am furious when I discover that Tommy, our tour manager, has been running a sweepstake, taking bets on who will get to shag me and Emma. Outraged at being cast as a broodmare for the boys'-club entertainment, I give him an earful and threaten to fire him on the spot, but he's one of those dyed-in-the-wool sexists who views every woman he speaks to as though looking down the wrong end of a telescope – tiny and harmless. He shrugs, 'Wassa problem?', his expression as ever like a dozy sheep, while various onlookers in the bar either stare at the floor, embarrassed, or titter like schoolgirls. Howard steers me off to placate me, muttering that he may be a prick but he *is* good at his job and since Emma seems to find the notion of men betting on access to her vagina rather amusing and flattering, I can sense myself being swiftly filed under the category of humourless diva.

Howard's right, there isn't much point in getting angry about Tommy's behaviour as he seems incapable of embarrassment. I'd witnessed his old-school attitudes way back at the opening of the tour in San Francisco, at the Miyako Hotel, where, warming to the Japanese vibe, he'd repeatedly barked 'Sa-ki!' at the bemused bar staff, while pulling his eyes into slitty slants. But his betting scheme has made me guarded and paranoid, recasting every innocent chatty exchange as a possible plan to win the jackpot. All of which goes some way to set the scene for my negative takeaway regarding Anthony Kiedis.

He is disarmingly friendly, keen to disabuse me of any negative impression I might have formed from the earlier strip-show misstep. I'm flattered that he bothers – the rest of his band don't pay us the vaguest interest. But, while my efforts are focused on manoeuvring past his hypersexualised public image, Anthony seems equally determined to centre it, albeit by finessing the dick-socked frat-lad persona into that of a sophisticated playboy. All my conversational gambits on neutral subjects are quickly steered toward ex-girlfriends, former conquests, female friends – a bragalogue of faceless females made distinguishable only by the multitude of ways in which they serve to illustrate Anthony's profound love and respect for, y'know, the whole *genre* of woman.

I found an interview quote from RHCP drummer Chad Smith describing Anthony as 'usually on the make. He really fancies himself a connoisseur of women.' And I can't deny that there were plenty who appreciated his efforts. When a gaggle of Warners staff show up at an East Coast date, several of the females get all a-twitter about Anthony recalling their past meetings in impressive detail, including food allergies and zodiac signs. I imagine him keeping a file of handy facts on every useful woman he's encountered, hastily consulting revision notes to flatter them with the impression that he's spent the intervening months obsessively dwelling on the memory of their last meeting. So, although his shtick grates on me, I've got to admit – the bloke puts in the hours.

If you're already familiar with the Lush song 'Ladykillers', you may be disappointed that my exploits with Anthony didn't climax to some unforgiveable sin (or even sex), but really it's all there in the lyrics. He didn't do anything terrible – he was just a bit of a twat. And on the exasperating-male-behaviour scale, he was less of a handful than Gibby Haynes, who joined the tour for a couple of weeks to perform 'Jesus Built My Hot Rod' with Ministry.

I saw the Butthole Surfers play some years earlier and was pleasurably blown away by their visceral chaos, but Gibby really isn't interested in my opinions about music and his exchanges with me consist almost entirely of tongue-lolling hubba-hubba leering that on the one hand is so over the top and cartoony you can barely take offence, but on the other, gets very tired, very quickly. I try to get past the salivating façade by holding an actual conversation, but all I get for my effort is a yeah-whatever eye-roll and the cut-to-the-chase line: 'How about we just go up to your hotel room – you can suck my cock while I lick your pussy.' I mask my mortification with a forced laugh and keep my distance from that point.

Look, there are benefits to having someone available on a tour who's made it transparently clear that they are up for it, in case the mood strikes. But, like I say in the song, I don't even think Anthony really wanted it, he just needed his bitch-magnet credentials bolstered. As for Gibby, Pete once found himself witness to one late-night hotel-room party where Howard was hoovering up the coke, Al was indulging in loud dirty talk on the phone to a sex worker in Hawaii and Gibby smashed every bottle and glass in the room, then rolled around in the debris howling in performative pain. So for all his talk, I'm not convinced Gibby has the sensitivity and application needed to perform cunnilingus to its desired conclusion.

———

The end-of-tour party has been scheduled to take place ten days before the final LA shows. The exciting prospect of a New Orleans jamboree has me picturing lavish offerings of fine food and generous cocktails, a banging dancefloor and maybe a surprise unannounced band. Certainly, given the recent mayhem of shenanigans in Atlanta just two days previous – where one of Soundgarden hurled a Fender amplifier from his fifteenth-floor suite, narrowly missing the Mary Chain, who were breakfasting on the veranda below; Al was chased by cops through the hotel lobby while dragging a large wooden duck; and half the guests were running around the corridors until dawn having had their drinks spiked with mescalin – all manner of lunatic debauchery is being cheerfully predicted. But like many much-anticipated parties, the reality is a letdown.

First off and unforgivably, there is no free bar. Rumours start circulating that the Chili Peppers, as tour headliners, have been granted control of the party's arrangements. I have no idea whether this is actually the case, although the band exude a proprietorial air throughout the proceedings and the demotion of booze down the priority list is seen as accommodating the current clean-living regime of some of their number.

After nursing a white wine for an eternity in the main bar, where everyone is politely standing about like businessfolk at a sales conference, I am pointed towards the back room where, according to Howard, 'it's all kicking off'. This hedonistic extravaganza consists of a motley collection of strippers – muscle-bound men in budgie smugglers and bare-breasted women in sparkly thongs, one of whom has a very large but thankfully sleepy snake draped around her shoulders – writhing along to some indeterminable thumpy music. Al, keen as ever to keep any kind of party going, however unpromising the circumstances, joins the bump and grind while sporting a George Bush face mask, a set of enormous plastic buttocks, a pair of strap-on tits perched atop his exposed hairy belly and a 3-foot rubber schlong dangling from the fly of his cargo shorts.

I have about two minutes to tire of this spectacle before Howard appears by my side, urgently requiring me to minister to Emma, who has apparently put her hand through a window. I rush back to the bar area and find her sitting in a booth cradling her hand: 'Are you okay? What happened?!' She flashes me a manic smile and squeals, 'I'm FINE!!! Look!', and promptly punches her fist through another window. Emma is chauffeured to A&E to get the lacerations in her hand stitched and the dismal party is hastened to its conclusion shortly after Al reputedly decks a member of Elvis Costello's Attractions and the police patrol arrives to clamp down on the non-existent mayhem. Most people mistakenly assume the cops are part of the strip show, which is probably the most amusing thing I witness all night.

As the tour moves on to Texas in its final week, many of the folk have tired of the relentless circus and are relieved to see the light of normality at the end of the tunnel. Others are part of the growing number of walking wounded, struggling through the remaining dates aided by crutches and plaster casts and the remainder (like me) feel the urgency of a final chance for havoc and ramp up the insanity for a last hurrah.

Ministry arrive at the Dallas gig encompassing the full spectrum of these moods. Al let off an industrial-size firework during their overnight drive, setting their bus aflame as it hurtled along the freeway. The raucous contingent of their entourage found this a hilarious wheeze, but the more level-headed members (and, indeed, the bus driver) are tiring of Al's antics. While everyone is encouraged to join in the fun by sticking paper plates bearing scores out of ten for the 'Ministry Trash Course' on the side of their crippled bus, Bill looks darkly unimpressed, his hands wrapped in bandages from trying to put out the fire in his bunk.

For myself, I receive some distressing news shortly after playing: one of Pearl Jam's people has knocked over my precious twelve-string during the set changeover and snapped the neck. They offer to whisk my treasured instrument to a distant workshop for mending, but I am struggling to choke back hot tears at the injustice of having my guitar options reduced to one (no back-up now if the other goes out of tune) as I dejectedly watch the Pearl Jam crew set up their fifty-plus axes across the side-stage area. There are failed efforts to cajole me into picking a temporary replacement – the only twelve-string option is a double-necked monstrosity that I can barely lift, let alone play – and I am left feeling decidedly uncool and prima-donna-ish in what is quickly being framed as an over-emotional response. I grab a bottle of Cuervo Gold for comfort and race headlong into trouble.

I have a snapshot recollection of enjoying some friendly conversation in Soundgarden's elaborately pink-lit and rug-decorated dressing room and then having a shouting match with Fritz, prompting the standard 'Wow you're such a wild chick I bet you're a tiger in the sack' whooping from Gibby ('Oh, just FUCK OFF!'). The rest is a bit of a blur, but I later manage to trash my nascent friendship with Soundgarden by smashing a beer bottle in their dressing-room toilet while they are on stage and drunkenly self-harming in a futile effort to focus my mind.

Howard, whose own socialising has narrowed from the networking opportunities offered by the tour's professional personnel to a small pool of hard-core lunatics congregated around Al, is by this stage of the tour alternately out of his mind or tetchily hungover and has no patience for my antics. He growls at me to pull myself together, so I head out front to let off some steam by jumping up and down and screaming, 'Fuck you, Ice Cube!' (this is, by the way, a chant encouraged during his performance), while necking the offer of a handful of mushrooms from a friendly member of the audience.

My maelstrom of self-destruction reaches a peak during Ministry's bone-juddering set, when I make the rash decision to launch myself into the crowd. All caution and coordination gone, I bolt across the stage and promptly vanish from the 15-foot-high edge into a sea of revellers whose sensible reflex is to sidestep the large object hurtling at them from above. I've been told by those who were witness to the disaster that I eventually resurfaced, unconscious, held aloft and passed atop the crowd like a rag doll. It was difficult to tell the red hair from the blood. Once the assembled crew and security manage to claw me back to the safety of the backstage area, I am jolted back to sensibility with some smelling salts and stretchered off in an ambulance to the nearest hospital, where fifteen stitches are sewn into my forehead and I am reassured that, despite the neck brace I've been clamped into, I won't be spending the rest of my life in a wheelchair.

There is no question that I am a liability and a band meeting is called the next morning to establish this fact. Howard, though visibly relieved that my injuries aren't permanent, seems determined that we should take the next flight home, primarily concerned that the incident might reflect badly on him. He is, after all, our manager, tasked with some responsibility for ensuring Lush fulfil their on-stage requirements, otherwise why is he here? And yet most of the tour he's been actively cheerleading the rollercoaster of overindulgence and is usually more off his face than any member of the band.

Emma listens to his catastrophising with growing impatience and eventually puts her foot down, pointing out that, whatever bat-shit behaviour I've exhibited, it's hardly more condemnable than the many other insane stunts that have taken place elsewhere during the tour and, in any case, this isn't Howard's decision to make because the rest of us are determined to stay the course. This may be the first incident of Emma yelling 'YOU work for US' at Howard, who retaliates with 'We work for EACH OTHER', but I can't be sure. It certainly becomes a common exchange over the next years and usually ends with Emma having the last word: '*WE* pay *YOU!*'

By the next day, we are on stage again in Phoenix – me with a bandaged head and arm, Emma still sporting the dressing on her right hand from her bout of spontaneous vandalism in New Orleans and Bill drafted in on rhythm guitar, his performance made all the more impressive by having learned our entire set in one morning while playing with two broken fingers, an injury incurred during an earlier-in-the-tour stage dive to Lush.

———

Hand on heart, Lush were ill suited to open the rock-fest stadium tour that was Lollapalooza. On a vast stage where the glaring summer sun bleaches out any spectacle of atmospherics, our swirling guitars and pop-lilt harmonies risked evaporating into the sky, although I've since been assured that there was a healthy indie cohort who lapped us up, dancing and whooping on the grassy lawns beyond the bleachers. But being thrust out from the comfort zone of our indie bubble did us a lot of good overall, as did some time away from the insular UK scene. It boosted our confidence and added some gravitas – put us on the map, so to speak. And, despite becoming heartily sick of all the macho nonsense and losing my shit along the way, I really did have an absolute blast.

The tour closes with a three-date LA finale, bringing a stabilising influx of friends and family. Maxine and Melissa are over from London, staying at Mum's, and we enjoy a short few days' holiday, seeing the sights, before heading back together to London. At the final show of the tour, everyone is playing on everyone else's stage – Phil describes it as 'a deranged version of Live Aid' – and our own last gig closes with the eye-popping spectacle of Marky Ray, Turner and Mr Lifto invading the stage, stark naked but for some strategically placed gaffer tape. At this point, even the Jesus and Mary Chain can no longer withstand the tide of inter-band bonhomie and Emma and I are beckoned on stage to provide the 'hey hey hey' backing vocals to 'Far Gone and Out'.

During the (real) end-of-tour party, the hotel bar is packed with revellers as phone numbers are exchanged along with warm parting hugs and promises to keep in touch. Celebrations are brought to an abrupt conclusion in the early dawn, when someone has the bright idea of holding a lighter flame up to the ceiling of the party room, thus triggering the sprinkler system and an immediate evacuation of the entire hotel. It's an aptly idiotic end to a chaotic nine weeks and I wouldn't have missed it for the world.

41

TROUBLE AT HOME

Readjusting to home life after touring is a challenge. We've been on the road for the best part of a year and I'm used to living within the insular bubble of our entourage and having my routine dictated by the gig schedule. Pete once told me of a band who got so used to the pampering that they once insisted the driver go a mile up the road to turn the bus around so they didn't have to cross the street to get to the hotel. But it's also a relief to escape the treadmill and settle back into domesticity with John and the companionship of old friends.

Going to see bands has been an integral part of my life for a decade but I'm beginning to encounter a whiff of hostility as 'Miki from Lush'. Back in the fanzine days, if we recognised any indie celebrities in a gig audience, Emma and I might nudge and whisper or occasionally screw up our courage and approach them for a brief chat. Even if it was a musician from a band you didn't care for, no one invaded their space to give them grief. That would have been so *uncool*. Now I get blokes (always blokes) asking, 'Are you that bird out of Lush?', and, when I smile and nod in response, they sneer, 'Your band's fucking shit,' and howl with laughter at the 'gotcha'. A man asks for my autograph, then screws up the paper, chews it in his mouth and spits it at my feet with a look of triumph and disgust. At one show, a group surrounds me, baiting me to take a tab of acid that's clearly a cloakroom ticket, determined to paint me an idiot, however I respond.

This happens away from the nightlife, too, where boozy high spirits aren't an excuse. I get collared in a shop by a chatty bunch who afterwards hover in my peripheral vision, pointing and laughing hysterically. It's only when I'm back out on the street that I realise one of them has eased down the zip on the back of my dress, which nearly falls off me. And there's a thuggish, skin-head busker I regularly pass in Tottenham Court Road Tube who gives me wild-eyed manic stares and bellows, 'I fucking HATE Lush,' with an accentuating stab on his acoustic guitar – and thereafter, every time I walk past: 'You're still shit, love!'

I don't take it all lying down, but retaliating merely proves that the wankers have got to you. Gigs had always been my carefree social space but these experiences put me on my guard and make me defensive. So I stick to shows where I have a personal connec-tion – labelmates, people we've toured with, bands I knew from pre-Lush days. John has decided to branch out from PR and is managing the Verve (just 'Verve' back then, before they had to adopt the definite article to pacify the US record label of the same name), so I tag along to their gigs, as well as other bands on Savage & Best's roster – Elastica, Suede, Pulp and the Cranberries.

These are early days, so the Cranberries are still supporting Moose and Belly and there are no hints yet of their global fame to come. And while the seeds of Britpop are taking root, it's not yet a recognised phenomenon. It's true that Suede are getting the 'best new band' treatment and their debut album had just won the Mercury Prize, but Blur's *Modern Life Is Rubbish* hasn't matched the commercial success of the Madchester bands, Elastica are lumped into the New Wave of New Wave along with S*M*A*S*H and These Animal Men and Pulp are still a year away from releasing the breakthrough *His 'n' Hers*. There's an undeniable buzz in the air, but it's still 'indie' rather than mainstream, a familiar and friendly environment where I feel comfortably at home. Or at least I tell myself so.

John arranges a 26th-birthday bash for me at a bar in Camden. For the first few hours, I sit with the dozen or so mates who have turned up at the appointed time to celebrate with me. But we are a forlorn group in the party space and it's not until 11 p.m., when there are few other options for a drink elsewhere, that there's a rush of revellers and the place fills up. The night ends up a success, with Pulp DJ-ing and everyone drinking and dancing – the bands, the journos, a young new crop of 4AD staff, people from John's work world and the familiar hangers-on. But there's something jarring about celebrating my birthday with a roomful of acquaintances who are mainly here for the late bar. It feels fake and depressing to have to rely on people I barely know to signal my popularity and I wish I'd just gone to the pub or had a party at home with my friends. My real friends.

———

Emma and I spend the first half of 1993 writing songs for the new album. On tour, I might have the beginnings of a song, a half-developed idea strummed while sitting about backstage, but we don't immediately work them up as a band during soundchecks, so when the touring is over and I sit down to write at home, I'm either starting from scratch or fleshing out snippets. There's no predetermined 'concept' – each song is written as an entity in itself – and the overall mood of an album will develop organically in the recording and the mix. So we don't discard songs just because they don't 'fit' with the others, we *like* that they explore different aspects of our range.

I write 'Light from a Dead Star' ('LfaDS') from a chord that Johnny once taught me that he's figured out from the theme tune to '70s British sitcom *The Fall and Rise of Reginald Perrin*. It's almost impossible for me to play and I have to detune one of the strings to manage it, but as an arpeggio it has a haunting spy/horror-movie feel. The lyrics come easily – Dad, Mum and I get one of the three verses each, a sad song of broken love. I've spent a lot of time with John talking about my childhood and my feelings came out neatly in this song. He gave me the title, which matches the sense of a vanished past that still casts its effect.

Emma, too, has been inspired to write lyrics about family. Her father passed away in December while we were on tour in Japan and there was an enormous half-page obituary in *The Times*. Even Emma was surprised by the list of heroic exploits: Second World War missions behind enemy lines in preparation for the Normandy landings, an MBE for his intelligence-gathering in Korea, a research posting in Antarctica and an expedition to the Andes. A whole other life that Emma had known little of. So Emma wrote 'When I Die' about her father's death and when I listened to her typically crappy demo at home, I cried. So did Chris. It has the folky air of a madrigal elegy – a funeral on a crisp, English morning. Sorrow without melodrama; restrained, reserved and heartbreaking.

42

THE DIFFICULT SECOND ALBUM

Howard's ambitions for becoming a music-biz mogul have hit a wall. While Chapterhouse are about to release their second album, Moose have been dropped from their deal with Hut and have quietly severed all contact with their management, recording an EP on their own newly set-up label. Having blown his chance by turning down Pulp, Howard's big-time hopes rest on Lush.

Aware that Howard was used to hammering an expense account with little care for who would eventually pay, I refused his offer of having Lush's finances handled by his management company's in-house bookkeeper and insisted that I countersign every cheque myself. On tour, he once offered to pay for a band and crew dinner – 'I'll get this' – lapping up the thanks from the table until Emma pointed out that he was brandishing the Lush credit card, not his own, which meant *we* were footing the bill; and when I went through the payments of the Lollapalooza merchandise we'd sold, I discovered he'd charged his commission twice. He seemed to expect Lush to pay a percentage of his office rental, too, until I countered that, in that case, we'd start charging *him* 20 per cent of the band's running costs.

And Howard's obsession with America is beginning to grate. Once the songs are written and we are on the hunt for a producer, he proposes Bob Rock, John Paul Jones, Rick Rubin – basically, any big Stateside name that might impress Warners, however inappropriate for Lush. Emma suggests Bob Mould, whose music we all admire, but he has scheduled commitments and is only willing to record an EP and we're not prepared to fritter away half our songs yet again on piecemeal releases that detract from a full album. After a hunt through our individual record collections, we land on Mike Hedges. He's produced some of our best-loved bands: the Banshees, the Cure, the Associates.

Having failed to coerce us into using a heavyweight American producer, Howard decides the best way to convey legendary status on our next LP is to record at a residential studio. We do a tour of out-of-London premises where I am completely out of my depth and have no idea what I'm supposed to be looking for. After dropping in at Wool Hall, Tears for Fears' studio in Bath, I can recall nothing of the technical fixtures, only some anecdotes about a heavy-metal band nailing a mackerel to the floorboards.

A cool blonde in riding boots armed with a clipboard walks us around Peter Gabriel's Real World Studios. We're given a cursory recce of the facilities within our budget and then a look-what-you-could've-won glimpse of the main studio – a vast and sumptuous space that sits on a lake and has a control desk like the bridge of the starship *Enterprise*. Howard can barely contain his erection and is making mental plans to chisel more cash from 4AD. But I feel like I'm being shown around the grounds of an elite health resort and can't envisage how we'll bring our songs to life in this manicured, moneyed environment. In the end, we plump for Rockfield, in Monmouth, just across the border in Wales. It's unpretentious and a bit shabby (like its owner, Kingsley), which appeals to us – somewhere music is made rather than bragged about. The deal with Mike is a co-production, which means we demo the songs with Pete, working out the details and getting the songs up and running before the recording starts. Finally, in October 1993, all calendars align and we begin work.

Mike is personable and easy to work with. Though I loved *Spooky*, Robin's production was hit and miss – some of the tracks were fresh and lively, but others struggled to emerge from the swamping effects. Mike gives the songs room to breathe, rather than squeezing them into a shape that fits his particular sound. Chris is delighted to be playing on a regular kit, rather than the elaborate tech set-up endured on *Spooky*, and the studio control room has plenty of space for us all to lounge about on the sofa, absent-mindedly completing jigsaw puzzles on the coffee table while chipping in with ideas and encouragement when needed, all of us involved.

We work through seventeen songs with little fuss or friction, getting our performances down and methodically building the tracks. It helps that I'm more accomplished and confident with the vocals after a year of touring. But, while the mood is laid-back and relaxed, there's a lot of hanging about. Phil entertains himself by shooting miles of super-8 footage and Chris, at home in the rural setting, enjoys long rambles around the local countryside. Kingsley's daughter lets Emma and me loose on her horses – me clinging and terrified while I'm led around the stable yard, Emma tearing off across the fields, leaping fences. Friends and partners visit and we enjoy the odd night out with local heroes T'Pau and members of the Stone Roses posse, who are recording in the big studio next door.

Mike suggests we embellish four of the tracks with strings, hiring in Audrey Riley and Martin McCarrick to score compositions. It feels very grand to have professional musicians adding nuance and depth to the tracks and 'LfaDS' gets a long, atmospheric intro punctuated by a Pixiphone, bringing a twinkling, cosmic atmosphere that perfectly matches the song's title. 'Desire Lines' becomes a key part of our set and remains Ivo's favourite Lush song. We're delighted with how the songs have come out and, though none of us is convinced that it was worth the expense of a residential studio, we're confident that it's our best work to date. Now we just have to mix – which is where everything starts to go wrong.

———

Mike wants to mix in France. He relocated from Willesden to Normandy a couple of years ago and bigs up his renovated chateau, singing the praises of the expansive grounds, the commanding views, the charming nearby village of Domfront, the huge bedrooms with ensuite bathrooms and the heated pool. Emma and I are reluctant. We've been away for weeks in Rockfield and both of us miss London. Paris would be one thing, but I'm not a country girl and being cut off from everyone in the middle of nowhere holds no appeal. Moreover, John has been on tour in the US with the Verve and the band's busy schedule means he and I are spending less and less time together. But Mike plays his trump card – the wonderful vintage mixing desk, previously installed at Abbey Road, which he insists will make the album noticeably better than if we mix anywhere else. I can see the advantage of him working on familiar equipment, but we could do with some outside advice, a third party looking out for *our* interests, to counter Mike's one-sided arguments and point out that this arrangement holds a number of other advantages for him, beyond the purely musical, such as the healthy wad of money he'd be getting for our accommodation and the use of his own studio.

Howard is preoccupied with exploring fresh fields, setting up his own independent label, funded by London Records (Chris has suggested the name 'Wingnut' in reference to his jug ears, but he settles instead on Laurel). He pontificates that he might eventually be running a label as influential as 4AD, at which Emma snorts derisively, pointing out he is no Ivo and didn't even see Lush's potential until we started making records. But, in any case, Howard isn't the person to offer advice on the minutiae of mixing. He's probably just satisfied that the album might bear the legend 'mixed at Le Château de la Rouge Motte' on its credits, which sounds appealingly decadent and rock 'n' roll.

The person we really need to talk to is Ivo. We've relied on his focus and guidance from the start and his opinions, though sometimes brutally honest, are always thoughtfully considered. But his mind is elsewhere, too. He's grown disillusioned with running 4AD, been swept up in a whirlwind romance and marriage and is in the process of relocating to America, opening an LA office and delegating much of his role to others. To us, however, Ivo *is* 4AD and we miss his close involvement, which made us feel loved and looked after at the label. But Ivo isn't around, in body or in mind and I speculate that he's having some sort of mid-life crisis. It's actually worse than that and he's mere months away from a nervous breakdown.

With no one to dissuade us, we apprehensively fall in with Mike's plans. Best to keep him happy so he's fully on board. But Domfront isn't quite the idyll we've been promised. There's no doubting the weathered splendour of the chateau, but it's a work in progress and the communal areas are neither self-contained or purpose-built and we feel like in-the-way guests in someone else's home. There's nowhere for us to relax or talk or even think without being overheard or interrupted. Chris and Phil are convinced that the place is haunted, reporting terrifying dreams, night-time noises and apparitions, and, though we try to fill the interminable hours with countryside walks, it's January and freezing cold. I'm bored and homesick and the promised positives that were meant to outweigh the known negatives are nowhere to be seen. There's just nothing to *do*.

Mixing a record is a dull process if you're not either pressing the buttons yourself or you don't have a controlling interest in every minutiae of the sound. It involves hours of EQs and panning of individual elements before there's anything approaching an actual song to listen to and sitting in on the mix from the start makes me less able to provide fresh ears when things are starting to take shape. I'd normally take tracks home to listen on my familiar stereo, where I can compare the sound to records in my collection. But all I have here is a Walkman and Mike's conviction that the record is already sounding amazing.

When a first cassette of mixes is sent back to involved parties, none of us is prepared for Ivo's damning verdict: the songs sound lumpen and flat and the whole album will have to be remixed. The phone gets passed around the room as each one of us tries to fathom what's wrong, until I end up losing my temper. I have so much respect for Ivo and I fully trust his judgement, but *where is he*?! We are cut off and isolated and we need help, but everyone seems to have deserted us.

In lieu of Ivo, Tim Carr flies over on a rescue mission. He's regularly been a positive presence, turning up in times of trouble to infect us with his enthusiasm. But Tim can't offer much beyond optimistic good cheer and there's something a little 'off' about him, too. He's blathering excitedly about his big idea for the album: teaming up with hair-colour company Manic Panic to offer a free tub of Poppy Red with a promotional release of 'When I Die', retitled 'When I Dye'. Emma points out that it's a song about her father's death and the whole idea is in rather poor taste. Tim has a past plagued by addiction and we wonder if he's fallen off the wagon. So we crack on with renewed effort to fix the problems ourselves. Much of the grunt work is left to Mike's engineer Ian Grimble, who spends days 'sharpening things up in the basement'. Emma and I sit in on this mysterious process but it becomes clear that we're best off leaving him to it. Meanwhile, the depressing isolation and glum mood is sending us all stir crazy. I've had my songs home-demoed, demoed again, recorded, mixed and now remixed. I have no fucking idea what I'm listening to any more and neither does Emma. We sit around the kitchen table conducting heated character assassinations of our producer, manager and label boss, seeing neither hide nor hair of Mike, who spends the days with his wife and kids in a separate apartment. When he reappears at dinner, relaxed and jovial, Emma glowers with incipient rage.

The episode reaches its conclusion when Emma can no longer bear to even be in the same room as Mike. One evening, as she paces the room spitting a Basil Fawlty-level tirade, Mike sails through the door brandishing an antique hunting horn as a prop for some jolly 'I give you the horn' jokes, which sends Emma storming out through a second door. When Mike trails after her with a baffled expression, wondering what's wrong, Emma immediately reappears from a third door, gnashing with rage. I feel like I'm watching a Whitehall farce. When Mike comes back in, 'Ah! There you are!', she's off again and we hear her scream from a distant corridor: 'FUCKING HELL!!!' It's time to admit defeat and pack our bags.

———

Howard convenes meetings with potential candidates for the remix. He makes no disguise that his favoured option is Scott Litt, who has worked with REM, and downplays our preferred choice, Alan Moulder, making embarrassing jibes about 'indie enclaves' in reference to his work with the Jesus and Mary Chain. We dutifully jump through the required hoop and sit dolefully in a fancy west London studio while Scott bounces around the room, dad-dancing along to 'Kiss Chase'. He's a nice enough guy, but we're done with Howard's ideas, which are conceived entirely to kiss Warners' major-label arse.

The album is finally mixed by Alan, who is efficient and calm and works his magic. I have little to contribute since I am at this stage so exhausted and demoralised that I'm almost sobbing with relief and gratitude when the mixes are complete. But the ordeal isn't over yet as we have to compile the album and choose the singles, which turns into the usual too-many-cooks bollocks.

Tim Carr suggests we put two EPs out on the same day, in a kind of shoot-yourself-in-the-foot 'fuck the charts' gesture. I think the assumption was that 'Hypocrite' would get all the radio play and end up in the top twenty, while 'Desire Lines', at over seven minutes long, would likely miss the top fifty entirely but serve to showcase the album's more contemplative side. In the end, neither makes the top forty, which is the worst outcome all round and *Split* (the name inspired, once again, by Vaughan's artwork, while reflecting the two songwriters and the lyrics about broken relationships) peaks at nineteen. Not a disaster, but twelve places below *Spooky*, which isn't great either.

43

FUCKED OVER BY BLOKES

John Harris pens an in-depth feature in the *NME*, interviewing us separately to avoid the relentless in-joke banter that tends to interrupt anything useful we have to say. He delves into my child-hood and I am honest and he is sensitive. He's said that he will handle the child abuse with the tact and seriousness it deserves, but nods sagely when I say, 'You will, but then others won't' and agrees not to print anything too close to the bone. Chris and Phil are interviewed together and Chris shows a rare serious side by talking about the songs, but 'the conversation is swiftly railroaded into more of Phil's Felt stories'. Phil rarely gives anything of him-self away to the press and tends to trot out the same well-worn anecdotes about the bands he's previously been in. Maybe he knows from experience that oversharing can be unwise.

Harris also explores Emma's past and she explains that many of her lyrics on *Split* are about relationships. The pull-quote for the piece is: 'I've had a bad time with men in the past. Which is something Miki hasn't had. That is where we are really, really different. She's never been fucked over by a bloke.' I bristle at the implication that my troubled love life is a paradise of wine and roses, not least because Emma has been witness to my on-tour affairs and knows full well that it's caused all kinds of trouble at home. I suspect she resents me 'getting away with it', because John, though upset and humiliated, continues to put up with me.

A friend once observed that the two of us were like competitive sisters: if one of us had a lover, the other followed suit. I don't agree that it was purely competitive, but I'll concede that, if one of us hitched up with a bloke on tour, it felt more acceptable for the other to do likewise. And those were fun times. Laughing in the bar and cracking jokes about our pasts for our lovers' entertainment, shrieking, 'No! Don't tell him about that!', and collapsing in hysterics. If we were both in the same boat, it gave us something to bond over and we could confide in each other about how one or the other's affair was going.

But I was aware that a tour isn't the best environment to make sensible choices – there are too many excitements to cloud your judgement – so, if an affair went sour or if I got 'fucked over', then I'd just move on and find someone else. And, if I seemed to get less hurt than Emma, it was probably because I didn't expect much in the first place. I once got talked into joining a singer for drinks with friends he was meeting at his hotel. I was a big fan of the band and delighted he wanted to keep chatting. Sex was the last thing on my mind, but as the hour ticked by with no sign of his 'friends', he got increasingly huffy and non-communicative and I finally cottoned on that the entire story had been a pretext. It was the classic: he invited you to his hotel room, what did you *think* he was after?! I felt stupid for flattering myself that he'd actually enjoyed my company, so I fucked him just to avoid any grief. He was so pissed he could barely get it up, anyway.

Making things my fault gave the illusion of control. Emma, however, rarely blamed herself, claiming she'd just been unlucky in her choices. But, to me, this seemed hopelessly defeatist, allowing bad fortune and other people's failures to make her a victim of outside forces. There's no doubt that Emma got fucked over sometimes, but she'd been out with some terrific blokes. You win some, you lose some. But she seemed to think, because I didn't hurt in exactly the same way she did, that I didn't get hurt at all.

In the tour bus once, Pete suggested some kind of 'group therapy' game. There were about six of us in the back lounge having to list stuff like best/worst thing about yourself, then each person would say what they most admired about you or whatever. Chris was out the door like a shot, but the rest of us indulged and, in answer to what I'd change about myself, I said I wished I could stay faithful and happy with John. That I just couldn't seem to control myself and I hated it because I really did love him and I was hurting both him and myself. It was a bit awkward, because most of the other answers had been about losing weight or washing socks more often. But Emma seemed genuinely taken aback, perhaps for the first time considering that I had my own struggles and heartbreaks and my love life really wasn't worth envying.

The oft-spoken rule is what happens on tour, stays on tour. Our own crew has never judged me, but the wider industry is another matter. John is frequently, gleefully informed of my affairs, real or not. I received a frosty phonecall from him during Lollapalooza telling me that the Warners rumour mill was buzzing with tales of Al and me being at it like knives. Apparently, we'd been caught together in a hotel room, fucking in a bath of Champagne and high on coke. Frankly, I was as insulted by the banal rock cliché as by the complete fabrication of our sexual congress. A girl in a band dismissively tells John, 'Oh, everyone knows Miki and Jarvis Cocker fucked each other in Paris' (not true) and, when I angrily confront Jarvis, asking whether he's been spreading the story himself, he is so appalled that John – who has been tirelessly promoting Pulp – might be thinking badly of him that I'm told he doesn't leave his home for three weeks.

It grinds John down and he feels humiliated. In retaliation, he embarks on a fling of his own, but, in his case, everyone keeps loyally silent. It's easy for me to discover just by observing their behaviour around one another and I let it slide, aware that it would be hypocritical of me to complain. But my patience finally snaps at a party one night, where her guitarist boyfriend follows me around, repeatedly shoving me and whining, 'Your boyfriend's a wanker,' eventually pushing me down the stairs (well, okay, two steps), leaving me sprawling on the floor.

I put my foot down and insist John ends the affair. I wrote 'Hypocrite' because I can dish it out but I can't take it, but I'm also wound up by the double standard of being slut-shamed when blokes – particularly blokes in bands – are high-fived for the exact same behaviour. Girls want to live the rock 'n' roll dream, too, you know! I didn't join Lush to sit in a dressing room knitting bootees. And I've seen with my own eyes the girlfriends-of-the-band willing to ignore on-tour shenanigans. Why can't I have that, too?

John and I try to maintain our relationship when I'm on tour. He'll visit occasionally and I call him when I can, but I'm on the bus for days and when I do get to a hotel, the transatlantic calls are expensive and there's also a time difference to contend with. It's hard to say whether mobile phones and the internet would help. It's not just distance that separates us or the lack of technology to be able to connect – our lives are operating in completely different spheres. John conveys the news from home and whatever band gossip that's doing the rounds at work, but then worries that this all seems boring or is only making me homesick. I share (some of) the details of the tour, but it's really just gigs, injokes with the band and crew and endless travelling and promo. You kind of have to be here to get it. The distance makes it hard to read each other's mood, to know what the other wants to hear and a misfired conversation can make both of us uneasy for days. And, if things are bad with Emma, I feel even more anxious and isolated. It's not just libido that drives me, I need a stop-gap stand-in for John – some no-strings affection with a sell-by date built into the script.

Allow me a moment to psychologise while accompanied by the world's tiniest violin. It's easy nowadays to google the links between childhood abuse and promiscuity and the need for constant companionship and validation – someone by and on my side – is embedded in me, which I'd learned at an early age could be bartered for with sex. I don't expect much in return, just be friendly and distract me from myself. Or, when I was a child, keep me company and play Monopoly. But it's no excuse for the pain I cause John and while I tell myself I'm simply enjoying harmless flings when it suits me, my affairs are in danger of becoming just another self-destructive addiction. I can't tell if I'm living life to the full, being driven into self-destructive patterns by my fucked-up past or merely bored and seeking distraction. I need to get a grip.

44

DEAD IN THE WATER

The UK press give *Split* the usual kicking, complaining about the length of time it's taken us to release what they consider to be a disappointing album. There's some praise for individual songs, but the consensus is that the record is too long and too sprawling and lacks coherence. At least we're no longer criticised for hiding the lyrics, although John reports to me that a journalist explained, on their cool reception to the album, that everyone already knows Miki was abused as a child, implying that I'm expected to come up with less predictable traumas for each new release.

We play a short taster tour on the week of *Split*'s release, then head off to the US for two and a half months – effectively playing two tours back to back, the first half in 'intimate' venues, the second with Weezer along for support. In America, we're getting good reviews and plenty of press and appear on MTV's *120 Minutes* and the Conan O'Brien show. I hate to admit it, but I'm starting to understand Howard's obsession with the US since we're doing way better here than at home.

The LA show – usually a highlight of an American tour because Mum, local friends and the 4AD crowd are all there – is, however, a debacle. We're playing Prince's Glam Slam club and from the second we show up, I know it's going to be a difficult night. The stage is flanked by two tacky gold pillars of naked ladies crawling over each other and every décor detail in the room features the Artist Formerly Known As 'Love Symbol'. When I find myself inadvertently resting my feet on one of these signs, woven into the design of a balustrade, a burly bouncer with a headset admonishes me for disrespect and warns me that, if the Great Man himself deigns to drop by, I must on no account insult him by making eye contact. Thankfully, we're spared a royal visit, but this is not a welcoming space. On the third song of our set, the stage power goes out and the ponytailed club manager doesn't have a clue how to fix the problem. With the air-con dead, the temperature rises and we distribute our rider to the packed house of sweaty punters. The show has to be rescheduled for the following night and we lose a precious day off from the treadmill.

There's just enough time at the end of the US dates to nip back for the Reading Festival – Flaming Lips are also playing and Steven guests on drums for 'For Love' – and then we're immediately off to Europe for another month. Richard Hermitage, newly appointed as a chief exec at 4AD, tries to bargain down our tour support by asking whether we really need to carry the expense of our soundman, Pete. My terse answer is that we could save even more cash if we just left Phil behind and asked nightly if there was a bass player in the audience who knew the songs. To be fair, Richard isn't a bad bloke, but he has no fucking clue and God, I miss Ivo.

On the overnight ferry crossing to Bergen, we party and dance to a tacky covers band while surrounded by boogieing pensioners. As we drink our last tequilas at the emptying bar, I watch a white-haired grandma straddling and snogging the face off a paunchy septuagenarian in a booth. It's shocking but also rather reassuring to witness that you can get away with bad behaviour well into old age. In Prague, we try absinthe and Chris tries to blag his way into a club without realising it costs the equivalent of 5p to get in. Dad drives from Hungary to Vienna to see me play. He's forgotten to bring anything decent to wear and looks a bizarre sight with a suit jacket thrown over a Lonsdale sweatshirt and baggy-arsed trackies, but it's great to see him and I'm touched that he's made the effort. Robin Guthrie shows up in Rennes, wired but sweet and complimentary about the new songs.

But news from home is not good. Despite spending a cool couple of grand having a London taxi painted to promote the album, the 4AD marketing and promotions department hasn't managed to book us a single TV appearance or any further press at all. In Britain, the album is already dead. The scheduled release of 'Lovelife' as the follow-up single is scrapped and the UK tour is cancelled. All that time and effort spent on making *Split* and we've played a total of eight dates promoting it in the UK.

Emma calls Howard to complain that we've been let down by 4AD, who have dropped the ball, expecting the album to simply do well off the back of *Spooky* and what the fuck has *he* been doing as our manager to ensure that they do a proper job of marketing it? But Howard has never been willing to take blame, which he sees as a sign of weakness. It's become a standing joke between the four of us that he's always keen to take credit, but loath to share responsibility: '*We* were great' at every success; '*You* were shit' at any setback. He blames the songs, which apparently aren't good enough and need to be more 'relevant'. Never mind that pre-release he was raving about *Split*, convinced that it would set the world alight. Now he's citing the success of the Cranberries and Radiohead in the US, saying we should 'write songs like them'. Emma tells him to go fuck himself and hangs up.

But it's true that the landscape has changed. The chart-topping success of Blur's *Parklife* and Oasis's *Definitely Maybe* has ushered in a new mood of swagger, flag-wavingly British in defiance to American 'grunge'. *Split* is too fragile and introverted and out of step with the times. Which is ironic, because Emma and I are both dating men who operate at the beating heart of the tastemaking power base – you'd think we'd have noticed the change in wind direction. But Lush were never band-wagon jumpers and the music we made stemmed from our personal interests and moods. Once, this had been to our advantage; now it just makes us irrelevant.

After some last dates in Japan, we end the year with a secret Christmas gig at the Dublin Castle, encoring with our fun French version of 'Sunday Girl'. I'm hamming it up and make the comment that 'we're all Europeans now' in reference to the opening of the Channel Tunnel, which draws merry boos and cheers from the crowd. At the aftershow, I'm told by one member of the Britpop glitterati that it's a revelation to see me perform a song without the guitar and I should do it more often. He seems staggered that I've pulled off this feat and seems to think he's discovered some hidden talent I wasn't myself aware of. As if it's somehow a massive achievement to prance about throwing coquettish shapes while singing.

Howard makes it clear that, if the next album doesn't go top ten, we're fucked. And there's no Ivo to balance the argument. Even John and all our friends in the business, seem to agree. Like it or not, this is a ruthless new world and there's no room for 'it's all about the music' indie sensibilities. If we're not prepared to join the pack chasing commercial success, we may as well split up and call it a day.

———

Savage & Best are at the hub of this exciting time for music. They've effectively become the talent scouts for the entire record industry, every new band they promote snapped up and sent stratospheric as labels vie to have their own Britpop signing and ride the wave of success. But, while it's great to get free entry and hang out at aftershows for Suede and Pulp and Blur and Oasis and Elastica and Echobelly and the Boo Radleys and Salad and Powder and Menswear and all the rest of it, I can't get away from these fucking bands. Britpop is happening, not just out there but in my home.

When I get back from tour, there are two members of the Verve's entourage staying in our flat. They are sweet, but I am tired and I could do with some privacy. Richard Ashcroft regularly turns up to play his demos, poring over every detail with John. He barely acknowledges me, just grunts in response if I say hello. Another singer in one of Savage & Best's bands sits mutely at our dining table, smoking heroin. John waves away my concerned looks, so I shut myself in the bedroom and wait until he leaves. Meanwhile, John brims with insider knowledge of every bit of gossip and intrigue, the huge sums the bands are signing for and their chart positions, who's slagging off and shagging who – every spit and cough of what's going on behind and in front of the Britpop scene.

On tour in Sweden, I wandered into a Levi's shop and was confronted with a life-size cardboard cut-out of Richard Ashcroft advertising their latest line in jeans. I genuinely mistook it for a shop assistant. Not two years ago, everyone in the Seattle scene was appalled by the Marc Jacobs 'Grunge' collection and Kurt and Courtney burned the samples in protest at the commodification of their look. Now John is delighted at the coup, as it's suddenly 'cool' to have your image coopted to flog clothes. He and Savidge become founder members of Soho House, where soap stars and fashion designers hobnob with comedians and models, basking in the glow of how fucking marvellous they all are. I feel hopelessly out of step and my old 'indie' values are so (yawn) passé. Sell-out is no longer a dirty word but a baseline requirement.

But let's not pretend this is exclusively about my high moral values. I'm feeling sidelined and excluded. Half these bands are older in age than I am, yet they make me feel past it (Chris uses the term 'mutton dressed as Mod' to refer to the entire youth-obsessed trend of passing off bands knocking thirty as teenagers). And it's not like I'm boycotting the social life. I'm there with John, mingling at the events, desperate to keep up. Because I know full well that Lush are yesterday's news, consigned to the dustbin of failure and without the band, what value do I have? What on earth will I do for a living? Christ, even Emma has recorded with a dance act, the Drum Club. Her songwriting chops will guarantee her survival. I'm not sure John would even want me if I didn't hold at least some trophy appeal as he rises up the ranks of the movers and shakers.

But John and I are definitely on the rocks. We try to forgive and forget, but there's no space or time for us to move on and rebuild. One weekend, when we are on the verge of breaking up and John suggests we get away for some 'us' time, our country-side bolt to Wales is rather soured by having to spend an entire day at the Verve's residential recording studio. While I suspect that John has always rather enjoyed the kudos side of dating 'Miki from Lush', I loathe seeing him dribbling over these bands, massaging Ashcroft's already astronomical ego. I'm not sure I even like John any more, let alone love him. Which, unfairly, makes me feel less guilty about hurting him. But even Chris is growing concerned about my trashy reputation and wilful blind-ness towards anyone else's feelings. And, if Chris thinks I'm in the wrong, then I really am on a downward spiral.

45

GONE GEEZER

23 February 1995 – I'm still working on 'Ladykillers' and for the first time in fucking ages I'm feeling really good about a song. Not been out star-hopping and am going to less obvious gigs or not going out at all and just having mates over for dinner. Oh yeah, we sacked Howard. When I told Dave, he was overjoyed and said we should have invited him round to watch.

4AD treat us to a late-afternoon restaurant meeting to clear the air of past problems and re-establish some positivity. All the staff are here and Robin Hurley – an extremely likeable and capable chap who is now heading up the label's LA office – has flown over specially. There's a lot at stake, not least our future with the label and after some initial nervousness, it's acknowledged that 4AD are 100 per cent behind us and will market our next release competitively. We in turn declare that we want to co-produce the next album with our live soundman, Pete Bartlett. No fuss, no frills, no unnecessary big names. He's recorded with Kitchens of Distinction and knows his way around a studio. And no one knows our songs and our sound better than Pete.

Everything's going smoothly until Howard shows up an hour late. Bellowing to the table that he's been at the rugby all day, he's affronted by our refusal of some 'top-grade charlie' and announces that all the bands on 4AD are shit. 'Oh, COME ON, I'm only joking – for fuck's sake! Why's everyone looking so *serious*?!' We each get a matey c'mere-you-wanker bear-hug and he finally sits down, barking orders for Champagne and derailing any attempt at resuming our discussion. When Simon Harper – now a board member at 4AD – nips to the toilet, Howard is hot on his heels and we can hear him banging on the door: 'SIMON! Are you doing a line in there?! AHAHA! ARE YOU HAVING A WANK?!' Simon returns, composed, with a bemused smile: 'Howard's in a good mood, isn't he?' I think I can see smoke emanating from Emma's ears.

Simon calls Emma the next day and says, sorry, but there's no way the label can continue working with Lush if Howard is our manager. Emma arranges a band meeting and, in the hour before Howard's scheduled arrival, we discuss the inevitable. Only Chris is reluctant – he's got a soft spot for Howard and finds many of his bullish antics amusing, possibly because they've never been directed at him. When Howard arrives (on time, sober) he knows what's coming and gets in there first, saying he's got other fish to fry signing Menswear to his label. We're all rather relieved and during the resigned silence at this end to our working relationship, the plaintive break-up lyrics of Celine Dion's 'Think Twice' ring out from the radio, prompting everyone to burst out laughing.

I didn't see much of Howard after that. He must have done well out of Menswear, who had astronomical sums of money thrown at them from all quarters – famously, a half-million-quid publishing deal that worked out to around £70,000 per song. The trick back then, which I assume was Howard's ploy, was to sign some completely unknown band on a worldwide deal, then clean up with a massive US licence from an American label who were expecting a British invasion. The latter stage never materialised, but a lot of opportunists made a pile of cash while the bands got hyped, then vilified and finally chewed up, spat out and destroyed.

Oh and Howard got to realise his wet dream of having a band record at Real World. Menswear did their debut album there, which according to the band was a ludicrous waste of money and they'd have been better off 'banging it out in Camden'. But I'm sure they had some fun on the way. They certainly did better than one of his other signings, who released one single on Laurel and promptly vanished. Howard had boasted to me that he was plying the youngsters with drugs while promising the parents their boys were in good hands. Hey ho, the wonderful world of Britpop.

———

Finding a replacement for Howard is proving difficult. Tim and our friends at Warners recommend various options, all American, but we've had enough problems with Howard centring the US and it'll be even worse if we have a manager based there, too. But the lacklustre reception to *Split* means our profile is at rock bottom. Britpop wants fresh new bands who have sprung out of nowhere, not familiar old faces carrying the baggage of their past.

Robin recommends Cocteau Twins' manager, Ray Coffer, but I've never warmed to him, acting the Big I Am in a ridiculous floor-length ermine-trimmed purple velvet coat. And he gleefully fuelled Cocteaus' exit from 4AD to Fontana, which I felt was driven more by riches than nurturing their career. We need someone who cares about our music, not just a money man who babysits you by booking your holidays and finding a cleaner. Pete, too, introduces us to one of his friends, warning us that he's a bit 'old school'. No shit. 'Alcohol Terry' is a big, wide bloke in a suit who looks and talks like a throwback East End gangster. In any case, he too is only interested in the money side: 'Tell me how much you need and I'll get it. The rest is up to you.' Another dead end.

In an echo of our fruitless search for a singer, when we needed a replacement for Meriel, Phil suggests we manage ourselves – 'like Depeche Mode'. There's some sense in this – we could get a business manager to deal with the finances and make the creative decisions ourselves. But, when I point out that Emma and I have enough on our plates having to write the album, so it would be up to him and Chris to take on the tasks of holding strategy meetings with 4AD, flying over to enthuse Warners, negotiating tours with the agent and overseeing every album campaign, he looks at me like I've lost my mind. Hmm, thought not.

Phil's other favourite band-comparison mantra is 'Pulp split everything equally'. Like many of his observations, it falls some way short on detail. First off, in Lush, the *work* isn't shared equally. The songwriting rests entirely on mine and Emma's shoulders – it isn't a band process and it takes us months. In the studio, too, Emma and I do the lion's share, while the boys are free to go once they've played their parts. But I recognise that Phil and Chris are tied to the band, whether their time is used productively or not. And, though the deals we signed had originally seemed generous, they are per album – and we've taken a long time to put out each album. Emma and I aren't exactly rolling in cash – she's always needed a flatmate to help cover her mortgage and mine is split with John – but the boys are barely scraping a living wage.

Also, mine and Emma's income is boosted by publishing royalties in the form of quarterly cheques paid by PRS, a copyright organisation that collects from broadcasts – everything from TV and radio to venues and restaurants. While none of us makes a penny from the gigs, at least the promo brings radio and TV in the US, which will eventually filter through as royalty money for the songwriters. Chris and Phil are flogging their arses on tour, making nothing at all apart from £10 per-diems and a cut of the merchandise. They'd make a better income touring as our session musicians.

That said, it can take years for PRS money to be distributed and unless you've got a hit record or a lucrative ad campaign, it really doesn't amount to much. At this stage, my payments total around £500 a year (Howard once let me off his commission when I told him one cheque amounted to the grand total of £8.52). I assume Emma gets more, since her songs are most often singles, but really, it's negligible. The problem isn't so much that Emma and I are getting more than the boys, it's that the money we are *all* being paid doesn't compensate for the insane demands on our time and effort. Meanwhile, the crazy sums being thrown at new bands means that many of the musicians we knock about with are swimming in cash. The disparity in our circumstances is demoralising.

There are legions of sources you can google to discover how the music business fucks over musicians at every turn, how they are the very last to be paid in the vast chain of people involved in putting out a record or playing a tour who *all* take their chunk first and how the whole process of recouping a record deal means 4AD and Warners are raking in the profits well before we ever see a penny. The entire model is geared towards keeping the industry stable and artists disposable – wringing as much out of you as possible, in full expectation that you'll burn out and implode, by which time there will be a new prospect to replace you.

But what the fuck can we do about it? Phil got some cash-in-hand work at the *NME* and realised that, on second thoughts, being a bit skint and in a band is preferable to a nine-to-five job. Chris, meanwhile, dipped a toe in other projects, playing drums with Modern English, Moose and Hard Skin, all of whom encouraged him to jump ship from Lush and join them permanently. But these bands were making less money than we were, so while he enjoyed himself, it didn't solve his financial problems. So all hopes are pinned on the next record – that we might be able to capitalise on the new music boom, which has already leapfrogged beyond the narrow confines of the weekly music press. If we manage to get in the charts, the critics can go fuck themselves.

46

BOLLOCKS TO BRITPOP

In May '95, we begin recording *Lovelife* at Protocol Studios off Holloway Road. Pete had checked out a dozen other options but in-house engineer Giles Hall swung his choice with his calm and friendly demeanour and competent knowledge of the studio's every piece of equipment.

Giles is good mates with the Boo Radleys, who suggest that their own manager, Peter Felstead of CEC, might be a good fit for Lush. In a meeting at CEC's offices, Felstead is businesslike and professional, laying out the strategy he has in mind for the band. He's as opposite to Howard as you could possibly get – a bit dad-like and staid, to be sure, but it's a relief to find he doesn't seem to have a raging drug habit and isn't full of bullshit promises of overnight global dominance. We're a little worried, though, about the prospect of a contract, not least because it will entitle him to a 20 per cent stake in our back catalogue and he's charging us for gigs as well. We never had a contract with Howard and he waived any commission from tours (apart from merchandise, calculated separately) unless they made a profit. Ah well,

4AD will just have to give us more tour support – adding to our already enormous debt. And 4AD *love* Felstead. They eulogise about how easy he is to work with – such a refreshing change from most managers they've dealt with. Warners rate him, too, and it's a relief that after months of disruption and uncertainty, everything is falling into place. So we park our concerns – there's a six-month trial period before we have to scrutinise the contract, so let's worry about it later, after we've made the record.

I threw every trick I had up my sleeve at 'Ladykillers' when I wrote it. The sudden stops, the here-comes-the-chorus signals of 'I wanna tell ya', the mid-section breakdown with crowd-pleasing handclaps and the repetition of the song's title throughout the outro was my attempt at writing a hit. *Lovelife* was hailed/denigrated as a Britpop album, but 'Ladykillers' was my one conscious effort to give the rabble what they seemed to be asking for.

'Ciao!' was originally written for Chris to duet, since he'd expressed an interest and I pounced on the chance to get him more involved with the recording, but he got cold feet and John suggested asking Jarvis Cocker instead. The rest of Pulp are cautious, repeatedly wanting confirmation that we will never, under any circumstances, release it as a single. I only asked Jarvis as a mate – it didn't occur to me that I'd get accused of trying to cash in on their recent success. But Jarvis turns up, plays some pool, drinks some brandy and nails it in two takes, delivering the monologue he'd written for the song's middle section in his unique and brilliant style. Poor Ivo – no fan of Pulp to begin with – remains appalled that the song has anything to do with 4AD, but the Beautiful South like it enough to cover it, so I'll take that as validation.

Recording the album is immense fun. Pete's buzzing with ideas for embellishing the songs – riffs and tweaks and off-the-wall experiments – and we involve friends from all quarters to contribute brass, strings, percussion and backing vocals, which makes the sessions sociable and lively. Emma and I are getting on better than we have done in ages and I genuinely can't remember when I last had this much of a laugh in the studio. I cook meals for everyone and we drink and socialise during listening sessions. To be honest, I prefer it here to home and am in the studio almost constantly. Which is just as well, because there's an absolute truckload of work to get done.

The singles market isn't a level playing field. I've seen ours priced at £3.99, racked alongside others at £1.99. Major labels (and their indie subsidiaries) can afford to throw away singles as loss leaders for the album, but 4AD don't have the limitless funds required for that kind of push and likely see it for what it is – a race to the bottom. To coax our singles up the charts, 4AD have decided to splurge on formats, encouraging fans to buy the same record twice – perhaps three times – over. Both 'Single Girl' and 'Ladykillers' will have two EP versions, with differing sleeve designs, on both CD and 12-inch vinyl, as well as a 7-inch. To make this more than an empty packaging exercise, the separate formats will boast unique B-sides – three each for the two EPs and another for the 7-inch. That's seven B-sides, for each release.

The demand for extra tracks means the boys finally get to join in the songwriting – Phil brings in two instrumentals that we work up with some three-part vocal harmonies and I provide lyrics for a song Chris has been working on. By the time a third release is proposed – '500 (Shake Baby Shake)' – we've got one original song by Chris and are down to acoustic versions, remixes and two more covers – 'I Have the Moon' by Magnetic

Fields and 'I'd Like to Walk Around in Your Mind with You', a vintage record in Phil's collection that gives no clue to the artist other than the name 'Vashti'.*

We've provided twenty-eight songs for one album release (thirty-three if you count the acoustic versions and remixes) which is exhausting, but it's been an enjoyable and creative time and everyone – the band, Pete, 4AD, Felstead and Warners – feels buoyant that the hits are there and the campaign is primed for success. Emma and I fly to Cambridge, Massachusetts, to mix the album with Sean Slade and Paul Q. Kolderie and, with the release date for our first single planned for January 1996, we wait to see whether the year's intense work bears any fruit.

———

John and I have finally split. We spend several months in an unbearable cohabiting scenario, pursuing new relationships and timetabling our access to the flat. Occasionally, we have close and sorry conversations, but we no longer trust one another and it's difficult to get beyond the point-scoring. I get particularly hostile when people from his 'scene' poke their nose and opinions into my business. Some dimwit confronts me at a do, gesturing contemptuously at my new boyfriend, 'What's he got that John doesn't?', while a guitarist from one of Savage & Best's bands berates me for forcing John out of his own flat, wilfully

———

* We made every effort to track down the songwriter, but we didn't even have a surname. Singer-songwriter Vashti Bunyan had disappeared from making music in the early 1970s and says she only discovered our version when she bought her first computer in 1997. After contacting 4AD, she was delighted to receive her first royalties in over thirty years.

assuming that he'd paid for everything. At such times, I accuse John of bad-mouthing me for sympathy. But I'm taking it out on the wrong person.

There are entitled arseholes everywhere, throwing their weight around. At a Headcoats gig, Graham Coxon and his new squeeze Jo, from riot-grrrl band Huggy Bear – an unlikely combination if ever there was one – confront me, petulantly demanding: 'Why are YOU here?' Never mind that I've known the band's singer, Billy Childish, for over a decade and, if anyone's the fucking interloper, it's them. Their attitude is everywhere, erasing any history before their patronage, claiming bands, venues, entire genres of music have only existed in any 'happening' sense since the Britpop royalty 'discovered' them. And there's a cruel schadenfreude in the air, as bands failing to achieve the required top-five hit are dumped from their major-label deals and mocked for their failure.

Bands have always been competitive and often bitchy, but it's now *de rigueur* to trample everyone else into the dust to ensure your own supremacy. Everyone is picking sides in the Blur-vs-Oasis battle for number one, ignoring the fact that both 'Country House' and 'Roll with It' are the two worst songs either band has produced. The music is irrelevant, it's the conflict that everyone is enjoying. I get that in past times, there was an opposite snobbery about 'selling out' and commercial success was treated with suspicion as people vied to find the smallest, most obscure band to champion, however shit they were. But that was mostly the preserve of irritating contrarians. Now, the *only* barometer for taste is success and a record only has value if half a million other people like it, too.

I'm bitter, of course, because none of this works in Lush's favour. Our chart positions are viewed as feeble by bands hyped to the rafters with major-label money. I feel like I'm surrounded by trust-fund millionaires: 'My dear, you're just not *trying* hard enough.' Chris's self-deprecating brand of humour, too, is wasted in this environment of braying one-upmanship. When he jokes that he's just a crap drummer playing 'bog-standard indie shuffle', they take him seriously. Poor Chris, stuck in that loser band. As if he'd rather be in *their* band for any other reason than he'd appreciate a decent wage. The arrogance is astounding.

The drugs don't help, either. We play Féile festival, in Ireland, where Chris is overjoyed to be meeting up with a band he's close mates with. Their guitarist merely barks at him, 'Have you got any drugs?', and, when he offers her some coke, she sneers: 'No, I mean REAL drugs.' Meanwhile Chris has hooked up with a crowd of new friends whose defining characteristics are dressing like aristocracy– top hat, frock coat, silver-topped cane – and chopping out endless lines of charlie. Backstage, Terence Trent D'Arby is in the trailer opposite and his assistant pops into our Portakabin with the news that Mr D'Arby is requesting my presence. He's literally sitting on the steps not 10 yards away looking straight at me. I tell her that, if he wants to speak to me, he can get off his arse and come over himself.

Back in the pre-shoegaze days, the *Melody Maker* had labelled Lush part of the Scene That Celebrates Itself (STCI), because rather than clawing each other's eyes out, the bands – Moose, Chapterhouse, Ride, My Bloody Valentine, Stereolab, Silverfish and others – played in each other's line-ups, watched and enjoyed each other's gigs, lent our gear, offered supports, hung out together as friends and seemed part of a community. Sure, there was a hint of cosy backslapping implied in the moniker, but the spirit was genuine. This new environment is completely baffling to me: where friends you haven't seen in months act like you're a random stranger to ponce drugs from and musicians treat other musicians like handmaid groupies; where someone whose only claim to fame is designing a T-shirt swans around oozing celebrity entitlement and every no-mark hanger-on acts like they're Johnny fucking Rotten. I mean WHAT THE FUCK is going on? I've been subsumed in music since my teens and found my tribe, my family. Now it's been hijacked by elitist dickheads.

I know from friends outside the industry and people I've since met that Britpop was a wonderful experience in their lives and the vibrancy of the music provided an exciting soundtrack to the heady and optimistic times. But I'm on the inside, feeling like I'm back at school, trying to fit in with people I don't even like. And splitting with John has lowered my status, so several people I once thought of as friends no longer give me the time of day or are openly rude. It's making me chippy and hostile and often a bit of a cunt. So apologies to anyone I met during this period, who I may have been unkind and obnoxious to. It's a poor excuse, but at this stage I feel the best way to survive is to give as good as you get.

47

LADETTES

'Single Girl' and 'Ladykillers' chart just outside the top twenty, which is enough to secure us appearances on *Top of the Pops*. We nip back to Elstree for filming between gigs on our small-venue 33-date UK tour and the next night, the queue for the show stretches around the block. It's a welcome boost to our spirits, since our tour money has been cut to the bone – while our support band enjoy suites at the Hilton, we're staying in out-of-town B&Bs. But we're used to putting in the hard graft. There's a promised tour later in the year, when we'll be playing bigger venues.

PR company Hall or Nothing are handling our TV appearances and we do the rounds: *Live & Kicking*, *The White Room*, *Hotel Babylon*, *The Big Breakfast*. Davina McCall interviews us for some show I can't even remember the name of – conspiratorially matey when the cameras are on, completely blanking us when they are off; and Julian Clary does his camp, catty act on his latest BBC vehicle, taking the piss out of my undyed roots. Emma and I chat with two comedy puppets, Zig and Zag, on *The Big Breakfast*; and are friendly and girly with presenter Katie Puckrik on *Pyjama Party*, where two drag queens plaster us with a home-made face pack. I drew the line at the vagina-tightening yoga they'd originally wanted us to participate in and while the crowd of nightwear-clad women whoop it up for the cameras for the closing credits, Emma and I choose to sit and chat unobtrusively, unwilling to throw our remaining dignity aside by party-dancing for the sake of a late-night ITV appearance. But it's all just dumb fun and it's great to finally be getting some TV attention. I just hope that all this nonsense eventually pays off.

Lovelife comes out in March and charts at number eight. We're happy to have bounced back after *Split*, but, in this climate, any-thing outside the top three is considered a bit *meh*. The press cov-erage is mixed – some dismiss us as desperate has-beens trying to hitch our wagon to Britpop and even the positive takes are all 'back from the dead' backhanded compliments trumpeting that we've *finally* released something worth listening to. Everything we did before this moment is garbage; any previous failure to reach the top ten recast as 'the wilderness years'. Whatever, I don't let it get to me. The press are championing so much utter drivel right now that their opinion has become largely irrelevant. We play along, for the sake of the coverage, posing for a feature with Champagne bottles and striking 'aving-it-large poses; told to jump up and down or snarl or 'look excited', depending on the narrative devised by the editorial and PR geniuses. Press is press, so I focus on the positives.

The video for 'Single Girl' is a *Four Weddings* pastiche and fea-tures two of the hit film's lesser-known cast. We invite our mates along to act as extras, including old schoolfriends, the Savage & Best crowd, even pals from the Staverton Road days. For 'Ladykillers', we are flown to LA for a two-day shoot involving multiple sets and a host of actors and extras. It's all terribly glamorous and jet-setting. The video for '500 (Shake Baby Shake)' requires me to sit at the wheel of a Fiat 500 bouncing along to the music while the rest of the band play characters from car adverts of the time – Chris as a hip priest, Emma as a flash rich bitch, Phil as a playboy gambler. Unfortunately, I've only just passed my driving test and instantly plough the lovingly restored vintage vehicle into a ditch. But most of the action is filmed with the car on the back of a flatbed truck, so I can concentrate on tilting my head from side to side in time with the music and looking inane. Chris isn't entirely keen on poncing about in a surplice but we're playing the game now, so just do what you're told and try to enjoy it. I'm actually finding some of the 'acting' rather fun.

Many of the TV appearances are just me and Emma and she no longer seems to mind my encroachment – perhaps because she's getting way more attention than when we were insisting on more equal representation among the four of us. I'm not sure how the boys feel about it – they barely feature in the first two videos. No one's complaining, though, so I assume that things are fine. Anyway, it's all for the greater purpose of selling more records. When I get recognised at my local newsagent's by a schoolgirl, who tugs her mum's arm in whispered excitement, I take it as a sign that Lush is reaching a new audience. I'm also inwardly touched, remembering myself at that age and the thrill I'd get of seeing 'someone off the telly' in an everyday environment.

Emma also seems to be having a whale of a time in the thick of the Britpop ligging scene. This may be an overstatement, since I am less enamoured overall, but I am happy to dine out on her gossipy reports – to listen and laugh at the good times or commiserate and support for the bad. One night, a group of girls freak her out with some hostile comments in the toilets of a club. I act the mouthy bitch and warn them to leave her alone, but only discover later that one of them at least had acted with some justification since she'd previously walked in on Emma glued to her boyfriend. But I'm happy to be her attack dog if it keeps me in her good books. I think most of these people are wankers anyway, so it's no skin off my nose.

When John and I split up, Emma only found out two weeks after the event, when Peter Felstead rang her to ask if I was okay. Emma had no idea what he was referring to and was shocked at the news. It just felt easier to let her hear it from someone else. I've long accepted that she isn't the person I turn to for comfort. She might nod in sympathy, agree that it sounds really bad or ask if I'm okay, but she's more interested in hearing the details than giving anything back. It's what she expects in return, too. I learned from experience that the blow-by-blow accounts of her own – often very entertaining – dramas are delivered for her own purging. She doesn't want to know what you think, she just wants you to agree.

I put way too much pressure on our relationship in the past, crowding Emma with my expectations of being best buddies, together through thick and thin. I forced my friendship on her, expecting her to reciprocate, so we could grow closer. But that was never what Emma wanted and I didn't account for that. I needed to tone it down, to just accept our friendship for what it is. Far better to expect less, to let her come to me when she needs me. I have other friends I can rely on for support and a shoulder to cry on.

———

I'm going to be thirty next year and, for the first time ever, I'm feeling my age. Even the blokes I'm hooking up with are now often a couple of years my junior. Maybe that doesn't matter. After all, it's never bothered Emma and Phil often dates women who are a decade younger than him. Chris, too, is seeing a 21-year-old. She seems terribly young and I'm not entirely sure I approve, but my sex life is a car-crash so I'm hardly in a position to criticise his and they seem to be a good match. In any case, I first met the girl as a teenager sporting a T-shirt bearing the legend 'Fucked by Fabulous', so I assume she's no vulnerable flower.

Fabulous were a made-up cash-in band consisting of *NME* staff and masterminded by James Brown, who I've known since the days of *Alphabet Soup*. The groupie merch was just one element of the band's bad-boy image and hyped-up exploits that their press friends splashed over the pages of magazines and tabloids. For James, it paved a direct path to *Loaded*, a men's magazine positioned directly in opposition to political correctness and a publication that is now fanning the flames of lad culture.

I can't take it seriously and I realise I'm not meant to, but I mean not in the way I'm not meant to. The girls with their tits out, the iconising of machismo – it's all meant to be *fun*. Yet the joke for me is that the James I knew was a skinny-arsed brat who would have shat himself at the thought of a shag and once bored me with a description of his technique on cunnilingus – writing the alphabet with your tongue, apparently – which I took as a dead giveaway that he must be fucking hopeless at it. Lauding him as the Hugh Hefner of Britpop seems ludicrous. I wouldn't mind if these boys just wanted their fun and admitted they didn't have a clue, but it strikes me that the women are being reduced and boxed in, made lesser, to make the boys look more. 'Fucked by Fabulous' – not even 'I fucked Fabulous'.

James does in fact offer Lush the chance to plug *Lovelife* in *Loaded*, but only if Emma and I strip down to bikinis. It takes me a moment to realise he's actually serious. And why shouldn't he be? Sarah Cracknell was happy to press herself against a mirror in a bra and Anna Friel, celebrated for being one half of the first lesbian kiss on the soap *Brookside*, had no problem posing in a silver swimsuit. None of the other girls have an issue with baring the flesh, so why shouldn't he assume that I'm up for it, too?

Emma and I do a photo shoot for *Dazed and Confused* and are presented with a rack of clothes picked out by a stylist. This sounds glamorous, I know – *ooh! Lovely special clothes selected by an expert!* But the reality is often some snarky girl choosing outfits based on her own fashion-victim style and diet-obsessed size. Or, worse, a bloke who has his own ideas of how a woman should look. Nothing fits Emma as she's a UK 12, which in this insane environment is seen as a plus size, despite being under the average. The photographer picks me out a black top and a leather mini. It's only when I put them on that it becomes apparent that the skirt is the width of a football scarf and barely covers my arse. As we walk to the proposed location, through an office of men tapping away on computers, I tie my jumper around my waist to cover my rear and make sure I walk bolt upright, lest the skirt ride up any further.

The snapper's brilliant creative idea is to have Emma and me pose in a toilet cubicle. We position ourselves in our usual stance, but now he's telling me to stick one leg against the door or push my hip out and stretch an arm up the wall. Any shift in my posture has the microskirt riding up, so I cautiously comply only as far as dignity will allow. When he indicates that he wants me to bend over the toilet, legs splayed and look back at him over my shoulder, I realise that this whole set-up is an elaborate ploy. The magazine isn't interested in Lush, they just want some wank fodder for their readers. The guy didn't even have the balls to be straight with me from the off, coercing me instead like some violated innocent in the plotline of a rapey porn flick. I firmly tell him no and we finish the shoot. The piece ends up relegated to an eighth of a page with about forty words of text.

This kind of sexist bullshit is becoming commonplace and reframed as 'edgy'. I'm recommended a hot new photographer who is hailed as a visionary genius for shooting underage models in white underwear having a pillow-fight on a bed. I pontificate sarcastically that me and Emma could dress up as cheerleaders and this nonce could photograph us in a locker room through a peephole drilled in the wall. A mate of Emma's brings us to a private drinking club and tells me if I flirt with the owner, I'll get free Champagne. This is all apparently totally cool and I'm uptight for thinking otherwise.

At one of the Soho House soirées, while I order drinks from the bar, a drunk comedian slurs at me to either suck his cock or fuck off. As I stand chatting to friends, Alex from Blur is sprawled on the floor making 'phwoarr' noises and sinks his teeth into my arse. The *Carry-On* Sid James impersonations are a common theme. I fall into conversation with Keith Allen and try to ignore him sweeping his eyes around my body, twitching with overheating gestures and tugging at his collar to show he's letting off steam. Another comedian sharing a cab ride for convenience suggests he come in for a bunk-up, despite having spent the entire night excitedly chatting about his imminent fatherhood.

Liam Gallagher circles me, wondering aloud when I'll be ready to fuck him in the toilets. Look, I know I'm hardly Mary Poppins, but this isn't flirting, it's harassment. It's constant, relentless sexualisation. And there's a nasty edge to it, implying that it's me, not them, who is asking for it.

I recall Suzanne Vega once pointing out that Madonna may be breaking boundaries, but every teenage girl who dresses like her is still treated like a slut. I'm experiencing a similar uncomfortable side effect with the supposed androgyny of Britpop. While Justine from Elastica and Sonia from Echobelly and Louise from Sleeper, wearing ungendered suits or jeans and T-shirts, get treated as one of the boys, my long hair and short dresses are now a signal that I'm absolutely gagging for it. Sure, I could get a crop and stop wearing a skirt, but that's no different to saying, 'If you don't want the grief, dress like a nun.' I've been doing what I do for years and now I'm being reframed as happy to be objectified.

I've been reading feminist texts since college, however unfashionable that might be right now (and, to be fair, Chris has always found it a bit tiresome). My education, both at PNL and from the politicised bands I've followed, has taught me precisely to see through the 'harmless fun' to the misogyny that drives it. I'm not militant about it. I don't crucify people for crossing a line, I just recognise there is one. And I need to know someone well enough to accept that they're 'just joking'; I'm not going to swallow it as a lame excuse from a bloke I've just met.

I tag along to the *NME* Brat Awards and the only women to take the stage all night are some semi-clad dancing girls and Candida Doyle, keyboard player in Pulp. Of the seventeen categories, with ten entries each, there are just seven women included and four of those are in the solo artist category: Madonna, Björk, PJ Harvey and Alanis Morissette (Paul Weller won the award). It strikes me that the claim that Britpop celebrates sassy women in bands is a veneer. I saw it before with riot grrrl, where (in the UK, at least) the press consisted mainly of pitting women against each other, slagging off everyone from Babes in Toyland to Throwing Muses (and Lush, obviously) for being the 'wrong type' of woman. It spawned a host of 'women in rock' debates that to my shame, I got dragged into, bad-mouthing Kylie Minogue when it was the men comparing every other female musician disparagingly to her sexy pop-poppet image that I should have attacked. I'm not going to be fooled again.

The female-led Britpop bands sold a negligible fraction of what the successful bloke bands did. Sure, the girls got a fair bit of attention, but it's the blokes who ruled the roost. I'm now a 'ladette', a sub-category of 'lad', trying to fit in with and be fancied by the boys. My drinking pints and swearing and interest in football are no longer things I do purely for my own enjoyment; they've been fetishised as attributes for ideal girlfriend material. *Lads! Why go out with a high-maintenance prom queen who makes you mind your language when you can have a bird who doesn't mind you getting pissed while watching the footy? AND you get to shag her after.* I'm supposed to be flattered that my normal behaviour is now framed as a male fantasy, as though that's the peak of any woman's dreams and achievement.

I told a fair few people to fuck off during that time, which only made them laugh all the more ('Ooh! Feisty!'). And, though most of the men were nothing like as bad as this, few objected to the behaviour. There wasn't much solidarity between the women, either. Feminism was just an empty 'girl power' slogan that seemed to be more about celebrating your girly BFFs and being 'allowed' to get your tits out than treating women as equals. So sorry for being a party pooper, I know a ton of you had a blast, but I fucking hate Britpop and I'm glad the whole sorry shit-fest ended up imploding. I just wish it hadn't done so much damage while it lasted.

48

SUCKING CORPORATE COCK

We headline the US on a 4AD tour with Mojave 3 and Scheer, named Shaving the Pavement for some obscure reason known only to Ivo. It's a lot of fun and at the LA aftershow, Chris and I are beside ourselves when we get to chat to John Lydon and Paul Cook (the Ex Pistols, Chris calls them). But it's Lush's sixth visit to some of these venues and, though I always get a buzz off the gigs and we're playing better than ever, it's become clear that while we do great on either coast, we're just never going to draw the crowds in the rest of the States. It's not for want of trying. We've played almost 200 shows over seven tours in America and done every in-store signing and one-man video show and late-night college campus radio interview asked of us. We've autographed every album sleeve and shaken every hand and complied with (almost) every desperate scheme dreamed up by the Warners marketing machine.

Tim has moved to a new job at Dreamworks and, though he is still around to mediate, he no longer holds the same sway and we're getting the distinct feeling that the label is losing interest.

We're told we have to film a whole other video for '500' as the UK original's references apparently don't work for the US. So we head out to the desert to enact some inexplicable narrative featuring a little girl in a pink plastic wig, with the band playing on a dusty open-air stage backed by a billboard. Much of the action features me prancing about like a tit and my diary entry notes: *Been rolling about in the sand for this poxy video. The more of a moron you act, the more they like it. Whatever.* It remains Emma's most loathed Lush video.

Warners also want us to do separate promo shots for US press since the UK ones are too 'London'. They pick us some 'very now' photographer who carries a young make-up artist/stylist, clearly more used to working with lithe and malleable young models than two female musicians pushing thirty. It's the usual story with the outfit selection – all geometric one-shoulder semi-transparent body-con wear and nothing in Emma's size. The girl is making me up with rectangular blocks of solid black on my eyes that look like Groucho Marx moustaches. I don't understand why, since the make-up she's done for Emma's is completely normal. Does she think that as the singer I need to be made to look 'special'? Maybe she's unfamiliar with working on Japanese eyes? I ask if she can tone it down a bit, but she seems to take this as an insult and I suddenly see myself through her eyes: a past-it nobody, trussed up like a tart with stupid red hair and an ugly non-model face that she's having to perform miracles with to make me worth photographing.

The two Warners staff accompanying us are busy gossiping together at the front of the dressing-room trailer and have barely said hello. They've failed to show up to several of our press bookings already, simply ordering a cab and leaving us to it. I am invariably friendly with everyone we work with, but being chatty and accommodating doesn't cut it any more. If you don't throw your weight around and show everyone who's boss, they'll simply treat you like a sap. I am weary of being a 'product', made to look ridiculous and expected to perform like a pet poodle to fit whatever narrative the next photographer or video maker has conceived. We're a band with an identity, but that no longer seems to matter. I'm struggling to hold back the tears and Emma is baffled that I don't just tell everyone to fuck off. 'You don't have to do this shit!' she screams. 'THEY work for US! These are OUR photos!!!' She's right and suddenly everyone is alert and ministering. The girl fixes my make-up, the Warners people hover nervously and the photographer is polite and undemanding as I struggle to mask my inward despair. I cover the humiliating clothes in every picture by wearing a huge fluffy white coat, which they let me keep after the shoot.

We fly to Atlanta to play a one-off gig coinciding with the South by Southwest (SXSW) Music Seminar in Atlanta. We're supporting Ben Folds Five, another of CEC's bands, handled primarily by Felstead's US partner, Alan Wolmark, who whether through genuine lack or by design, exhibits absolutely no sense of irony, responding to Chris's wisecracks with utmost seriousness. I realise that it's now recognised that the music biz deliberately hires artist-facing staff that the band can relate to, the better to lull them into trust, but I miss working with people who I have a connection with. At least it made the exploitation more enjoyable.

Wolmark treats us to a tour of SXSW's Convention Centre HQ, where the foyer is a hubbub of music industry bods sporting laminated name tags and glossy brochures. He's eulogising about the event and completely blind to our growing unease at the sterile corporate environment. I'm sure that there are plenty of great conversations taking place about 'format capitalisation' and 'maximising the brand', but for Emma and me, this is an unsettling exposure to how little music – and the artists that produce it – matters. We're just 'product' and 'units', objectified and interchangeable, like gambling chips that have no intrinsic value until they're cashed in at the bank.

Wolmark leads us into an empty hall filled with hundreds of seats, each bearing a goodie bag and a programme listing the afternoon's invited speakers, while Ben Folds Five are setting up their gear on a stage, alongside a three-piece suite arranged around a coffee table. It transpires that they will be playing the incidental music as various corporate bigwigs with 'head of' job titles drop by to share their expertise and pontificate on the biz. Emma sneers, 'You mean, they're like the house band on a chat show?', to which Wolmark's face lights up in enthusiastic affirmation, stating that come next year he'll be putting Lush forward for something similar. Emma's seen enough and spits, 'Over my dead body,' storming from the room and leaving Wolmark wondering what he's possibly said to upset her. I agree, if he thinks we're going to whore ourselves out for this corporate wank then he's sadly mistaken.

Despite Warners being lukewarm about *Lovelife*, Felstead hasn't given up and we're back two weeks after the Shaving the Pavement tour playing a string of radio-station-sponsored festival gigs. The theory behind these events is that the broadcast organisation gets to boost its profile and listening audience by hosting a multi-band extravaganza; the punters enjoy a day of music in the sunshine; and the bands get to play in front of a festival crowd while getting plenty of local airplay. Win–win all round, right? Except the entire set-up is more like a big-budget talent night where the bands are random fodder for filling a bill. And Pete can't make it – his daughter is barely three months old and he needs some family time – so we're minus our front-of-house soundman and most sensible on-tour ally.

The KROQ Weenie Roast takes place in an LA stadium where the rigorously imposed timetable of performances is fine-tuned to facilitate live interviews with MTV and no allowance is made for any delays. Bands perform on a revolving stage, each act setting up behind the scenes while the other plays to the crowd. We are on after the Fugees and before Goldfinger, but the Fugees have turned up late and have been warned that their set will be cut short. We sort out our gear to the sound of 'No Woman, No Cry' being performed behind us and are signalled by the KROQ crew to plug in and get ready. As Lauryn Hill launches into the opening lines of 'Killing Me Softly', currently number one in the charts across the globe, an appreciative roar goes up from the crowd – and at that precise moment the stage begins to revolve. Honestly, if it was up to me, I would have let them play their whole set. But the crowd is now booing us and we are stranded front of house while the Fugees and the festival personnel are involved in an almighty row backstage. So I just yell into the mic, 'Oh, for fuck's sake, give us a chance,' and we launch into our set and manage to make it through unscathed.

While nothing else matches the *Spinal Tap* comedy of the Weenie Roast, the rest of the shows are hard work. The whole point of these dates is to try to flog Lush to a wider audience, but things have changed in the five years since we supported Jane's Addiction, when their stadium audience was happy to listen and mosh to an unfamiliar new band. There's now a macho element who will only sanction music that's specifically aimed at them and they're not going to risk looking like pussies by tolerating two sappy English girls who aren't even making the effort to act sexy. I do my best to gee and corral – as the singer, I feel it's my job to win over an unwilling crowd, rallying our cause at the mic. But it's an uphill struggle and exhausting work and I get little thanks for my efforts. Emma is furious that we're even doing these dates, so my attempts at trying to make the best of things aren't helping her argument that the gigs are a waste of our time.

Agawam, Massachusetts is a nightmare from the start. The crew set up our gear on a stage already littered with debris from the previous band, who suffered a relentless assault of missiles. During the opening song, a furious moshpit of stripped-to-the-waist jocks starts punching the shit out of each other and the shower of plastic bottles is so relentless that I'm struggling to get near the mic. No one from the festival organisers or the radio station does anything to calm the situation and the security merely stand around with crossed arms looking tough.

Three songs in, a bottle hits its mark and explodes in a shower of water over me and my guitar, closely followed by a boot that narrowly misses Emma's head. She dumps her guitar and stomps off stage and the rest of us follow. I'm a bit 'the show must go on' about setbacks and hate to let the bullies win, but Emma is livid that I'm even trying to calm the situation and Tommy, our tour manager, does nothing but dither about, failing to even challenge the event organisers – which is, after all, his fucking job.

Emma briefly returns to the mic: 'It's a shame some people have to ruin it for everyone else.' But the jocks are chanting 'FUCK YOU' and there's little point in trying to continue.

I'm told later that, when Stabbing Westward took the stage, they slagged off the 'assholes' for 'throwing shit', adding Lush were the best band on the bill so it was their loss. This show of solidarity perks me up a little, but for Emma, whose twenty-ninth birthday takes place during a dismal three-day bus journey across the entire width of the country, it's the last straw.

49

END OF THE ROAD

Diary entry, 9 April 1996, quoting Irvine Welsh, *Marabou Stork Nightmare*: *I went through a phase where I fucked loads of women. This was after I discovered that all you had to do was be what they want for about twenty minutes . . . Each time you went through that bullshit act to get closer to them, you got further away from what you wanted to be. At the time, it made me feel good about myself.*

My diary pages read like a nervous breakdown – self-loathing lows, then momentary highs from some chance encounter, convincing myself that I'm having fun when clearly I'm not. Then overwhelmed by guilt, shame and self-pity again. I don't know who I am any more. It's all self-delusion and desperation. I can't even be bothered to be nice to the men. What difference does it make? They come, they go – nothing ever changes. I sound as fucked-up as when I was a teenager. Except I'm not a teenager, I'm less than a year away from being thirty, so there's no excuse.

The photo albums tell a different story. I look confident and happy. We all do. Except one giveaway snap that shows me grinning but with fresh scratches on my arms. So I'm grateful for the gigs, where I can lose myself in a performance and socialise outside the confines of the band. Even then, there's something manic and unhinged about my behaviour. But at least it distracts me from how shitty and hollow I feel the rest of the time.

I can't find a way out of this mess. Lush is my life, but I've got less and less connection with the people in it. Emma is mostly distant with me, but after wasting a decade of my life trying to figure out how to please her, I'm happy just so long as I'm not in the firing line. Phil is amusing enough, but there's no depth to our friendship. I often find him catty and shallow and he thinks me boorish and insensitive. And Chris – well, I love Chris and when John moved out of my flat, he moved in. It's a temporary arrangement that means he can save paying any rent until we're done touring for the year, so it's mostly just a matter of storing his stuff in my front bedroom. It's great having him around, but he spends most of his time at his girlfriend's place and they're bang into the party scene, which I find way too druggy and full of wankers.

Away from the band, I spend most of my time with close friends – old friends mostly from pre- and early Lush days. I still see John, but being around his crowd puts me on edge. The whole music scene has become an environment where everything you do or say becomes gossip, which makes me wary and uptight. I'd dreamed of 'making it' in a band, but now I'm here, I can't handle it. I'm just keeping my fingers crossed, hoping it will all get better on its own.

When we went on tour, I needed to find a cat-sitter. Moose was living on a friend's sofa and jumped at the opportunity to have my flat to himself, rent-free. When I get back, the inevitable happens one night, but he has known me for seven years and we are clued up to each other's mistakes and misdemeanours. He's got a questionable reputation himself – after splitting from his partner and their son two years earlier – so neither of us judges the other. We both acknowledge that we're hopeless fuck-ups and neither of us – or anyone else for that matter – thinks it's likely to last. Which, in a funny way, rather takes the pressure off.

I don't fully realise it at the time, but Moose is my lifeline. I've got so used to affairs that flare with passion and end up going nowhere that it takes me a while to recognise I've fallen properly in love. That the ease and happiness I feel in his company is genuine and not just the usual temporary distraction I consumed like a drug. He's effortlessly good at stopping me from overthinking and catastrophising – over the band, the scene, what other people think. Ignore the wankers, enjoy the music, drink the beer. He gives me perspective on what's important and what isn't.

Since I was a kid, I thought that the best way to get through difficult periods was to fake what you want to be: happy, confident, fun. With Moose, I don't have to. He doesn't demand anything of me and doesn't want to change me. It's the first time in ages that I don't feel the real me is a disappointment I have to hide behind the bulletproof 'Miki from Lush' exterior. It's such a relief to drop the bullshit and be completely honest.

———

Relations between Emma and Felstead are not good. He's pushing for us to tour America again, but Emma has had her fill of managers with dollar signs in their eyes. She's raging that we're wasting our time banging our heads against the wall – we'll *never* break America. We're not Garbage or the Cranberries or No Doubt – we just aren't the right kind of band. We should be concentrating on Britain and Europe, where the album at least has done well. And she's overheard his business partner slagging her off and calling her moany and difficult. So fuck him, fuck them – we should sack them and move on.

I know she's right, but move on to what? It took us six months to find a manager and how will we cope on our own? There's no Ivo or Tim or anyone looking out for our career. Phil chips in, saying he wishes we'd never got rid of Howard and Chris and Emma are nodding in agreement. *Seriously?!* Has everyone conveniently forgotten what a fucking *nightmare* that was?

We're no longer capable as a group of having a constructive discussion. I'm not sure we ever were. I've grown inured to Emma's rages, which always boil down to personal insults and demand absolute agreement without offering any solutions. I've been on the receiving end of enough of them to know how unfair they can be. She's ranting and wailing in disbelief – WHY aren't we as angry and outraged as she is?! But I don't know *anyone* who's as consistently angry and outraged as Emma. Phil loves to pile in with complaints but is mute when it comes to acting on them. And Chris's entire personality is go-with-the-flow – it's hard to tell what he really thinks as his opinions are delivered via self-effacing jokes.

My entire childhood was spent making my parents – and myself – feel fine about their every terrible decision. Making the best of whatever madness is happening around me is part of my character. Conversely, Emma grew up relentlessly kicking against her parents' values. She is inherently suspicious of people's motives and bristles at anything that threatens to impinge on her perceived best interests. If I could have my time again, I'd sacrifice a chunk of money on a band therapist. Not because I have blind faith in the profession, but it might at least force us to put in the effort to understand each other's motives – and strengths and weaknesses – a little more. Instead, there's just bad-faith second-guessing, spiralling and consuming any common ground.

Our divisions are Felstead's gain and we end up with the worst of all compromises – back to the US for the third time in six months. Elvis Costello had been offering us a support (we'd covered one of his songs at his request for his own use and I recall some mention of Beck), but I can't even remember why those options were dismissed. Either would have been infinitely preferable to the one we agree to with Gin Blossoms, a band I know nothing about but who Felstead seems to think will be our golden ticket to wider exposure.

But before that there's at least some respite. We're playing a few weeks of European and UK festivals and Pete is back on board, which lifts everyone's mood. In Paris, we get a rapturous reception, the crowd jumping up and down singing along to the opening riff of '500'. Chris gets to see his beloved Nick Cave headline in Milan and after playing T in the Park in Scotland, we hang out in the bar singing Abba songs accompanied by Neil Hannon from the Divine Comedy on piano. We watch John Lydon winding up the crowd when the Sex Pistols play on a beach in Belgium and catch up with a host of old friends after headlining the packed tent at Phoenix.

Moose and I decide to drive to the gig at the Benicassim festival in Spain. It's a mad non-stop journey made intense by insane mistral storms across France, but we make it in time for the gig, ending the night dancing to the Chemical Brothers. Emma and Chris have known Moose for as long as I have, since Lush's early days, which makes hanging out together a laugh. Then we take off for a week together, driving up the French coast – camping by beaches and forests, swimming in the rain and drinking wine in our tiny tent.

But the idyll is short-lived and, by mid-August, Lush are back in the US. We're third on the bill to Gin Blossoms and Goo Goo Dolls and even my reality-denying efforts can't override the complete mismatch. Emma is having screaming rows with Felstead and the rest of us agree that we're unlikely to gain a single new fan from these gigs. At least we're all on the same side again, though the incessant conflict and the pointlessness of the shows is grinding everyone down. We slot in some dates with Eels, who are completely uninterested in mingling with us, so there's not even any sociable distraction from the misery.

It's a shame because live, we're at the top of our game. Moose joins the tour for a week of our own gigs and is staggered at how good the shows are. We play some sold-out West Coast dates with Imperial Teen, who are a great band and old-school friendly; and have a fine time catching up with all our friends (and Mum) in LA. Ian Astbury joins us on stage to sing 'Ciao!', though there's some confusion at the soundcheck rehearsal where he comments, 'It's a bit skiffle, isn't it?', and, it transpires he thinks we'll be playing a cover of the Cult's 'Edie (Ciao Baby)'. Chris is laughing so hard he can barely play the drums.

So it's not all doom and gloom. I have photos of us out and about, checking out the tourist sites of Washington, DC and boogie-boarding in California. Chris's thirtieth birthday is celebrated in front of a packed house in San Francisco with an encore of Elvis impersonators singing 'Happy Birthday'. During our first trip to Hawaii, tagged on to the tour as a much-needed treat, we spend a day at a friend of Mum's North Shore beach-side property and accept a no-refusal-possible invitation to take part in Don Ho's show at the Waikiki Beach Hotel, singing the backing vocals to 'Tiny Bubbles' in front of an audience of pensioners. Finally, it's off to Japan to play two shows in Tokyo, where I manage to slip away for a home-cooked dinner with three generations of my family. The pages of happy, smiling photos give no indication of the problems below the surface and that this would be our last ever tour with the four of us.

50

DARKNESS FALLS

The tour was planned around returning for Maxine's September wedding. Marriage has never appealed to me, but I am sentimental and excited by other people's nuptials and spent the year looking forward to celebrating with my best lifelong friend and her partner Barry, a thoroughly good bloke with an easy charm and humour who had slotted seamlessly into our social group. It's a wonderful day and a great party – some unadulterated joy in these stressful times. I take it as a hopeful sign that now the US tour is out of the way and the European dates are on the horizon, everything will get better.

But, while I am enjoying the love being back home with Moose and my friends, Chris and his girlfriend have split up. He feels depressed and abandoned, inconsolably sad. We sit up late, night after night, in his cluttered temporary set-up in my flat. He doesn't blame her for leaving, since he is living in someone's front room, going nowhere, hardly a catch. I try to contradict the hopeless narrative – we've been away on tour for most of the year and, Christ, she's twenty-one, barely an adult. She's not dumped him because he's a loser, she's just young. It's a huge ask to expect her to wait around at the mercy of his schedule.

Look, things will get better, they always do. He's understandably sad about the end of a relationship and exhausted by the tour, but we've only been back a couple of weeks. He just needs to be patient, spend some time away from the maelstrom. And the set-up in my front room is temporary. The album has done well, there's some extra merch money from the tour and, after the European dates, scheduled from the end of October, he'll get a flat and be up and running again. Chris, you're a great bloke, good-looking, smart, funny and you *are* a catch.

But Chris is struggling to feel good and he's always relied on feeling good. I'm used to his dark moods but he's crying, really sobbing. I've not seen him like this since back when our relationship was falling apart, when we were just kids and bereft at our loss. I keep him company, sleep next to him, comforting and reassuring. But none of my usual efforts are working. He feels embarrassed at being so hopeless and keeps apologising for boring me with his problems. Melissa is heading off for a spell and Chris takes up the offer to flat-sit, needing some alone time to think and regroup. A friend of his who struggled with a difficult period herself recommends visiting the doctor for antidepressants. Chris gets a prescription of Prozac and temazepam and is recommended a course of counselling.

I don't have a diary that covers this period. My bag got stolen one night in the pub – a couple of years after these events, when I'd started a regular office job. There was nothing of any value to the thief – my purse of cash and cards was in my pocket – but the bag's contents were irreplaceable. The diary had Chris's letters stored in it, which I carried about like a talisman. I hunted through the bins in the local area and reported it to the police, but I figured the thief just ditched the lot in the river. So I can only piece together the events from my own memories and other scraps of evidence and recount the truth as I recall.

I know Chris, Moose and I went to see a Holly Golightly gig on 2 October, where Chris was anxious that the medication wasn't working. But he'd only been on it a couple of days and the doctor had warned it could take up to a fortnight before he started to feel the effects. I'm not sure if he was at Suede at the Kilburn National on the 10th. Uppermost in my memory at that show was that, when I joined Emma to say hello and chat, she barely met my eye and, by the aftershow, she was scowling and stropping off with an exasperated huff if I even looked like I was about to approach her.

Shortly after, Emma called a meeting, offering no clues, but I could tell what was coming. In my memory, Chris was going to head up to the Lakes immediately after the meeting and we walked back to Melissa's flat so I could get her keys off him. In any case, Emma said she had an important announcement – she wanted to leave the band. When I replied, 'I know,' she hotly demanded I reveal who'd told me, but I said it didn't take a genius to figure it out from her behaviour towards me.

We manage, finally, to have a sensible conversation about Lush and its future. Emma is sick of touring the US, hates Felstead – who she accuses of treating the band as a cash cow and a means of furthering his own reach in America – and feels we are just puppets with no control. She has no enthusiasm for writing another

Lovelife, pandering to commercial pressures to churn out the hits. Personally, I don't entirely agree with her reasoning – *Lovelife* has been a success and I have some sympathy with Felstead's drive to keep us relevant in America. Our Stateside popularity has helped us survive the incessant critical pounding we get in the UK and there are plenty of British bands who envy our success there. As a manager, he would have been negligent to ignore that. But he's been dismissive about our complaints and the radio festivals and Gin Blossoms dates were a mistake. We should indeed have been capitalising on the album's popularity closer to home.

However, this isn't the time for a debate. Emma is clearly at the end of her rope and she's not trying to start a row. She points out that Suede have gone on to succeed without Bernard Butler and Lush could do similar. But however difficult my relationship with Emma over the years, I've never had any desire to pursue a solo career and I can't for a second imagine the band without her. No Emma, no Lush – and I will comply with whatever Emma wants to keep the band together. Meanwhile, we all acknowledge that Chris needs some time to recover, so we'll rehearse a stand-in drummer for the European dates. He can return as soon as he feels ready: before, during or after – it's entirely up to him and the door is held open. Everyone has his best interests at heart and we only want him to get better.

Maybe Emma only agreed to continue with Lush for the sake of moving the discussion on and she still fully intended to leave after the European dates. But she wasn't the type to mince words and, in that meeting, there was nothing stopping her from insisting that no, this was definitely the end. In my recollection, she was pleasantly surprised by my response – that if she never wanted to set foot in America again and planned to record an album of

Gregorian chants, I'd go along with her wishes. It would be a crying shame not to make another Lush album – after all, the music was still great and, performing live, we were better than we'd ever been. I wasn't going to sacrifice all that for the sake of a fucking manager – we would find a way to ditch Felstead once the gigs were done. So that's how I remember it being left. Tentatively hopeful and everyone agreeing that it was worth another roll of the dice.

Chris and I do a last recce of Melissa's flat and hug good-bye on the Bayswater Road. He's a bit deflated but smiling that 'yeah, I'm sure it'll all be fine'. I'm optimistic, too – tell him not to worry about Lush, everything will be taken care of. He just needs to concentrate on getting better. It's hardly surprising he's run down after the year we've had. And he agrees – he'll see his family and his friends, recharge in the Lakes. That always does the trick.

I call and we chat. He doesn't sound good. He says that coming home hasn't worked and he's still feeling depressed, but I say he's only been back all of two days. Has he called any of his mates? No, he doesn't want to see anyone while he's feeling down, he'd be lousy company. He's missing the point – I know how much he loves his old friends, they'd be a tonic, I'm sure. But he wants to wait until the pills start to work their magic. Then he'll be better at socialising.

He admits he hasn't been taking the temazepam, prescribed to tackle his insomnia – it's one of the recreational drugs that's doing the rounds, so he associates it with ketamine and diazepam and ecstasy and heroin and whatever other crap's out there. I'm alarmed and tell him he can't possibly get better if he isn't sleeping and there's a world of difference between a GP prescribing drugs and some arsehole at a party dishing them out. He doesn't want to do the counselling either and, though therapy has never held any appeal for me, I point out that Phil has had sessions and swears by them. I make a mental note to get Phil to call Chris and try to convince him.

Look, I'll get the train up. I can be there by tonight. But he laughs and says no, don't be ridiculous. And I don't want to bully or crowd him. He promises he'll start taking the sleeping pills and, yes, he'll give his mates a call. It's fine, he's just exhausted. Sleep will help. Yes, definitely, I say – sleep will make all the difference.

I call the next day and speak to his mum. No he's not there right now, he must have gone for a walk, which is a good sign because at least he's getting out in the fresh air. She says he's been a bit quiet but is generally okay and we swap notes on what Chris has said about why he's so down. I tell her about him not taking the sleeping pills and we discuss ways to convince him about the counselling sessions. We both agree he's not forthcoming about his feelings and a professional would be better equipped to draw him out. I say I'll call tomorrow and speak to him again. I can come up and visit, if it helps. And she says, yes, it might. Let's see what Chris thinks.

But Chris is already dead. He's hanged himself from some scaffolding around the back of the barn, out of sight and hard to find, where his dad will discover his body some hours later, wondering why he still hasn't returned from his walk.

Phil calls me with the news. I'm struggling to breathe. No no no no no – and the overpowering impulse to run from the room, from the house, away from Phil's words. Please just make it unhappen.

Everyone is in blank shock. Was there a note? No. Any signs? Nothing to indicate anything like this. No one has a clue. Most can only speculate a perfect storm.

We can go and see Chris in the chapel of rest, but I want to remember him alive not dead. At the crematorium, the coffin is wheeled in and it's too much – him lying inside, so physically close but so absent. 'When I Die' is played during the service and Emma is hunched and sobbing – my arm around her, hugging her to my side.

Chris's family hope that we'll continue with Lush – giving us their blessing. But I knew from the second he died that there was no future. All that time squabbling with Emma, accepting all the difficulties because I needed her. But I needed Chris more. He was the happy soul of Lush and without him it's pointless and empty.

51

ENCORE

After the funeral, Moose and I retreated to the cocoon of home. We'd been a couple for mere months, still in the throes of romance, and this terrible event – it might have ended us. But Moose looked after me, kept me company, gave me space – whatever and whenever I needed it. It helped that he had known Chris for years, too, and felt the full weight of the tragedy.

I slept with Chris's hoodie on my pillow, breathing in the remnants of his scent. Then I'd wake in the night, confused about why and the realisation would come like a blow. Over the weeks, then months, I moved through the stages of grief – shock, denial, pain, guilt, anger. But even the first signs of acceptance felt like a betrayal, the fading of immediate and all-consuming pain like losing Chris all over again. And so it progressed – good days, bad days.

Despair is exhausting and eventually the tears dried up. I'd gone to a few gigs, hoping it would lift my spirits, but it was too soon. Others had moved on, which made me feel alienated and upset. So Moose and I stuck to a tight-knit group of close friends, spent weekends with his son, Joe, and travelled to visit friends and relatives: Dad in Hungary, Mum in LA, the folks in Japan and up to the Lakes to see Chris's family. New memories to replace the bad ones.

It took fourteen months to make public that Lush were officially splitting up. I'd resisted the announcement, angry about the obituaries that speculated that the band's disappointing career was somehow responsible for Chris's suicide. Let them wait for ever, what do I care? Like I give a shit that the press and the industry need their coda. Eventually Emma pointed out that it wasn't fair on the fans and I said, 'Fine, do what you like.' She needed a line drawn under Lush, having started a new band, Sing-Sing. I went along to a couple of their shows, grinning like a maniac to mask my discomfort. I felt like the first wife, replaced by a younger model.

I made a half-hearted stab myself. 4AD had given Emma and me some money for equipment to write solo music, so I bought a sampler, gave a chunk of cash to Phil (too little, too late), then piddled about with a couple of projects that came to nothing. I couldn't muster the enthusiasm. It would only be less-than-Lush. I needed something completely new, where I wasn't constantly reminded of the loss.

I wish I had known the heightened risk of suicide in men hitting thirty. Statistics have a way of cutting through the individual personalities and it might have helped to have had that possibility in my mind. I only say this because there was little awareness at the time. We all assumed suicide only came after prolonged and obvious suffering, with unignorable cues signposting the danger. We'd focused on Chris getting better, not ensuring his safety – relying on his optimistic disposition to get him through a bad spell. I'm older now and understand more about depression. Chris had always been a happy person and being unable to shake the feelings of despair must have been unbearable for him. And I miss him very, very much. Whatever joys I've experienced since his death – and there have been many – would be improved with Chris in the picture. The memories of his face, his laugh, his demeanour, how it felt to be in his company – even twenty-five years on – are crystal clear. And I believe, with intervention, he would have got through the tunnel of that dark period and come out the other side. Maybe not intact, maybe changed, but alive.

As for Emma, if it weren't for the band, we probably would have lost touch decades ago. Even after Lush, when we weren't in each other's faces all the time, the relationship remained fragile and spiky. Too much baggage and our patterns were hard to break. We fell out a couple of years after Chris's death. She was going through a tough time and I thought I was helping, but she sent me a shitty email at work, accusing me of saying something unspecified but apparently unforgiveable. It wasn't the first post-Lush blow-up, but I was done with grovelling to her for every perceived misdemeanour. We didn't speak for five years and then we did and then we had the Lush reunion in 2016 and then we fell out again. But that's a whole other story, with an ultimately happy ending: forming Piroshka (with Moose, Justin Welch and Mick Conroy), continuing to make music, hooking up again with Simon Raymonde of Cocteau Twins and putting out two albums on his Bella Union label.

But for all the conflict, I miss Emma, inasmuch as we share a lifetime of history. Memories are brought alive by the people who were present when the events happened. Many of mine died with Chris and now many more are flat and dull without having Emma to chime in and animate them. And whatever the fall-out, I still love her songs and mine wouldn't have existed without hers. I needed her for Lush and she needed me. And that was the problem all along. For Emma, it was only ever about the songs and she could write those on her own; she could have recorded them with a better singer and got all of the attention and rewards. But a band is more than just the songs. It's personality, it's romance, it's a spark. And she couldn't do that alone. Just as she needed Ivo and Robin and Pete and Howard and Chris and Steve and Phil and the whole cast of characters who put in the work to make a success of Lush, she needed me to support and enthuse, to bounce off and compete with, to perform her songs and love them and help make it all happen. She may have resented it, but she wouldn't have been anywhere near as successful, or had half the fun, without the rest of us. Without me.

Emma had been ambitious for Lush from the very beginning and I'd tagged along because it seemed like a laugh. There was no grand plan, I just wanted to be with my mates, getting praise and attention for doing something I loved. It was a happy accident that I turned out to be any good at it. Making records, signing to 4AD, touring around the world and all the rest of it were unexpected bonuses – exciting opportunities I grasped. But, if I'd been surprised by my luck, I had equally under-estimated the negatives.

People think the toughest time for a band is at the beginning, when you're struggling to make it. But it's easy when you are young and full of hope and have nothing to lose. Far harder when you're already on the ladder and scared of falling off. I never much minded the workload, but the financial exploitation, the bickering with Emma, the anxiety and the relentless lack of fuck-ing respect ground me down. And finally, I ended up in a place that felt hostile, where I barely recognised myself, nearly all the good people gone. But you can't expect good times without the bad – neither makes sense without the other – and I learned that hard work and a hopeful spirit can get you a long way towards your dreams (I'm hearing Chris now, chiming in: '*Wise words, mate*'). Emma and I were never great musicians and couldn't rely on showing off virtuoso performances to carry a song. In punk-rock style, we used the best of what we had and threw everything into the writing. I remain proud of those songs, our legacy.

In 1997, I took a correspondence course for proofreading. I was an English lit graduate, after all, so it seemed a good fit. Chris's aunt recommended me for mentoring with an editor and I quickly progressed under her tutelage to paid work. Then a journo friend got me freelance stints in the TV listings department at IPC, where I eventually got a staff job. It was a revelation to discover that an office could be so much fun – gossipy and social, with pub lunches and after-work piss-ups – and I was getting paid twice what I'd been earning in the band for half the work. No sleep-less nights panicking about Lush – 6 p.m., job done – my home life blissfully separate. And I was good at it. Another career I'd lucked into – I've been a sub-editor now for over twenty years.

I was thirty-four when my daughter was born and her brother followed three years after. I was nervous about having children, worried I might mess them up, but becoming a parent was full of excitement and emotion; hard work, too, but hands-down the best thing I've ever done. And their school life immersed me in a whole new community of families and new friends. Unlike Mum and Dad, who had moved far from their own homes to start a family, I live a ten-minute bus ride from Staverton Road. I've lived here since 2005 and have no intention of ever moving. In that respect, I didn't inherit my parents' adventurous spirit, but it probably makes a difference being the one who was left behind. After the years of disruption, both through childhood and in Lush, I've finally found my home and my family.

Becoming a parent made me more forgiving with my own. I'd been angry that they'd failed to protect me from the abuse, then left me to fend for myself. I felt like I'd been saddled with fuck-ups that it was going to take me a lifetime to deal with, just to catch up with being 'normal'. But that kind of thinking just makes you feel hopeless and, now I'm a parent, I know it's impossible not to make mistakes. And Mum and Dad gave me plenty of other advantages in life. They were exciting people to be around – magnetic, outgoing personalities who seized opportunities and enjoyed life to the full. Though it wasn't easy bouncing between them, I'm grateful I had both – however incompletely. And I always knew I was loved. It sounds like a low bar but I promise you it isn't. Love is rare and not to be taken for granted.

But I'm aware that it's not enough on its own, either. I only need to look at my children, see a photo, hear their voices or even think of them, to be flooded with affection. They are so easy to love, but far harder to nurture and, in that respect, I feel I've done better than either of my parents. I'd spent all my life chasing love, always wondering if there was a more perfect version around the corner that would magically make everything alright. Having kids taught me that simply feeling love isn't enough, that it needs care and attention and effort – compromises to be made, demands to be met, the right environment – to thrive.

I sent my children to local state schools, despite Mum offering me the funds to send them private. I don't have a go at people who choose that route (though, maybe, don't call yourself a socialist if you do) – everyone wants the best for their kids. But I was stung by my time at Queen's and had no desire to send my kids into an environment where they'd be judged on their family income. I wanted for them what I'd had in Windsor, living in a community of families where they could walk to their schoolfriends' homes; but also a life in London, where they'd be free to enjoy the diverse social and cultural opportunities I'd enjoyed as a teen. And I'm not much enamoured of the outward trappings of wealth. I had enough of that with Ray. I prefer to cook at home and stay in with friends and family; I rarely buy new clothes and I still cut my own hair (badly). Family holidays with Moose and the kids were mostly spent in campsites, driving around a beat-up campervan – our own version of going on tour!

In the end, I'm just as good or bad a parent as anyone else I know: one day patting myself on the back, glowing at doing a fantastic job; the next filled with anxiety, thinking I've made some godawful mistake, but then I fix it. Or try to. It's the trying that's important. With family, with friends, with anyone you love.

I'd never worried about finding a man – they're everywhere! It's just finding the right one that's difficult. My parents were never short of lovers, either, but Mum was content with playing the foil to self-centred men, which I discovered in my teens I wasn't cut out for. I am more like Dad – I want intellect, humour, tolerance, companionship, entertainment and attention from a partner. In many ways, I'm as selfish and unreasonable as he was.

And we shared the common bruising of Nora's abuse, so, even without the permissive playground of the rock 'n' roll environment, I suspect I'd have been as promiscuous. Except Dad never found his peace, running from his past rather than confronting it, and he blew his opportunity, losing my mother and her love and the happy family he could have had. Whereas I recognised that Moose being the father of my children made him irreplaceable, that no one else would do. I know that sounds unromantic, but there's more to love than romance. Wanting to make our relationship work – needing it to – made me try harder.

A friend (ex-friend, actually) once commented that I must not be that committed to Moose since we aren't married. Like I need a certificate to prove how much I love him. But you know what? Now that it doesn't matter, because we are already tied together by years and children and a home and a life, maybe now I will. Because then it will be for the hell of it. That – and for love.

ACKNOWLEDGEMENTS

This memoir would not exist without Pete Selby approaching me with the idea and pooh-poohing my 'but I'm not a writer' objections. Massive thanks to him and to my agent, Jane Turnbull, for their enthusiasm and patient nurturing and to everyone at Bonnier Books – with special mention to editor Melissa Bond – and to publicist Dusty Miller for making this book happen.

Huge hugs to Maxine Lynch, Bunny Schendler, John Best, Steve Rippon, Pete Bartlett, Geoff Stoddart, Dave Baker, Mike Pettifer, Ivo Watts-Russell, Richard Smith, Brigitta Boszoki, Peter Pallai and my mother, Yasuko, for rambling and immersive chats and email chains about ancient history, all of which helped me to relive the past. Lucy O'Brien, Liz Evans, Dominic Wills and Gill Wood provided invaluable guidance and feedback with the manuscript, while Bill Spandagos's brilliant Lush site, Light from a Dead Star (lightfromadeadstar.org), was permanently open on my browser throughout, helping to sort my scattered memories into a coherent timeline.

I raise a glass and drink good health to all the fans who cherished Lush, bought our records, came to our gigs and have kept our music alive for (gulp) over thirty years. Your support made everything worthwhile. And a toast, too, to the whole gallery of people within these pages. Whatever your contribution, you are part of my story and the tapestry would be less colourful without you.

Kisses to all who put up with me blathering on about my past and agonising over the 'writing process' and to those who have shared my ups and downs over the years: my NW London community and my further-flung friends; everyone involved in the Piroshka entourage; muckers from the IPC and Dennis years; people I got to know through gigs and music and social media and interviews. I'd name you all, but we'd be here all day – if I see you and you have a copy, I'll write your name in biro at the bottom of this page.

Finally, love to my family: my parents and the *kazoku* in Japan; and Moose, Stella and Ivan, who mean absolutely everything to me.